Law and Order vs. the Miners

LAW AND ORDER
VS
THE MINERS

West Virginia, 1907 — 1933

Richard D. Lunt

ARCHON BOOKS

Hamden, Connecticut

1979

LS

Library of Congress Cataloging in Publication Data

Lunt, Richard D.
  Law and order vs. the miners, West Virginia,
1907-1933.

  Bibliography: p. 183.
  Includes index.
  1.   United Mine Workers of America — History.
2.   Trade-unions — Coal-miners — West Virginia — History.
I.   Title.
HD6515.M616W44   331.88'12'23309754   79-16043
ISBN 0-208-01811-5

Endleaves: Firearms confiscated from Cabin Creek miners, 1912-13. *West Virginia Collection*, West Virginia University Library.

For my mother and father
Pearl and Herbert

Contents

Acknowledgments

The initial research for this study was made possible by a growth and development leave granted by Rochester Institute of Technology.

The professional staffs at the institutions where I did my research were of immense help: Library of Congress; National Archives; New York Public Library; New York State School of Industrial and Labor Relations, Cornell University; University of Virginia Library; West Virginia Collection, University of West Virginia Library.

Dennis R. Nolan, professor at the Law Center of the University of South Carolina; William Preston, professor at John Jay College of Criminal Justice, The City University of New York; and James William Hess, archivist at the Rockefeller Archive Center, North Tarrytown, New York, have read the entire manuscript. Stanley I. Kutler, professor at the University of Wisconsin, Madison; and Salvatore Mondello, Thomas J. O'Brien and John Sanders, professors at Rochester Institute of Technology have read portions of the manuscript. I am indebted to all these individuals for their criticisms and suggestions. The final product, of course, is my responsibility.

Ann Pompili provided valuable assistance by typing the manuscript. Susan Hubregsen drew the map of Southwestern West Virginia.

Richard D. Lunt

Introduction

In the name of law and order, coal operators, aided by state police and United States troops, drove the United Mine Workers out of West Virginia in the 1920s. The Mine Workers' defeat in West Virginia signaled defeats in other states and the near destruction of the union. A Mine Workers' lawyer in West Virginia remonstrated:

> We all favor, or should favor, law and order based upon justice. I desire, however, to register my protest against the use of the term "law and order" as a smoke screen behind which to hide oppression, lawlessness and the invasion of personal rights guaranteed by the Constitution.[1]

The defeat of the Mine Workers in West Virginia in the 1920s was but one of many for the coal miners going back to John Bates, who, in 1849, unsuccessfully led the Pennsylvania anthracite miners into a strike. John Bates's successors, notably Daniel

Weaver in the 1860s and John Siney in the 1870s, fared little better. For a few years their burgeoning national unions gave hope to the miners that justice might some day be won, but depressions, the greater unity and wealth of the mine operators, and the law joined forces to destroy their unions.

The law joined forces with the operators because American society, or at least those persons in it who customarily made the legal decisions, believed that the employers' property rights were more important than the workers' personal ones. When union organizers tried to proselytize miners, the operators required the miners to sign individual employment contracts forbidding them to join miners' associations. (Later, miners would loathsomely call these "yellow dog" contracts.) When the unions struck their mines, the operators went into court claiming that the unions threatened their properties and won injunctions from sympathetic judges to halt picketing. The operators also petitioned obliging state legislatures to pass laws allowing them to appoint their own police to protect their mines from union organizers and picketers. When all else failed, the operators persuaded compliant governors to impose martial law on strike zones. Under martial law, state militia protected the mines and sometimes military commissions tried and convicted strikers.

After John Siney closed the office of his national union in 1876, some miners, most prominently the Molly Maguires in Pennsylvania, fought back. They roughed up strikebreakers, derailed mine cars, and took potshots at foremen and superintendents. The operators responded by bringing in Pinkerton's National Detective Agency. James McParland, an undercover agent for Pinkerton, infiltrated the Molly Maguires and slyly urged them to undertake even greater deeds of violence. He later informed on and testified against them in court. Fourteen Molly Maguires were hanged as a result of his treachery.

In the 1880s some miners joined the National Trades Assembly under the Knights of Labor. Others joined the Amalgamated Association of Miners of the United States, and when it was defeated in the strike of 1883, its successor, the National

Federation of Miners and Mine Laborers. Finally, in 1890, various factions of miners came together in a national convention at Columbus, Ohio, and established the United Mine Workers of America.

The preamble to the 1890 constitution opened with the article of faith that has guided and sustained miners from the beginnings of their union movement to the present:

> There is no fact more generally known, nor more widely believed, than that without coal there would not have been any such grand achievements, privileges and blessings as those which characterize the nineteenth century civilization, and believing as we do, that those whose lot it is to daily toil in the recesses of the earth, mining and putting out this coal which makes these blessings possible, are entitled to a fair and equitable share of the same.

The miners were right. The mining of coal did make possible the industrial revolution, and late in the twentieth century coal still plays an important role in meeting our nation's energy needs, as other sources of energy either are approaching exhaustion or are still in the early stages of development.[2]

Until the advent of mechanized strip mining, the way coal was mined was for men to descend into the ground to undercut, drill, and blast the coal away from the tunnel face and load it onto cars for shipment up to the surface. Coal dust sifted into their clothing, covered their skin, and finally reached their lungs. For decades the official line was that coal dust was a healthy influence — it helped combat silicosis — but meanwhile uncounted thousands of miners died. Not until the 1960s did the medical profession recognize that "black lung" disease, pneumoconiosis, had afflicted the miners. In 1968 it was estimated that at least 125,000 miners had black lung disease.[3]

But the great killer was mine accidents. In the last 100 years of coal mining 120,000 men, an average of 100 every month, year in and year out, have died violent deaths in the mines. The greatest cause of death was falling tunnel roofs, but death could also come from exploding pockets of methane gas ignited by electrical sparks or the miners' explosives. The largest loss of men occurred in December, 1907, in Monongah, West Virginia, when 361 men were killed in a single explosion. However, the Monongah tragedy did not result in noticeably increased safety precautions.[4]

The men who became coal miners could not help but be affected by their daily trips into the dark tunnels of the earth. Away from the sun, fresh air, and the safety of the surface, they were entirely reliant on their own resources for survival. Should they, or a company engineer, make a mistake, injury or death awaited them. Forever brooding over the possibility of injury and death that was all too frequent in their underground world, they viewed the outside, normal world with hostility and defiance.[5]

The newly formed United Mine Workers of America reversed years of miners' defeats with a victory in 1897 against bituminous operators. The agreement, signed in January, 1898, established the Central Competitive Field, composed of bituminous coal fields in Pennsylvania, Ohio, Indiana, and Illinois, and provided for the introduction of the eight-hour workday and negotiated wage scales. The agreement also included an understanding that the Mine Workers would organize the rich and rapidly developing West Virginia coal fields, since much of West Virginia's lower priced, nonunion coal moved into the Midwest markets of the Central Competitive Field. If the profit motive of the operators in the Central Competitive Field led them to press for this understanding, the UMW had an even stronger motive — survival. Left unorganized the West Virginia coal fields eventually would destroy the Mine Workers' agreement with the Central Competitive Field, and thereby the union itself.[6]

But West Virginia coal fields were especially difficult to organize. The mountainous terrain isolated mining camps, making miners completely dependent upon the company. They lived in company houses and traded at the company store with company script. There were company schools, churches, and doctors. To break the company's control over the miners would require supreme union effort.

Nevertheless, the Mine Workers tried to organize some of the West Virginia coal fields during 1901 and 1902. A major effort was made in the northern section of the state, where the Fairmont Coal Company had a near monopoly on coal production in the extensive Fairmont Field. The Mine Workers also initiated a lesser effort to organize the Kanawha Field in the southern section of the state. The union sent in national organizers and allocated special funds for strike maintenance. Initially the organizing effort against the Fairmont Coal Company appeared successful. But the company eventually thwarted the Mine Workers' victory by obtaining a sweeping injunction which prevented union members from assemblying at or near company property. Although the UMW failed to organize the Fairmont Field, in the southern Kanawha Field the UMW was successful, securing union contracts for its men.[7]

The Fairmont Coal Company's defeat of the UMW through the labor injunction encouraged West Virginia operators to explore the possibility of using even more potent injunctions against the union. For many years employers had used individual employment (yellow dog) contracts which forbade employees to join unions. But the courts did not consider these valid contracts meriting injunctive relief against third parties (unions) interfering with the contractual relationship between owners and employees. In 1907 the Hitchman Coal & Coke Company challenged this prevailing legal interpretation. It sought an injunction against the United Mine Workers, arguing that its individual employment contract merited injunctive relief. A sympathetic federal district court judge accepted Hitchman's interpretation and issued the injunction.

Although the Supreme Court upheld the *Hitchman* injunction in 1917, government policy during the First World War temporarily prevented other operators from using the *Hitchman* contracts to stop the UMW from organizing their mines. But after the war, 316 operators in southern West Virginia won court protection for their individual employment contracts in the *Red Jacket* case. The *Red Jacket* injunction became the operators' wedge in their successful postwar drive to eliminate the UMW in West Virginia, and they thereby almost destroyed the national union as well.

But the adoption of *Hitchman* contracts does not wholly explain the operators' victory. The First World War also was a major factor. The war artificially expanded coal production, which led to the coal recession in the postwar years. When the recession hit, operators laid off miners and cut wages. The UMW tried to hold the line, but hungry men were eager to take the union miners' jobs at lower wages.

In addition, the First World War was the first "total war" in history; it mobilized the entire population and economy. In order to win the war, President Woodrow Wilson turned his back on reform and established a marriage of convenience with business. The federal government viewed strikes and criticism of the war, for whatever reason, as treasonous acts. The Justice Department arrested union organizers under dubious authority and the United States Army occupied strike zones in clear violation of the Constitution. The operators could not have been more pleased; the federal government was giving the *Hitchman* decision the kind of support, albeit indirect, that mattered. Apart from their impact on the labor struggle in West Virginia, these violations of citizens' rights constituted one of the major, tragic chapters in the history of civil liberties in America.

In 1920 the miners elected John L. Lewis president of the United Mine Workers of America. During the bleak decade of the 1920s, Lewis bided his time and concentrated on building a highly disciplined organization, ruthlessly purging subordinates who would not accept his leadership.

The decade ended with depression sweeping the nation. The Depression radically changed the political climate. A nationwide anti-injunction movement prodded Congress into passing the Norris-LaGuardia Act in 1932, which declared that individual employment contracts could not be enforced by the courts. The next year Congress passed the National Industrial Recovery Act, which guaranteed the right of employees to bargain collectively. Immediately after the NIRA became law in June, 1933, John L. Lewis sent organizers into the bituminous coal fields of West Virginia and other Appalachian states. By September, 1933, the Mine Workers had signed the first Appalachian agreement with bituminous operators.

The history of the miners' struggle for unionization in West Virginia involved many individuals — among them labor leaders, coal operators, sheriffs, intellectuals, judges, legislators, governors, army officers, attorney generals, and presidents. Much of the history will be told here by the participants in their own words. Original spelling has been retained unless confusing. Occasionally editorial changes have been made to achieve clarity, such as rearranging the sequence of quoted passages and changing verb tenses. The usual editorial indications — *sic*, brackets, and ellipses — generally have been omitted.

Chapter One

ORGANIZE

"To Hell with Judge Dayton"

After the Nick Heil baseball team had finished playing the first game of a double header at the Heil grounds Sunday afternoon, Thomas Hughes, state organizer of the United Mine Workers of America, delivered an address about the conditions existing at the Hitchman mines. The address was ably rendered and he was loudly applauded by the assembled fans. For three weeks past Hughes has been organizing the men and it is stated that he is meeting with deserved success. [*The Wheeling Intelligencer*, October 8, 1907.]

The United Mine Workers (UMW) had been trying to organize the Hitchman mines since an unsuccessful strike in the spring of 1906. Two weeks after Hughes's appearance at the baseball game, on October 23, 1907, Judge Alston G. Dayton issued a temporary restraining order to prevent the UMW from organizing the Hitchman Coal and Coke Company mines. The mines were located near Wheeling in the northern panhandle of West Virginia. The restraining order enjoined peaceful persuasion, including talking to the miners in their homes or on the streets. The order immediately attracted ·the interest of other West Virginia coal operators, for it could very well be the weapon they needed to block the Mine Workers' plan of organizing all the miners in West Virginia. But litigation progressed slowly. Dayton did not enter his final decree until January 18, 1913, at which time he granted the Hitchman Company a perpetual injunction.[1]

President Theodore Roosevelt had appointed Dayton to the United States Circuit Court (later District Court) for northern West Virginia in 1905. The appointment was Dayton's reward for supporting the president's big navy program in the Naval Affairs Committee in the House of Representatives. Dayton was a man of strong feelings. A prohibitionist, he once instructed a grand jury investigating liquor excise tax evasion:

> No honest, upright man, with the fear of God in his heart, would engage in the liquor business, knowing that it makes your boys sots and gutter grovelers, and prostitutes out of your daughters.

In a white-slave case Dayton became so anxious to jail the accused procurer that he denied defense counsel a one-day continuance to locate witnesses. The circuit court of appeals remanded the case to him for retrial.[2]

The Hitchman trial was a burden to Dayton:

> From the start it was very well understood between counsel and the court, that the issues presented were very important, if not new, and that the case would be a test one of the right and obligations of this Labor Organization, and the record would be most carefully made up in full expectation that it would be finally passed upon by the Supreme Court. I took in open court all the evidence; and upon a record of more than 8000 pages, with briefs filed of many more hundred pages, after nearly a year of the hardest study I have ever subjected myself to — for the first time in my life I dropped on the street in a dead faint by reason of the mental strain — I rendered my judgment sustaining the bill and the injunction prayed for.[3]

Dayton found the UMW guilty of violating Hitchman's individual employment contracts, which required its men not to join a union. In Dayton's mind the preeminence of property rights in Anglo-American law supported this judgment. In addition, Dayton considered the United Mine Workers an unlawful organization per se because it was a monopoly in restraint of trade under common law and the Sherman Antitrust Act. It was clear from the evidence, wrote Dayton, that the Mine Workers attempted to destroy Hitchman's business through work stoppages, or strikes, in pursuing its goal of organizing all mine labor (i.e., monopolizing it):

> The UMW struck the Hitchman mines from April 16 to June 12, 1906, some 50 working days, at a loss estimated from $300 to $700 per day, and with then no promise of let-up before plaintiff's final ruin should be accomplished. What excuse is set up for so foul and injurious prostitution of this organization, claimed to be in existence for philanthropic and lawful purpose, to a conspiracy so glaringly designed to injure and destroy?
>
> Actuated by a natural sympathy for labor and an earnest desire to uplift and aid it, which we all have, many sincere, but misguided, persons would concede to it an estate superior to and above that possessed by other classes in this republic of liberty and equal rights.

While sufficient precedent existed for Dayton to reach his judgments, nevertheless they represented new steps in the development of the law.[4]

The circuit court of appeals unanimously overruled Dayton on May 28, 1914. Judge Jetter C. Pritchard wrote the decision. Hitchman's individual employment contract did not impress Pritchard. He pointed out that this contract was not really a contract at all, since Hitchman's employees could quit at will or be fired at will. As for Dayton's judgment that the UMW was a monopoly in restraint of trade under common law, Pritchard acknowledged that the common-law view of property rights in

1914 supported Dayton's judgment, but he argued that it was time for common law to change:

> The growth and development of the common law occurred when property rights were recognized as paramount to personal rights. At that time there was little, if any, concert of action on the part of the laboring people, owing to their helpless condition. Their domination by the landowner and capitalist was absolute in most respects, and as a result they were as helpless as those held in slavery before our great [Civil] war.[5]

Moreover, Pritchard did not believe that the UMW was a monopoly in restraint of trade under the Sherman Antitrust Act. Pritchard wrote that it was absurd for Dayton to argue that the UMW's goal of controlling the labor market in the coal industry also meant that it wished to destroy Hitchman's business. Dayton had relied on the Mine Workers' strike against Hitchman as proof of the union's malicious intent, but Pritchard countered with the argument that, logically, the union would not want to use its strike weapon to destroy Hitchman's business because that "would necessarily defeat the very object for which this organization was established, to wit, the procurement of steady employment at remunerative wages." Pritchard pointed out that without the power to strike the United Mine Workers would have no power at all:

> If Hitchman has a perfect right to refuse to employ union labor, is it not equally true that the UMW may by the employment of legitimate means, do that which is necessary to keep its forces together?
>
> If the courts of this country should by injunctive relief protect the mine owner in the enjoyment of his property rights, and restrain the laboring people from organizing their forces by declaring such organizations unlawful, would not the mine owner then be in a position to control the situation so that he who has to toil for his daily bread would be placed in a

position where if he exists at all, he must do so at such wages, and upon such terms as organized capital may see fit to dictate?[6]

Following the court of appeals' decision overturning Dayton's judgment, Hitchman petitioned the Supreme Court to hear the case. The Supreme Court was not to make its decision until 1917.

Until May, 1914, when the circuit court of appeals overruled Dayton's *Hitchman* injunction, the individual employment contract remained a legally valid one and the UMW an unlawful organization. The UMW's uncertain legal status accurately reflected its weak position in West Virginia.

[The UMW had attempted to unionize the West Virginia mine fields in 1902. But only in the Kanawha Field in southern West Virginia had the UMW obtained a contract for its men. By 1912 even this gain appeared threatened. On April 19, 1912, operators in the Paint Creek subdistrict of the Kanawha Field refused to renew their contract. The Paint Creek miners went out on strike. A few of the operators sought court injunctions to prevent the UMW from organizing their mines. Undoubtedly more would have done so if Dayton's order on January 18, 1913, granting Hitchman a perpetual injunction, had been entered prior to the Paint Creek strike. All of the operators hired Baldwin-Felts armed guards to evict striking miners from company houses. The miners retaliated by arming themselves and by erecting tent colonies near the mines. They also petitioned Governor William E. Glasscock to remove the Baldwin-Felts guards. Glasscock recalled the situation:

> They complained that their men were being beaten, that they were compelled to leave the territory and to do whatever the guards wanted them to do. They demanded that I get rid of them. I told them that under the law I had no authority to go up there and just take a man by the nape of the neck and say you get out of here.[7]

So the miners took the law into their own hands and fought back against the guards. No arrests were made on either side. The local law enforcement officials hesitated to interfere with either the operators' business practices or the miners' defensive reactions. In July, after two men had been killed, the sheriff asked Glasscock to order the National Guard into Paint Creek. Although Glasscock complied, at the same time he rebuked the sheriff for not arresting the wrongdoers. When the sheriff continued to procrastinate, Glasscock requested the Kanawha County Court to convene a special grand jury to indict the gunmen. The court never met.[8]

In marked contrast to his immediate predecessors, also Republicans, who had provided West Virginia with fifteen years of conservative government, Glasscock aspired to reform West Virginian government so as to meet better the wishes of miners and other workmen who, disillusioned, were turning from the Republican and Democratic parties to the Socialist party. In the 1912 election in Kanawha County, for instance, Socialist candidates for local offices received nearly one-third of the votes cast. In the same election Glasscock broke with the national Republican party and supported Theodore Roosevelt, the Progressive party candidate, for president.[9]

On August 3, 1912, the strike spread to neighboring Cabin Creek. The next day, Sunday, the UMW held a rally at the state capitol in Charleston. Six thousand miners and their supporters attended. The featured speaker was Mother (Mary) Jones, "the white-haired angel of the miners," who traveled across the country from one Mine Workers' strike to another. A miner who heard her speak in West Virginia said, "she could permeate a group of strikers with more fight than could any living human being." Mother harangued the throng:

> No church in this country could get up a crowd like this. Why? Because we are doing God's holy work; we are breaking the chains that bind you; we are putting the fear of God into the robbers. All the churches here and in heaven couldn't put

the fear of God into them, but our determination has made them tremble. I don't know who started the racket, but I know Mr. Operator began to shake; and the marrow in his back melted and he had to run into the cellar and hide.

Let me say to you, my friends, let me say to the governor, let me say to the sheriffs and judges in the state of West Virginia, this fight will not stop until the last damn guard is disarmed. Talk about a few guards getting bullets in their skulls, the whole damned lot of them ought to get bullets in their skulls.[10]

Glasscock attempted to mediate the dispute, but the operators refused to cooperate for fear of giving tacit recognition to the UMW. Meanwhile violence continued. The local sheriff would not arrest offenders, and the National Guard legally could not arrest them without a declaration of martial law. Believing he had no other recourse, Glasscock declared martial law on September 2, 1912. The militia arrested miners who had committed criminal acts and tried them before a military court. The militia also rounded up all the mine guards and ordered them out of the strike zone, causing operators to complain bitterly about Glasscock equating the actions of their mine guards with those of the miners. The National Guard quickly ended the violence.[11]

With the mine guards removed Glasscock again tried to mediate the dispute. He pleaded with the operators to reconsider their position:

Unfortunately we have no law in West Virginia that authorizes the appointment of a board of arbitration. But there is nothing in the law of our land that prevents a man from being a patriot, and to refuse to try to make some agreement that will save life and property can not be justified, in my opinion, by either law or good morals. If you are not willing to meet the representatives of the United Mine Workers of America, whom will you meet and what plan have you to propose to settle our present troubles?

To which the operators replied:

The present trouble was brought on by persons outside our employ for the purpose of compelling "recognition" of the UMW. As is its custom, the UMW will accept nothing but an unconditional surrender to its demand. We submit we can not be accused of lacking in patriotism or good citizenship if we decline to surrender to the UMW, on the ground that if we do not its adherents will endeavor to destroy our property and kill or cripple our employees who are willing and anxious to work. We stand for law and order; the UMW does not. That organization has virtually invaded the State of West Virginia and is carrying on war therein; and it should be taught that such methods will not be tolerated.[12]

Glasscock tried another, more indirect, approach at ending the strike. He arranged for a state-wide industrial conference made up of representatives of boards of trade, civic organizations, and labor organization. Its intention was to propose broad-ranging solutions to labor-capital disputes. On September 2, 1912, five hundred representatives met in the West Virginia House of Delegates in Charleston. Before any business was discussed, the coal operators' representatives took the floor and announced they would withdraw from the conference if representatives discussed recognition of the UMW or if anyone (meaning UMW president John P. White) was allowed to participate who was not a citizen of the state. The coal operators' threat destroyed Glasscock's conference. Within the hour it adjourned.[13]

In August, over operators' objections, Glasscock had appointed a Mining Investigation Commission to determine the facts about the cause of the strike, the practices of the mine guards, and working conditions. The commission held public hearings in September and October and issued its report in November. It gave comfort to both sides. It accepted the operators' contention that the main cause of the strike was the UMW's effort to organize West Virginia's mines and that successful organization would put West Virginia's operators in a disadvantageous economic position, since the operators in the organized four competitive states were closer to the major coal markets. The commission also agreed with the miners that they had a right to organize and suggested that the district union meet in convention with West Virginia's operators and agree on a wage scale and conditions of employment "wholly independent of dictation from, or interference by, operators of competitive states or other outside influences." At first glance this recommendation appears naïve, considering that it ignored the miners' reliance on industry-wide agreements to prevent competitive undercutting of wages. Nonetheless, it represented a realistic compromise, for it was to move the miners one important step toward their ultimate goal of organizing the entire industry without at the same time imposing "unconditional surrender" on the operators. The commission also condemned the operators' use of guards as "vicious" and asked the legislature to outlaw it. In addition, the commission called for a workmen's compensation act and a law similar to the Canada Industrial Dispute Act of 1907, which did not deny the right to strike or lockout but did require public hearings on labor disputes and good-faith labor-capital negotiations before a strike or lockout could be called.[14]

Since his imposition of martial law had effectively restored order, Glasscock lifted martial law in mid-October. Simultaneously the operators started to bring in "transportation," an euphemism for strikebreakers. One supplier for the Cabin Creek Coal Association was George Williams, a "production and industrial engineer," in New York City. He advertised in *The New York World* for workers:

> Miners and laborers for coal mine — blacksmiths, track layers, drum runners, motor runners, trappers, greasers, slate men, tipple boys, mule drivers, tipple bosses, and men. Good steady job all the year around; family men of all nationalities preferred. Transportation furnished; long contract; also strong men used to pick work can make $6 per day. Strike on.

Homes all furnished. All the coal you want. Apply early. Call Mr. Williams, 458 West Broadway.

Williams explained his company's function:

We are not strike-breaking agents. We are fighting them on scientific methods, by using sociological facts. We understand labor is nothing but a commodity, and it is governed, not by trades organizations, but by supply and demand. I know this much, that if labor is in demand, union or not union, you are going to get good prices. If it is not in demand, union or not union, you are going to get lower prices. In the wintertime I can get a half a million men for any kind of work — strikes or any kind — because outside work is closed and people are starving in the big towns.[15]

Williams, and other suppliers, shipped "transportation" into Cabin and Paint creeks in special trains. When the striking miners met the trains and tried to turn the "transportation" back, violence erupted. The operators appealed to Glasscock for protection. Glasscock would not permit Baldwin Felts guards to return, but he did allow the operators to hire "watchmen" whom the National Guard had cleared. Most of the watchmen, it turned out, were militiamen who had been on duty in the strike zone. They easily shifted their allegiance to their new employers, serving them as loyally as they had the state. Violence continued until November 15, when Glasscock reimposed martial law. On December 11, Glasscock lifted martial law again. The pattern of events repeated itself, and Glasscock imposed martial law for a third time on February 10, 1913. Several incidents led to this third imposition. One of them involved operators who ran an armored train called the "Bull-Moose Special" into the miners' tent colony at Holly Grove. The train was equipped with iron-plate siding and machineguns manned by guards who fired away at the miners' tents, killing one person and wounding one other. The miners retaliated by attacking mine guards at Mucklow. The result was sixteen more dead on both sides. During the third period of martial law Glasscock arrested eighty persons, including Mother Jones who had urged the striking miners to defy "Crystalcock's militia."[16]

During January and February, 1913, Glasscock tried to push his industrial reform program through the state legislature. The legislature defeated two of his proposals, one of which would have provided for an arbitration board in labor-capital disputes and the other of which would have outlawed improper lobbying practices. His third proposal would have outlawed the mine guard system, but the legislature only went so far as to remove legal support for it. Under the act operators could still hire watchmen, but these watchmen no longer possessed authority to arrest offenders. Glasscock's fourth proposal provided for workmen's compensation for injuries sustained on the job, and it passed without serious modification.[17]

Henry D. Hatfield succeeded Glasscock as governor on March 4, 1913. A surgeon, he had founded West Virginia's first miners' hospital in 1899 and continued as its director for twelve years. Meanwhile he entered Republican politics. In 1911, he was elected president of the state senate. His fairness and effectiveness as presiding officer led his party to nominate him for governor in 1912.

Hatfield believed in extending democracy. He endorsed adoption of the state referendum and advocated women's suffrage. He held the major political parties responsible for the nation's industrial unrest because they had failed to pass reform laws the people expected:

> The great tendency of the American people now is more toward constructive socialism than ever before. Public opinion is the mind and the conscience of the whole nation, and the parties and their representatives, to a great extent, have not kept inviolate the promise made by them. The unrest that exists today is directly traceable to this fact.[18]

Two weeks after his inauguration Hatfield inspected the strike zone. "No one will be mistreated," he told the operators and striking miners. "Everyone will get a fair and square deal. But, my friends, there must be law and order." Two days after his inspection he released twenty-five of the eighty prisoners detained under martial law. "To my mind it is infinitely more important that peace be restored and law and order permanently established than that past offenders be punished."[19]

Since the strike zone had become relatively peaceful, Hatfield could have given up the authority of martial law, but he chose not to. He believed, in part, and the state supreme court of appeals agreed, that he needed his authority in order to end the "insurrection." Violence had persisted for nearly a year, and only during the three periods of martial law had peace been regained. Hatfield also believed that more than suppression of violence was needed. He perceived that peace had been maintained under martial law because the operators had been denied the coercive power of either Baldwin-Felts mine guards or privately hired watchmen to break the strike, so he concluded that lasting peace would be achieved only if he removed the operators' coercive power. And the only way he could accomplish this was to continue martial law until the operators agreed to settle their dispute with the striking miners.

Hatfield did not formulate this strategy consciously. But his actions and his public statements indicated that this was indeed his strategy:

> The mine guard system must be changed. No one doubts the right of a man to protect his property, but at the same time, there are the rights of man, which must be guarded and protected so that oppression will not be the cruel barrier which the laboring man is brought to face. Radical changes must be made in order that oppression may be eliminated and equal rights given to all.

The executive committee of the Socialist Party of America sent its president, Eugene V. Debs, and two other representatives to West Virginia to make an on-the-scene inspection. The committee came away persuaded that Hatfield was committed to winning unionization for the miners. However, local Socialists denounced the report of the Debs committee. The editor of the *Huntington Socialist and Labor Star*, Wyatt H. Thompson, charged that the report was a "weak mass of misstatements" and "a sickening eulogy of dictator Hatfield." The West Virginia Socialists were convinced that Debs had betrayed them. The striking miners, too, initially complained about Hatfield's actions — especially his retention of martial law after his inauguration, since most of the people the militia had arrested in the past were strikers and their supporters. But later, after discovering that under Hatfield's implementation of martial law they could freely campaign for their organization, the miners endorsed it.[20]

In April, Hatfield began pressuring the operators and the Mine Workers to reach a settlement. The operators would not budge from their position that to negotiate with the UMW would amount to granting it recognition, which they were not prepared to do. Furthermore, they argued, that since the UMW was an illegal organization — they cited Dayton's *Hitchman* decision of January 18, 1913, to support this assertion — they were absolved of any responsibility for meeting with it. Hatfield replied that "the case of the *Hitchman Coal & Coke Company vs. John Mitchell and others* tried by Judge Dayton furnishes some interesting information that it is claimed would tend to bear out the statements made by the operators." Thereafter Hatfield ignored the argument of the operators, emphasizing that "industry owners cannot do without the services of the laboring man, nor can the laboring man exist without the employer." He concluded that the laboring man does have a right "to meet and discuss conditions and organize into an association or union for his welfare and protection."[21]

The operators' refusal to negotiate directly with the United Mine Workers forced Hatfield into the role of mediator. The UMW leaders had informed Hatfield that they were prepared to settle the strike without insisting on recognition of the union, provided "there be no discrimination against mine workers for joining the UMW" and that a commission be selected to arbitrate disputes between the miners and the operators. When the operators refused to accept these conditions, Hatfield offered a compromise which amended the statement that "there be no discrimination against mine workers for joining the UMW" by deleting the phrase "for joining the UMW," and replaced the arbitration commission with his promise "to use all the means at my command to see that each and every proposition so acceded to is carried out in its fullness."[22]

The operators accepted Hatfield's compromise, which included, in addition, less controversial concessions to the miners of a nine-hour day, the right of the miners to hire their own check weighman, and a semimonthly pay day. In convention, the rank-and-file miners rejected the compromise negotiated by their leaders. Hatfield went to the convention to plead for acceptance. He conceded that he had not been able to gain union recognition, but he argued it was beyond his "power to dictate to the owners of industries whom they shall employ, and upon what terms." He then proceeded to dictate to *them*, threatening miners who did not accept this agreement and who continued to violate the peace, with prosecution under martial law. To prove his intent, he allowed the National Guard to search, without a warrant, the office of *The Labor Argus*, a socialist newspaper that opposed Hatfield's compromise.[23]

The miners capitulated. But they unilaterally interpreted the key clause that "no discrimination [shall] be made against any miner" to mean no discrimination against UMW members. The Hatfield Agreement, as it was called, went into effect May 1, 1913. Hatfield inspected the strike zone to see if the parties were adhering to its provisions. He found that the striking miners were willing to go back to work and that in most instances the operators were rehiring them. On June 12, 1913, Hatfield lifted martial law.[24]

After the strike settlement there still remained 150 members of the UMW whom the operators refused to rehire, claiming they were "ringleaders in the recent rioting." This angered radicals in the union, and they persuaded the membership to go out on strike despite the pleas of the district president and the international board representative. Hatfield resumed negotiations with the operators and the United Mine Workers. On August 1, 1913, he obtained a permanent settlement granting the miners the explicit right to join the UMW without discrimination. The settlement also guaranteed union members the right to hold their meetings on company property and provided for the appointment of a board of arbitration to settle future labor disputes. Two operators granted, in addition, full recognition to the UMW, including the checkoff under which the operators deducted union dues from the miners' wages.[25]

In the spring of 1913, UMW organizers also began to move into the neighboring New River field. The New River operators filed an injunction suit modeled on Dayton's *Hitchman* injunction in the Fayette County Circuit Court. Their intention, should it prove necessary, was to initiate contempt of court action against the union. When the UMW called for a strike on July 1, 1913, Hatfield pleaded successfully for a postponement, giving him time to negotiate an agreement between the union and the New River operators which provided for no discrimination against miners who joined the union. It is not known why the New River operators did not go ahead and initiate contempt of court actions against the mine workers instead of negotiating an agreement. Most likely they decided that Hatfield, who controlled the state militia, would not enforce a court order in such a way as to break the strike.[26]

After the Paint and Cabin creek settlement of August 1, 1913, UMW representatives began to organize UMW local unions throughout the Paint and Cabin creek valleys. The following spring the miners in the remainder of the Kanawha Field, which the mine workers had organized back in 1902, struck for and won the checkoff. By the summer of 1914, there were over 16,000 union miners in West Virginia. In addition, mine guards had completely disappeared from the Kanawha Valley and its tributaries south of Charleston. D. C. Kennedy, of the Kanawha

Operators Association, commented:

> There was no longer any necessity for mine guards. When that
> contract was made, it took away the question for which the
> miners were fighting: that was, organization. Whenever you
> establish that there is not anything to fight for.[27]

The operators regrouped for hopefully another round in the
struggle. In September, 1913, they formed the Coal Operators
Protective Association and pledged $1,000,000 to protect their
coal properties against "the Socialists, otherwise known as the
United Mine Workers of America."[28]

What Hatfield really had done was to use the authority of
martial law to achieve a labor settlement in conformity to what he
thought the law on property rights should be and in defiance of
the intent of Dayton's *Hitchman* decision. The fact that Dayton
had not issued Hatfield a court order removes an admittedly
crucial element. But it still does not diminish the importance of
Hatfield's action. Any legal system is very much open-ended. In
their decisions judges state what the law is; and if the executive
branch chooses to implement these decisions, the law is enforced.
Hatfield chose to ignore the intent of the *Hitchman* decision and
brought about peaceful change. Thomas Haggerty of the
international board of the UMW, who was directly involved in
the events, appreciated the significance of Hatfield's actions. He
concluded that Hatfield had done "the very best an able, honest,
strong man can do to correct wrong." The circuit court of appeals
decision overruling Dayton came after the Paint and Cabin creek
settlement. It chose not to undo what Hatfield had accomplished.[29]

Most contemporary observers were struck not by Hatfield's
use of martial law to disarm the operators but his, and especially
his predecessor's, use of martial law to punish striking miners.
Their concern focused on the trial of civilians by the military
commission in violation of the state constitution, which declared
in article 1, section 3, that "the provisions of the Constitution of

the United States and of this State are operative alike in a period of war as in time of peace." Glasscock and Hatfield had ignored article 1, section 3 because they believed that their proclamations of martial law automatically suspended the state constitution. The state supreme court of appeals upheld their position, ruling that the governor's actions under martial law were not reviewable by the courts. In particular, the Supreme Court held that the trial of civilians by military commission, or punitive martial law, was justifiable even when the civil courts were open. The Supreme Court noted that the civil courts were not functioning properly. Justice Ira E. Robinson did not agree with the majority and dissented, stating that only qualified martial law, in which civil courts continue to try offenders, was justified in the existing circumstances. Several official bodies joined Robinson in criticizing the governors' use of punitive martial law, the most influential of which was the United States Senate subcommittee of the Committee on Education and Labor.[30]

Hatfield had succeeded in bringing about peaceful change because a consensus had emerged for the establishment of new rules within which the warring industrial parties had to confine their struggle — specifically, that there should be no discrimination by operators against miners who wished to join the UMW and that the operators should not use force to prevent organization of their mines. This consensus developed partly in response to the chronic pattern of labor violence in West Virginia, and partly in response to emerging political pressures on behalf of reform. There were many individuals besides Hatfield who defied and subverted the intent of Dayton's injunction.

Glasscock's and Hatfield's detention of Mother Jones had backfired, making her into a vociferous martyr. With the assistance of sympathetic guards, she communicated her plight and the miners' cause to allies in the outside world. She signaled to the guards by clinking beer bottles together. One of the guards would crawl under the floor to a hole covered by a rug, pick up her messages, crawl back, and then smuggle them out to the recipients. One of her messages went to Senator John W. Kearns, a friend of the UMW, asking him to sponsor a Senate investigation of the West Virginia strike. He agreed. *The Masses Magazine* supported her request for a Senate investigation and called a mass meeting at Carnegie Hall in New York City to publicize it:

> NOW THEREFORE, it is UNANIMOUSLY RESOLVED by this large and representative assemblage gathered together to honor "Mother" Mary Jones at Carnegie Hall, New York City, May 25, 1913, under the auspices of THE MASSES MAGAZINE, and mostly composed of members of the following organizations, parties, trades and industires, to wit: The New York Socialist Party; the Central Federated Union, representing the Garment Workers, Painters, Carpenters, Typographical workers, and all other trades; The Womens' Trade Union; the Young Peoples' Socialist Federation; the New York Daily "Call"; the Jewish Daily Forward; the Volkszeitung; The Masses Magazine; the Woman Voter, and others,
>
> First: That the President of the United States be, and he is hereby requested, to take immediately whatever steps may lie in his power and influence to further and advance the purpose of the resolution introduced into the Unted States Senate by the Hon. John W. Kearns, Senator from Indiana, calling for a comprehensive and fearless investigation of the strike conditions in West Virginia;
>
> Second: That the said resolution has the hearty endorsement of this assembly, consisting of more than 5,000 representative citizens, who demand, in the name of humanity and liberty, the immediate carrying out of the purpose of the said resolution.[31]

The operators opposed the investigation, claiming it would ignite new disorders. In contrast, Hatfield said he would be "delighted" to have a Senate investigation. The operators lost out to national public opinion, and on June 10, 1913, a subcommittee of the Committee on Education and Labor came to West Virginia to hold hearings. Its report blamed the violence on the refusal of the operators to recognize the miners' union and on the equally strong determination of the miners to organize the mines. The subcommittee avoided taking a position on Dayton's *Hitchman* decision, since it had been appealed. Two of the five senators on the subcommittee, in separate reports, suggested government ownership of the mines in order to solve permanently the labor-capital conflict. As discussed above, the report also criticized the appointment of a military commission to try civilians.[32]

The operators in West Virginia depended on immigrant labor from Europe and migrant labor from within the United States to man their mines and to undercut the UMW. In 1911, the federal Bureau of Immigration unofficially adopted a policy of steering immigrants away from West Virginia because the coal fields were predominately open-shop, although officially the bureau reported that the unsafe conditions of West Virginia's mines had led it to adopt this policy. As a result, in 1912, only one-half of 1 percent of the experienced European miners came to West Virginia. The operators complained, but they were unable to change the policy.[33]

The Justice Department, of all the federal agencies, gave the miners the most immediate help. In his *Hitchman* decision, Dayton had ruled that the UMW was monopoly in restraint of trade to control labor in the coal industry under the Sherman Antitrust Act — "an express conspiracy under contract with coal operators in Ohio, Illinois and Western Pennsylvania to suppress and destroy the mining of coal in West Virginia." On June 7, 1913, the day before the Senate Education and Labor subcommittee came to West Virginia to begin its hearings, a United States grand jury in Charleston, West Virginia, returned an indictment against John P. White, president of the UMW, and eighteen other officials of the international union and local

District No. 17 for conspiracy to restrain trade in the Paint Creek and Cabin Creek strikes. Under the Sherman Antitrust Act only the federal government, not private corporations, could initiate suits against alleged violators.[34]

The indictment had political ramifications beyond West Virginia. Congress was then debating the Sundry Civil Appropriations bill, which included a provision that Justice Department funds could not be used to prosecute labor unions for violating the Sherman Antitrust Act. While President Woodrow Wilson did not desire to prosecute labor unions for restraint of trade, nonetheless they still remained eligible for prosecution as the courts had interpreted the act, and Wilson did not want to go on record as unwilling to enforce the law. Therefore, he had opposed the limiting provision.[35].

Attorney General J. C. McReynolds annouced that he was taken completely by surprise by the West Virginia grand jury indictment, and that he had not ordered it. He assured a disturbed senator: "You need have no apprehension that this Deparment will feel constrained to take the position that a labor union, the object of which is to better conditions and advance wages, is in and of itself a violation of the anti-trust law." He demanded an explanation from the United States attorney in Charleston, accusing him of violating a directive requiring Washington's approval before prosecuting under the Sherman Antitrust Act. The United States attorney lamely replied that he had "forgotten" the directive. A Justice Department informant provided a more reasonable explanation. He reported that the law firm representing the operators had prepared the indictment and compelled the United States attorney to present it to the grand jury.[36]

On instructions from Washington, the United States attorney continued the case, and a year later a newly appointed United States attorney withdrew the indictment, stating that the government possessed insufficient evidence to prove its case. The new United States attorney explained the government's position:

Even if there were a technical violation of the Sherman Anti-Trust Act, I think this indictment should be nullied, because the troubles mentioned occured in 1912-1913, involving a strike and other serious difficulties between the miners and operators of the Kanawha Valley, and these matters have been settled. A prosecution, therefore, even in case of a technical violation, would serve no useful purpose; but, on the contrary, would only engender strife and bad feeling.[37]

The Justice Department dealt operators another blow. In May, 1913, miners accused the operators on Paint and Cabin creeks of peonage, and the Justice Department ordered its agents to investigate the accusation. While they found no evidence of peonage in Paint and Cabin creeks, they did find evidence of it in neighboring Mercer County and indicted a mine superintendent and two mine guards.[38]

Events finally brought Dayton into direct confrontation with union miners. The confrontation grew out of an attempt by the Mine Workers during 1913-14 to organize the West Virginia-Pittsburgh Company mine at Colliers, located in the panhandle of West Virginia not too distant from the Hitchman operation. The West Virginia-Pittsburgh Coal Company had unilaterally repudiated its contract with the Mine Workers four years earlier. On September 4, 1913, Van Bittner, president of District No. 5 of the UMW, met with the manager of the Colliers mine and asked for recognition of the union. The manager replied that the company had individual employment contracts with its employees which prohibited them from joining the UMW. Bittner countered that, if necessary, the UMW would call a strike at the mine to support its demand.[39]

Ten days later the UMW struck the mine. James Oates, a Mine Workers organizer, arrived with a thirty-five-member brass band. Joined by 124 UMW members and sympathizers, the troop marched to the mine, stopping just short of the company's property, and held the first meeting of the Collier's local union. Oates rented a one-eighth acre of land (surrounded on two sides by company property) from Meyer Schwartz, who owned a store adjacent to the mine. Then Oates erected two tents and placed over them a large sign, reading HEADQUARTERS OF THE UNITED MINE WORKERS OF AMERICA. Fannie Sullens, a woman organizer in the garment trades in St. Louis, joined Oates: "My job was to distribute clothing and food to starving women and babies, to assist poverty striken mothers and bring children into the world, and to minister to the sick and close the eyes of the dying." On the morning of October 6, 1913, fifty strikers marched to the mine pit mouth. Harry Lucas, a mine guard, ordered them to leave. They refused, and instead exchanged threats and gunshots with him. Lucas received three bullet wounds. The sheriff arrested several strikers and detained them in jail.[40]

A week earlier, on September 29, 1913, the West Virginia-Pittsburgh Coal Company had obtained from Dayton, without notice to the UMW, a temporary restraining order preventing the union from organizing its mine. Dayton's order repeated nearly word for word his *Hitchman* injunction, prohibiting all peaceful attempts to persuade employees of the company to join the UMW. Dayton only added to the Colliers restraining order a prohibition against violence.[41]

In keeping with the procedural rule requiring argument within ten days of the restraining order, Dayton scheduled a hearing for October 9, 1913. Requests by counsels on both sides led to delays until December 1, at which time Dayton granted the company a temporary injunction, to replace the restraining order. The Mine Workers appealed the temporary injunction.

The company also petitioned for a contempt of court ruling against eleven defendants, including Oates and Sullens, for violating the restraining order. Dayton obliged the company and more, ordering the contempt ruling transferred to the law side — instead of remaining a civil proceeding between the company and the union, disobedience of the court order would now become a crime against the United States, with implications for surer punishment. After transferring the contempt ruling to the law side, Dayton found the defendants guilty of violating his restraining order. He explained that his decision was based on his earlier *Hitchman* judgment, in which he had determined that the Mine Workers was an "unlawful organization" and "that until the higher court determined otherwise it was unlawful for them to try to unionize these mines."[42]

Dayton sentenced the eleven defendants on December 1 to up to sixty days in jail, with the length of the sentence of each depending on his or her particular contempt action. He also chastised Fannie Sullens, warning her not to emulate Mother Jones. As for UMW president John P. White, who was not present, Dayton exlaimed, "If I only had John P. White here I would give him a year in jail." After sentencing the defendants, he offered to pardon them if they would promise henceforth to obey his injunction. Through their attorney they agreed.[43]

Two days after Dayton pardoned them, the convicted organizers and strikers attended a Mine Workers rally in Wellsburg, a short distance from Colliers. *The Wheeling Majority,* a labor newspaper, reported the event:

> A magnificent mass meeting in Wellsburg Wednesday afternoon proved the solidarity of the striking miners and also proved the sympathy of the people of Wellsburg and Follansbee is on the side of the brave strikers and their families.
>
> No arrests were made, although it was freely predicted that the meeting, which was held in the Barth Opera House, would be construed a violation of the injunction granted the company against the United Mine Workers by Judge Dayton and that those participating in the meeting would be jailed.
>
> The advice of the attorney was to the effect that none of the organizers, or of those who had been cited for contempt of court should speak, and although the strikers and their leaders felt in their hearts that the injunction was so palpably unjust and unreasonable and so subversive of all human rights that it should be ignored, they submitted to the advice of the attorney, and it was agreed that Walter B. Hilton, editor of *The*

Wheeling Majority, being neither a United Mine Worker, a "foreign" citizen, or in contempt of this particular case in court, should speak. He made "a few remarks." ...

Immediately afterward Fannie Sullens took the platform. The chairman had, in accordance with the advice of the attorney, declined to introduce her, but she said that she had talked from platforms all over the country, and that she refused to recognize Judge Dayton's right to deny her what the constitution of the United States already granted her. "I am free and I have a right to walk or talk any place in this country as long as I obey the law. I have done nothing wrong. The only wrong that they can say I have done is to take shoes to the little children in Colliers who needed shoes. And when I think of their little bare feet, blue with the cruel blasts of winter, it makes me determined that if it be wrong to put shoes upon those little feet, then I will continue to do wrong as long as I have hands and feet to crawl to Colliers."

Tony Amicone, who had been sitting down in the audience, was so fired by the thought of the wrongs of the miners by this time that he, too, could not restrain from leaping to the platform and giving vent to his feelings. "It is like the old story of the mice and the cats," he said, and he told the story of the mice that held a convention and decided, for their protection, to put a bell upon the cat so that they could hear her approaching, and how the scheme was thought good until no mouse could be found who would put the bell upon the cat. His point was that if the cat of capitalism had to be belled, and if it required the sacrifice of some of the workers to protect the others, then it was time that some should go to jail to do it. "And another thing," he shouted, "have they enough jails to put all the workers in?" He concluded by talking also in Italian.

Frank Ledvinski, a National organizer of the United Mine Workers, then so far forgot his coolness and self possession as to climb upon the stage and make a speech. He spoke in most "incendiary" language, language that would unquestionably be held in a capitalist court to be inciting to riot and to the violation of "sacred" contracts, for he said that the people had a right to even overthrow their own government if they saw fit. ...

> After Mr. Ledvinski had spoken in their own language to the
> Slavic and Polish, the audience was requested to turn out in a
> body that night and attend the revival service at the Tabernacle
> now being conducted in Wellsburg.

After the rally Oates erected three more tents on Schwartz's
property. And when the coal company tried to starve out the
strikers by denying them use of the only road into the area,
claiming it was a private right of way, the strikers hiked in and
waded across a creek to reach the tent colony.[44]

Dayton issued a second contempt of court ruling on January
17, 1914, against those who had not kept their promise to obey his
injunction. Dayton asked the United States attorney, Stewart W.
Walker, to appear at a hearing on January 27, 1914, to try the
accused. Dumbfounded, Walker wrote the Justice Department:
"I know nothing whatever about these contempt cases, as they
have grown out of some civil litigation. I do not deem it necessary
for me to appear on next Tuesday at Philippi in these hearings,
unless you so direct." The Justice Department replied that unless
Walker had been consulted regarding the institution of contempt
proceedings he should use his discretion about appearing. The
department added, "It is obviously not your duty to appear in
civil contempt proceedings in cases where the Government is not
a party. The Department sees no objection to your informing the
courts that you desire to be consulted before such proceedings
are instituted."[45]

Walker finally decided to send his assistant to the hearing. At
the hearing Meyer Schwartz, who had rented his land to Oates,
and Paul Scoric, a striker, were found in contempt of court and
sentenced to sixty days in jail. They appealed Dayton's decision
and obtained a release by posting a $1,000 bond. A hearing for the
other defendants was rescheduled for March 17, 1914.[46]

Shortly thereafter, the Ohio Valley Trades and Labor
Assembly of Wheeling began an impeachment campaign against
Dayton. The Trades Assembly had been an independent labor
organization, but in 1915 it affiliated with the American

Federation of Labor (AFL). The leading spokesman for the Trades Assembly was Walter B. Hilton, a Socialist and editor of the Trades Assembly newspaper, *The Wheeling Majority*. Hilton relished the fight with Dayton. Among other things, Dayton recently had issued an injunction, later overturned, against some of Hilton's labor activities.[47]

On February 8, 1914, before three thousand spectators in the Market Auditorium in Wheeling, the Trades Assembly "indicted" Dayton for "misuse of the power of injunction, and high crimes and misdemeanors against labor and the citizens of the State." Hilton addressed the throng:

> The laboring classes in this vicinity are going after Dayton in a manner which will brook no delay.
>
> We are not doing this because we want him to lose a certain job; but because we believe his decisions have been so prejudiced as to be contrary to the justice and fairness which we inhabitants of the land are justified in expecting.
>
> There is a higher law than the law of any statute book, or the opinion of any judge. That is the law of public opinion, the bar of public conscience, and they are amenable to it in all their acts as you and I must be also.[48]

Following Dayton's "indictment" Hilton and a committee traveled to Washington to deliver President Woodrow Wilson a petition, signed by six thousand persons, asking to investigate Judge Dayton's conduct. Wilson sent the petition to the House of Representatives for consideration of possible impeachment proceedings against Dayton.[49]

Meanwhile, the West Virginia-Pittsburgh Coal Company had hired strikebreakers from Kentucky. Tension mounted. On February 13, 1914, Harry Lucas, the mine guard whom the strikers had wounded on October 6, 1913, shot and killed James Moore, a striker. The coroner's jury ruled that Lucas had killed Moore in self-defense. Because the hearing had been held in the West Virginia-Pittsburgh Coal Company office and union representatives had not been permitted to attend, the strikers disputed the jury's finding. James Oates and Fannie Sullens carried Moore's coffin to Wellsburg and paraded it through the streets. Overhead the strikers carried banners:

THIS MAN ASSASSINATED AT COLLIERS

ANOTHER YOUNG LIFE SACRIFICED
FOR THE CORPORATION CREED

OUR BROTHER MURDERED BY THE HIRED THUGS
BUT NOT FORGOTTEN BY US[50]

On March 17, 1914, James Oates and Fannie Sullens, along with other defendants whose contempt hearing had been rescheduled from January, appeared in Dayton's court in Philippi. Only at this time did Dayton inform them of the specific charges against them. Two of the defendants could not understand or speak English, and Dayton denied their requests for interpreters. The lawyer for the company added insult to injury by telling the immigrant defendants that they should "go back to the old country" if they didn't like the wages here. At the emotional climax to the hearing, Dayton cried out from the bench: "I will not permit the United Mine Workers of America to exist within my jurisdiction as I consider their organization a criminal conspiracy!" He found the defendants guilty and released them on bond until sentencing on April 17, 1914.[51]

One of Dayton's objectives in the contempt hearing was to force removal of the tent colony from Schwartz's land:

At times processions of from 100 to 150 men were led to and gathered in these tents. One was led by an associate of Hilton's who went there with his body of men on Sunday, as he said, to "hold prayer meeting," while some of the men in it in profanation and ribaldry sang "Nearer My God To Thee," the others sang, "Hail, Hail, the Gang's All Here." Fights, shooting, drunkenness, profanity, and the grossest obscenity constantly prevailed in and around these tents, while the most wanton and degrading exposure of the person by their habitués

was common before the women and school children of the
Company's employees only a short distance away, the tents
being erected within three feet of the Company's ground.

Dayton won from defense counsel a promise to remove the tents.
Exactly what the defense counsel promised is unclear. At any
rate, on March 25,1914, the United States marshal, assisted by
Harry Lucas and another company employee deputized for the
occasion, tore down the tents and burned the wooden shacks. The
strikers moved to another location, understood by defense
counsel as beyond Dayton's prohibited zone, and pitched their
tents. The marshal and his deputies drove them from this
location, too. Later that same evening some of the strikers
returned. Thereafter the Mine Workers maintained at least a
symbolic force on the new site, although the marshall continually
threatened eviction.[52]

Frustrated by the strikers' persistence, the United States
marshal asked the Justice Department for the authority to
employ enough deputies to control the wholesale violations of
Dayton's injunction. Attorney General McReynolds replied that
the alleged facts should be submitted to the United States
attorney, who would consult with the courts and then wire his
and the court's joint recommendation. McReynold's cool
reception apparently killed the request. Newspapers also
reported speculation from court officials close to Dayton that he
wanted the Justice Department to bring in army troops and
instigate deportation proceedings against alien strikers who
repeatedly violated his injunction. Nothing came of these
proposals either.[53]

On April 14, 1914, a crowd of union miners gathered at the
West Virginia-Pittsburgh Company mine and began to abuse
strikebreakers. When a company official warned the union
miners that any action against the strikebreakers was prohibited
by Dayton's injunction, a striker replied: "To Hell with Judge
Dayton. He can't do anything with us. Let the old ———— put
us in jail if he wants to. The union will take us out." Soon union

miners and strikebreakers were brawling. The union miners were victorious, driving the strikebreakers from the mine all the way to the Colliers railroad depot. The next day, April 15, 1914, the United States marshal, again accompanied by Harry Lucas, arrested nine ringleaders who allegedly had instigated the melee.[54]

Dayton gave the newly arrested men a quick hearing on April 17, and sentenced them along with James Oates, Fannie Sullens, and the others who had been convicted in March. In all, Dayton sentenced nineteen strikers and organizers to jail. He gave the leaders six-month sentences and the others sentences ranging from one to five months. Dayton set bail bond at $500 per month. The UMW had already spent $10,000 on this contempt case, and it was not able to collect enough cash to post bond for its convicted members until July.[55]

After arriving in prison, James Oates, Fannie Sullens, and a few of their associates applied for a presidential pardon. When their application reached the Justice Department, the pardon attorney followed normal clemency procedure in contempt cases and wrote Dayton, as the trial judge, for his approval. Dayton refused, and in a long letter in which he reviewed the history of the *Hitchman* case, the Paint and Cabin creeks strikes, and the Colliers strike he explained why:

> A sense of duty compels me to say that I cannot recommend the granting of such pardons. An examination of the two published opinions that I have rendered in the case of the Hitchman Coal Company v. John Mitchell, et al. will fully show that I have had no personal prejudice or feeling of antagonism against labor unions, but after months of the hardest study I have ever given any question, I felt compelled to hold the United Mine Workers of America to be an unlawful organization and conspiracy both under the common law and the Sherman Trust [*sic*] Act.
>
> From the decree entered in this cause an appeal was taken to the Circuit Courts of Appeals. Instead of awaiting the legal determination of their rights in this case, this union

determined to continue its efforts, if not to increase them, but in the Southern District of this State. The result was the troubles on Paint and Cabin Creek in Kanawha County where it required two declarations of martial law to restore law and order.

Pending the appeal in the Hitchman case a bill in equity was presented to me by the West Virginia-Pittsburgh Coal Company against certain officers and organizers of this Union, setting forth not only such conspiracy but further charging an attempt by personal violence, intimidation and coercion to compel the unionizing of this Company's mines and the joining of said union by its miners, who were under personal contracts with the Company not to do so. The evidence clearly showed the guilt of a number of the parties so arrested and sentences of imprisonment were imposed upon them.

Under these circumstances, it seems clearly my duty to say that these men are not repentant, that they are persistent, deliberate and wilful violators of the law. In my judgment the crisis in West Virginia has not passed, but on the contrary it is my deliberate opinion that while, by means of this injunction, law and order have been substantially obtained in this section so far, at a loss not exceeding two or three thousand dollars in the destruction of property and loss of one life, that if these parties are pardoned and thereby given the opportunity to further disregard the law and its enforcement that it will be utterly impossible to control the lawless elements and a repetition of the Paint and Cabin Creek troubles in Kanawha County may be expected to arise at Colliers.[56]

On May 28, 1914, nine days after Dayton wrote the above letter, the circuit court of appeals reversed his *Hitchman* decision. At the same time it modified his December 2, 1913, Colliers injunction against UMW members to permit peaceful persuasion to join the union. However, the court of appeals upheld that part of the Colliers injunction which restrained violence.[57]

The court of appeals decision prepared the way for settlement of the Colliers strike. All previous efforts to bring the parties together, including a quiet effort by Governor Hatfield, had failed. Hatfield had not felt free to intervene directly because a federal court had issued an injunction in the dispute. The settlement came on June 12. While no contract was signed between the UMW and the West Virginia-Pittsburgh Coal Company, the settlement nonetheless provided: (1) that the company would rehire all former union employees as long as they had not violated any laws; (2) that the wages and working conditions of the union's Pittsburgh district would prevail at the Colliers mine; and (3) that the miners could have a checkweighman in accordance with the laws of West Virginia. Three years later the company recognized the Mine Workers as the miners' bargaining agent and signed a contract with it.[58]

After the court of appeals decision on May 28, 1914, the contempt proceedings based on the West Virginia-Pittsburgh Company's first petition (November 11, 1913) against Van Bittner, John P. White, and others were dismissed. Meanwhile, Oates, Sullens, and two other organizers, Frank Ledvinski and Hiram Stephens, appealed their contempt conviction based on the company's second petition (January 17, 1914). In its May 28, 1914, decision, the court of appeals remanded the contempt cases back to Dayton for rehearing, since Dayton had taken "judicial notice" of his findings in his *Hitchman* decision, which the court of appeals had reversed. At the rehearing the crucial evidence against the defendants came from a company detective, who testified that they had advocated violence in strike meetings. The defendants claimed the detective was an agent provacateur who had incited them into making their incriminating statements. Dayton didn't believe them and again found them guilty of contempt. In May, 1915, the court of appeals upheld their conviction.[59]

The court of appeals also upheld Dayton's January 27, 1914, conviction of Schwartz and Scoric. Violence was not the issue here, only their technical disobedience of Dayton's injunction. Schwartz and Scoric had promised to obey Dayton's decree and had not formally challenged the validity of the injunction order on the grounds that it was too broad.[60]

On June 12, 1914, Congressman M. M. Neely of Wheeling rose in the House of Representatives to initiate impeachment proceedings against Dayton, charging him with "high crimes and misdemeaners." The Ohio Valley Trades and Labor Assembly had distributed ten thousand postcards addressed to Neely urging him to take this action. The House Committee on the Judiciary assumed jurisdiction. Supporters and opponents of Dayton lobbied the committee. On February 8, 1915, with only a month left in the Sixty-third Congress, the committee voted to hear testimony on the allegations against Dayton and appointed a subcommittee to hold hearings. [61]

The subcommittee heard testimony in Parkersburg and Wheeling, West Virginia, and in Washington, D. C. Included among the charges against Dayton was that he had conspired with corporations and individuals to remove his predecessor, Judge John J. Jackson, from office. While the subcommittee did not find that Dayton had entered into a conspiracy to remove Judge Jackson, it did discover that Dayton was fully informed of the efforts to remove Judge Jackson and "gave aid and advice" to those seeking to remove him. A second charge brought against Dayton accused him of improper judicial conduct. In connection with this, the subcommittee discovered that Dayton had written a "to Whom it may concern" letter on his judicial stationery asserting his belief in the integrity of a coal company offering stock for sale. In fact, there was some question as to the value of the company's holdings. Moreover, the company's intention was to open up a coal-mining operation very near to coal lands in which Dayton had a financial interest.[62]

The most serious charge brought against Dayton, however, accused him of favoring coal companies involved in litigation with the United Mine Workers. In support of this the subcommittee discovered that Dayton held stock in coal-mining operations within his judicial district, creating a serious conflict of interest. In addition, the subcommittee found that during trials of labor union members Dayton's

> manner and language toward the defendants was that of hatred and bitterness. At times during the Colliers trials Judge Dayton was very impatient of hearing what the defendants had to say, his manner was heated and impassioned, he was laboring under emotional excitement, and his conduct generally was that of one who had prejudiced the cases before him.
>
> Judge Dayton has said that in certain cases under what he called the old constitution and by-laws of the United Mine Workers of America the members thereof were criminal conspirators, and, having formed that opinion, which is very positive with him, he has steadfastly maintained it; and it is in evidence that he has said in a certain case that if the evidence disclosed that the defendant was a member of the United Mine Workers of America, he wanted no further evidence to determine guilt and impose punishment as for an alleged contempt of court.[63]

While the subcommittee members unanimously agreed that Dayton had not adhered to "the high standard of judicial ethics which should crown the Federal judiciary," they recommended by a two-to-one vote that no further action be taken toward impeachment. On March 3, 1915, the full committee on the judiciary accepted the subcommittee's recommendation by an eleven-to-four vote, ending all possibility for impeachment in the Sixty-third Congress. Hilton vowed to start impeachment proceedings over again in the next Congress. [64]

Impeachment always has been a difficult procedure to accomplish. Throughout American history the House of Representatives has impeached only nine federal judges and the Senate has convicted only four of them. Two other contemporary "injunction judges," as organized labor called them, Judges Cornelius W. Hanford and Daniel Thew Wright, did not possess Dayton's stamina. When threatened with impeachment, they chose to resign rather than fight.[65]

Residents of Follansbee were greatly surprised yesterday afternoon when they appeared in the downtown section and saw, hanging from the arms of a telephone pole, Judge A. G. Dayton, in effigy. Nothing could be learned concerning the matter other than it was rumored that the stuffed "image" was placed there earlier in the day by a number of boys and men, sympathizers of the striking miners of Colliers. At a late hour last night the effigy was still hanging from the pole and no one had volunteered to remove it.

Feelings against the action of the federal judge runs high in this vicinity. [*The Wheeling Intelligencer,* February 12, 1914.]

During the Colliers trials in March and April, 1915, Dayton received anonymous notes in which persons threatened to kill him unless he resigned. The United States marshal in Philippi received permission from the Justice Department to hire bodyguards to protect Dayton. Dayton believe that these threats were part of a conspiracy to intimidate him, and he relayed his belief to the attorney general.[66]

Tom L. Felts, of the Baldwin Felts Detective Agency, showed Dayton a letter in August, 1915, from his brother A. C. Felts, in the agency's Denver office:

Dear Tom:

The Governor has just informed me that he has learned from a reliable source that the United Mine Workers have employed several pretty girls, and that these girls are going to make an effort to become friends with Judge Dayton while enroute to San Fransisco. They claim he is going to San Francisco alone, leaving his family in the East. Their plans are to have him caught in a compromising position. The legal authorities in Denver are in sympathy with the United Mine Workers, and it would be no trouble to have him arrested if there were the slightest grounds or provocation for same.

The Judge might not consider it a compliment to himself for us to go to any great trouble to give him the information, but I think he should at least have the information, as it will show to him that these people are laying for him and if they do not succeed in catching him in one trap, they will, no doubt, endeavor to spring another.[67]

Dayton sent the attorney general a massive document on September 20, 1915, which included evidence and arguments to demonstrate the existence of a conspiracy against him. It all began, Dayton wrote, after he issued his *Hitchman* injunction in 1907, when a resolution was introduced in the United States Senate requesting an investigation to determine if he had exceeded his judicial authority. At approximately the same time, Samuel Gompers appeared before the House Committee on the Judiciary to attack his *Hitchman* injunction. More recently, the central figures in the conspiracy, according to Dayton, were Hilton and other leaders in the Ohio Valley Trades and Labor Assembly who had tried to get him impeached. The attorney general promised Dayton he would assign an agent to investigate.[68]

A year passed, and Dayton received no reports from the Justice Department. Meanwhile, there was renewed speculation about impeachment proceedings against him. Dayton again wrote the attorney general:

> The facts remain that I have been threatened with assassination, have been subjected to every possible false and slanderous charge, found groundless upon investigation, and if these newspaper reports are true, am I from year to year, to be pursued with relentless malice until "they get me" because I have simply done my duty and enforced the law to the best of my ability as I am sworn to do. I am entirely unable against such odds to defend myself. I have a great personal anxiety because of the effect this persecution has upon Mrs. Dayton, threatened with a disease that necessitates freedom from nervousness and worry but that I know is my own burden to bear.
>
> It has impressed itself upon me that this persecution has gone so far, that I may properly appeal to the Executive Power through your Department to relieve me from further defense by having its own careful investigation of the facts concluded.

The assistant attorney general replied that the investigation has been interrupted and was not yet complete. He added that the investigations to date had "failed to disclose anything to prove that the interests aligned against you have adopted any method of injuring you, personally or officially, which would bring them . . . within the scope of federal law." Neither the Justice Department nor Dayton's opponents in the House of Representatives took any further action.[69]

When the United States Supreme Court declined to award a writ of certiorari reviewing the conviction of Oates, Sullens, Ledvinski, and Stephens, UMW president John P. White wrote President Woodrow Wilson urging him to pardon them. After reading White's letter, the president "felt inclined" to do so. His attorney general advised him to award a sixty-day respite from imprisonment pending a decision, during which time the Justice Department could investigate to make certain that the "dignity of the courts" would not be undone by granting the pardon. The president agreed.[70]

President Wilson's inclination to pardon the union organizers needs to be viewed in the context of labor's increasing demand for reform of labor-capital relations.

When Samuel Gompers attacked Dayton's *Hitchman* injunction before the House Committee on the Judiciary in 1908, his appearance was a part of labor's larger anti-injunction campaign that had been underway for several years. Labor had organized the campaign to counter the open-shop movement fostered by the Anti-Boycott Association. President Theodore Roosevelt supported labor's campaign by delivering five successive messages to Congress in which he asked for legislation to end the abuse of injunctions. Dayton's *Hitchman* injunction especially had incensed Roosevelt, ending Dayton's hope that Roosevelt would appoint him to the circuit court of appeals. Despite Roosevelt's help, labor's anti-injunction campaign failed to move Congress.[71]

But while Congress ignored labor, business responded by significantly reducing its use of injunctions. From 1901 to 1906 corporations increasingly had used labor injunctions, but after 1906 they used them much less frequently. Even so, injunctions remained a serious problem for labor.[72]

In addition, in 1912, the United States Supreme Court responded to labor's anti-injunction campaign by revising its rules of equity to eliminate unfairness. However, the Supreme Court's new rules only marginally protected labor from the abuse of injunctions.[73]

Labor won a significant victory in 1913, when Congress established the *Commission on Industrial Relations* to study industrial violence. But the victory was gained only be making important concessions in order to obtain enough Congressional votes, including an agreement not to study industrial relations in the South. The final report was published in 1916. Since the commission members could not agree, they wrote three different sets of recommendations. Three of the commission staff later became important figures in the miners' struggle against the labor injunction: Frank P. Walsh, who was commission chairman, and W. Jett Lauck and Edwin E. Witte, who were staff researchers.[74]

When Congress passed the Clayton Act in 1914 amending the Sherman Antitrust Act, Samuel Gompers believed that the Clayton Act would be the "Magna Charta" for the working man, freeing him to organize trade unions. But later judicial interpretations of the Clayton Act proved Gompers wrong. What Congress actually intended in writing the Clayton Act is unclear. Many contemporaries, inside and outside of Congress, believed that Congress ignored labor and only restated the courts' interpretation of the Sherman Antitrust Act to the effect that it applied to trade unions as well as corporations.

For instance, the seemingly unambiguous language in section 6 of the Clayton Act, which declared that "nothing contained in the anti-trust laws shall be construed to forbid the existence and operation of labor, agricultural, or horticultural organizations instituted for the purposes of mutual help," was weakened by the qualifying phrase "lawfully carrying out the legitimate objects thereof." And while section 20 of the Clayton Act forbade injunctions in all cases between employees, between an employer and an employee, between employers and employees, and between persons employed and those seeking employment, nowhere did the act specify cases between an employer and *his* employees. Whatever Congress's intention was in passing the Clayton Act, the effect was to leave labor in the same relationship to the law as previously.[75]

During the sixty-day respite President Wilson gave Oates, Sullens, Ledvinski, and Stephens pending his decision on pardoning them, the attorney general asked the United States attorney who had prosecuted the cases, Stewart W. Walker, for his recommendation. Walker replied:

> I have thought quite a good deal about what action I should take when the application for pardon should come to me. The ends of justice have been maintained, the dignity of the courts upheld and the rights of individuals in injunction proceedings determined. I do not believe that further good could be accomplished by demanding the pound of flesh, as it were, in incarcerating in jails further these four defendants. Whatever acts they committed were committed on their part believing that they were within their rights in so acting.

The attorney general also consulted with Dayton. This time, in contrast to his earlier opposition, Dayton acquiesced: "I desire to interpose no objection to the pardon of these parties. I am entirely satisfied to leave the matter to the judgment of the Department of Justice and to the President."[76]

The attorney general advised President Wilson it would be proper for him to pardon Oates, Sullens, Ledvinski, and Stephens. The president signed the order for their release. The attorney general instructed his pardon attorney that because of "the exceptional conditions" existing in these cases, he should inform the jail officials by wire that they were to release the union organizers immediately.[77]

Political action at many levels had been required to counter the effect of Dayton's *Hitchman* and *West Virginia-Pittsburgh Coal Company* injunctions. But in West Virginia the person who had been most responsible was Governor Hatfield. He had recognized a broad consensus for diminishing the operators' excessive power and had acted on it in settling the Paint and Cabin creeks strikes in 1913. The people indicated their approval in 1914 by electing large Republican majorities in both houses of the West Virginia legislature.

The next year West Virginia faced a financial crisis which ultimately became Hatfield's undoing. A recently enacted state prohibition amendment had eliminated saloon license fees, an important source of state income. Meanwhile, in recent years that state had increased its services. Since the state had to increase revenue, Hatfield proposed taxing out-of-state corporations that profited from West Virginia's mineral resources. The coal operators shrewdly fought Hatfield's proposal by allying with an anti-Hatfield Republican faction. Over this strong opposition Hatfield finally won legislative approval of a compromise tax measure.[78]

During the 1916 Republican primary the anti-Hatfield faction and coal operators tried again. They opposed Hatfield's choice as gubernatorial candidate, Ira E. Robinson. Robinson had been the Supreme Court Justice who had dissented in the martial law cases coming out of the strikes on Paint and Cabin creeks. The anti-Hatfield faction and coal operators backed A. A. Lilly. Hatfield warned Republican voters:

> This man Lilly is trying to deliver the state over to the predatory interests that seek to get a strangle hold on the natural resources of West Virginia, despoiling it of its wealth and robbing you and me of our natural inheritance. He would barter your birth right and mine to those whose only interest in West Virginia consists of what they can get out of it. Even now he has agreed on a division of the spoils with those who have gotten together the biggest slush fund ever raised for any candidate in the history of the state. I am reliably told they

have raised more than a quarter of a million dollars, and judging by the lavish hand with which they are disbursing that fund, it is evident that as much more will be supplied if necessary.

Robinson won the hotly contested primary by a hairsbreadth. In the November election the Democratic gubernatorial candidate to whom the operators had switched their support, John J. Cornwell, was able to defeat Robinson, although only by a slim margin of 2,755 votes. Cornwell had served as Dayton's attorney during the House of Representatives impeachment proceedings against him.[79]

A year later, on December 10, 1917, the United States Supreme Court reached its *Hitchman* decision. In an opinion written by Justice Mahlon Pitney, the Supreme Court upheld that part of the circuit court of appeals ruling which declared, contrary to Dayton, that the Mine Workers was a legal organization. The Supreme Court rejected Dayton's reasoning that the Mine Workers was a monopoly in restraint of trade under common law and the Sherman Antitrust Act.[80]

On the other hand, the Supreme Court overturned that part of the circuit court of appeals ruling which had disallowed Dayton's injunction. The Supreme Court declared that Hitchman's individual employment contract was a valid contract and that Dayton's injunction against the Mine Workers was a proper remedy. Up until this ruling, individual employment contracts had not presented a major threat to unions. Under past decisions, employers could require their employees to sign individual employment contracts not to join a union; but these had moral force only, since for all practical purposes they were unenforcible against workmen who signed them. But under the Supreme Court's *Hitchman* decision, injunctions sought by owners against third parties (unions) were allowable to prohibit them from interfering with the contractual relationship between owners and employees. This posed a serious threat to unions, because the courts now could effectively prevent them from organizing employees under individual employment contracts.[81]

Justice Louis D. Brandeis vigorously dissented from the Court's opinion. He agreed with Judge Pritchard of the circuit court of appeals that the individual employment contract was not a valid contract. Brandeis explained that the individual employment contract made it an unlawful act for the UMW to induce miners to leave the operator's employment without justifiable cause, although the miners were free to leave at their own will. Since the contract included no agreement as to the length of time it would be enforced, the contract added nothing to an ordinary agreement of a miner to work for an operator, under which terms the operator could discharge the miner without notice and the miner could quit without notice. The operators could fire the miner for breaking the contract, but that logically would be the limit of liability under the terms of the contract.[82]

Brandeis's reasoning was eventually to prevail, but not until the passage of the Norris-LaGuardia Act in 1932. Until then the judgment of the majority of the Supreme Court was the law of the land.

Chapter Two

WAR

*"There must have been some powerful
injustice that actuated them. . . ."*

On April 6, 1917, one month after Governor John J. Cornwell's inauguration, the United States declared war on Germany. Cornwell believed in the war:

> The war must be won. We did not want to go in it. We stayed out of it until Germany concluded we were cowards, unwilling to defend the rights of our citizens and our National honor.
>
> Hypnotized with chautauqua eloquence and pacifist pratings, we ignored or denounced the advice of Colonel Roosevelt and other men who saw the necessity of early preparedness for eventualities.[1]

Cornwell was at least partially right. Most West Virginians in 1914 did view the World War as none of their business. But gradually they became involved. One of the first indications was a riot in Salem in July, 1915, brought about by a few radicals raising a red flag. Reports of spies photographing the locks on the

Kanawha River prompted a Justice Department investigation in April, 1916.[2]

Organized labor in West Virginia opposed preparedness. *The Wheeling Majority* fought successfully the establishment of a new National Guard unit in Wheeling:

> There is at least one civilized spot in West Virginia where women don't raise their boys to be uniformed strikebreakers.
>
> Preparedness isn't worth the paper its defended on. Europe was prepared and she got what she was prepared for. It is a truism that this comes to every bully sometime.

After the declaration of war Cornwell undertook to educate organized labor to its responsibilities. Within a year he believed he had succeeded, except for the "socialistic and radical element, what I might term the Bolsheviki."[3]

Immediately on assuming office, Cornwell tried to push a series of "war measures" through the state legislature. Each bill ran into opposition from organized labor. Labor successfully defeated his proposal, which would have outlawed strikes for the duration of the war. But over labor's opposition the legislature enacted Cornwell's proposal for a compulsory work (vagrancy) law. The secretary of the State Council of Defense enthusiastically reported on its effectiveness in 1918:

> From an economic standpoint the enactment of the compulsory work law has been a signal success. It has paid many times over the cost of the special session of the Legislature which enacted it. I have advised you that 811 persons were arrested and 2,705 persons had engaged in lawful employment for fear of arrest. This is a total of 3,516 persons who have gone to work. Taking $500 as their average annual compensation in one year, these former idlers have earned $1,758,000. This is, indeed, a low estimate of the wealth created by the operation of the statute, for I am convinced that at least 5,000 persons in the State have been forced to find employment which would increase this newly created wealth or earning capacity to $2,500,000.

Operators discovered that the compulsory work law could be used to compel strikers, who were considered vagrants under the law, to work open-shop. Fred Mooney, secretary-treasurer of District No. 17 of the UMW, complained that the union spent more money trying to keep its membership who were apprehended under the compulsory work law out of jail than it did feeding strikers. In 1920 the state supreme court of appeals declared the law unconstitutional. Cornwell also successfully prodded the legislature to enact a special police deputy law that authorized sheriffs to appoint private citizens as deputies. Mooney charged that this law was used to appoint mine guards paid out of the public treasury.[4]

Cornwell urged the legislature to pass a red flag bill in 1918 which would make it illegal to display any flag or emblem supporting un-American ideas or to speak, publish, or communicate them in any other manner. The legislature passed the red flag bill over the opposition of the UMW, the Ohio Valley Trades and Labor Assembly, and other labor organizations. No legislator wished to go on record as acting soft toward radicals.[5]

Cornwell also fought for passage of a bill to create a state police force. It faced stiffer opposition. Organized labor sponsored meetings, collected petitions, and arranged marches to bring about its defeat. Cornwell countered by asserting that West Virginia would become a dumping ground for Bolshevists and anarchists if a state police force was not established. The Ohio Valley Trades and Labor Assembly objected:

> It is not the foreigner, not the Bolsheviki, not the I.W.W., not the anarchist, that are opposing this bill; the real Bolsheviki, the real anarchists, who are opposed to all government, actually want such laws passed, hoping that it will arouse hatred of government and will incite violence enough to overthrow government. Those who are urging you not to pass this bill are the bonafide labor organizations, who have been organized for half a century and more, educating themselves through their experience, learning through dealing collectively, lawfully, and orderly with their employers.

Cornwell finally won over legislators by suggesting that the creation of the state police force would make it possible to remove privately paid mine guards and unnecessary to use federal troops in industrial disputes. On March 29, 1919, the legislature enacted the state police bill.[6]

Labor did win passage of two bills it wanted: a child labor law and an improved state workmen's compensation law. Cornwell was not opposed to ameliorative measures that would lesson the hardship of the laboring man — he only opposed labor power:

> Labor organizations have had their way absolutely in Washington as well as in Charleston up until the last session of the Legislature, and they came very near to dominating the situation here then. The further difficulty was that the members of Congress and of the State Legislatures (especially the latter from Agricultural counties) lined up with the labor people on the theory they were fighting corporations. That was the case even here last sping in many instances. I believe that this attempt to destroy our Government and wreck the whole industrial and social system in this country will eventually be defeated and it will bring the American people to their senses.[7]

The Wilson administration planned the master strategy for winning the war. It believed that industry must play a key role, since it produced the immense quantities of armaments required by modern warfare. The administration organized major industries through agencies to which Congress granted emergency powers. The agency immediately affecting West Virginia miners was the Fuel Administration, established under the Lever Act of August 10, 1917. It had the authority to set prices, and for all practical purposes to set wages, and to prohibit strikes.

Harry A. Garfield, fuel administrator, met with bituminous coal operators from the Central Competitive Field and UMW officials and negotiated the Washington Agreement of October 6, 1917. The sweetener in the agreement provided for increased wages and prices over the temporary August, 1917, freeze. The bitter part of the agreement required that the operators and miners accept continued government control over prices and wages until April, 1920, or until the termination of the war, whichever came first. Under the Washington Agreement miners interrupting the operation of a mine or striking would be fined a dollar a day; operators closing mines or locking out men without just cause would be fined a dollar a day for each miner affected. Garfield made similar agreements with operators and miners throughout the bituminous and anthracite coal industry.[8]

The National War Labor Board was the most important federal agency that dealt with labor disputes. It was cochaired by William Howard Taft, the former president, and Frank P. Walsh, the past chairman, of the United States Commission on Industrial Relations. However, the War Labor Board limited its jurisdiction to labor disputes in industries not under direct government control. Therefore, Garfield had to establish a bureau of labor to resolve labor disputes in the coal industry. The War Labor Board and the Bureau of Labor devised the same policy on the issue of union recognition, decreeing that employees should not strike for union recognition and that employers should not discharge employees because they joined labor unions.[9]

In this connection, the Supreme Court's *Hitchman* decision upholding individual employment contracts and injunctions against unions violating them caused a problem for the administration. It finally decided that the paramount claims of public welfare during the war emergency justified superseding the *Hitchman* decision. It sought to encourage collective bargaining, although not to insist on union recognition. The administration defended its policy of encouraging collective bargaining against business critics by arguing that increasing war production required a degree of cooperation between employers and employees. Moreover, the administration pointed out to business critics that employees had made the considerable sacrifice of forswearing strikes for the war's duration.[10]

The United Mine Workers officially endorsed the administration's wartime labor policy. William Roy, president, and Frank Ledvinka, vice-president, of Sub-District No. 5, which had jurisdiction over the panhandle of West Virginia, advised their local union to support the government:

> We ask you to strictly comply with the terms of our Contract, especially that part pertaining to "stoppage of work."
>
> Let future history certify that the Mine workers of this country did their work nobly and well, and proved to the world their loyalty and devotion to their country, which means so much to all. It is our part of this great World Struggle.[11]

Measured by the primary goal of increased production, the Fuel Administration was very successful. It achieved the highest level of coal production in history, despite the fact that 80,000 coal miners entered the armed forces. However, in the bituminous fields the already excessive prewar mining capacity, much of it in West Virginia, was greatly expanded. This expansion, combined with the rapid adoption of machine mining, assured an industry-wide depression after the war.[12]

The wage increase Garfield granted the miners did not equal inflation in most instances. Jett W. Lauck, economist and secretary to the National War Labor Board, estimated that the wage increase for bituminous miners accounted for only one-fourth of actual price increases. Meanwhile, operators' profit soared. Tax return data revealed that from 1912 to 1918 operators' net income per ton climbed from 21.6¢ to 48.3¢, and the average earnings on captial climbed from 7.9 percent to 17.2 percent. By extrapolation from available data, Lauck estimated that from 1916 to 1919 all bituminous operators made a clear profit of $1 billion, approximately $10 per individual in the entire population of the nation. These excessive profits were the result of Garfield's policy to gain maximum coal production by guaranteeing a profit to even the most inefficient coal operators.[13]

While in some instances labor as a class appeared to improve its earnings as a consequence of the administration's policy, these improvements were due to special conditions that would not continue after the war: greater steadiness of employment, overtime opportunities, and large earnings from piece-work. In general, Lauck concluded that labor was worse off after the war than before it. By 1919, "in the distribution of income in the country labor received a smaller proportion than it did before the war, while capital — in the form of profits, interest and rent — received a very much larger proportion." Lauck's data contradict the usual interpretation that labor improved its economic position as a result of the war. But even Alexander M. Bing, in a cautious assessment of the impact of the war on labor, concluded that labor became bitter by 1919 as a result of its relatively poor economic treatment by the administration.[14]

The AFL grew from two to three and a half million paid members from January, 1917 to January, 1919. However, this growth was not real. Most businessmen reluctantly, and only for the duration of the war, tolerated increases in union membership. And some businessmen openly fought unions during the war. In West Virginia the Winding Gulf and New River operators unilaterally violated their contracts with the Mine Workers. When the Fuel Administration intervened and insisted that union miners not be fired and that all other outstanding issues be resolved in accordance with Fuel Adminstration policy, the operators challenged the right of the Fuel Administration to intervene:

> We have endeavored in every honorable way to co-operate with the Government. We, however, feel it is the duty of every one, and let us say a patriotic duty, to remember that we still have a Constitution that is the supreme law of the country notwithstanding the fact that many at this time are prompted from some cause or other to overlook this fact.
> Congress is wholly lacking in authority to vest power in the Chief Executive of the Nation to perform the functions of the Judiciary under the Constitution. This being true, this controversy ought to end here, and the Fuel Administration should not be called upon to perform a service that is clearly beyond the scope of any power that it can legally exercise under the Supreme Law of the Land.

Despite their protest, within a few months the Winding Gulf and New Rivers operators gave in and accepted the Fuel Administration's authority to resolve their labor dispute with the Mine Workers.[15]

West Virginia miners discovered that their patriotic desire to support the war by not striking conflicted with their natural reflex to strike for union recognition, higher wages, and better working conditions. Moreover, the war was an opportune time to strike. The demand for coal was high, and the usual labor surplus had dwindled because of the draft and the closing off of immigration. William Roy, president of Sub-District No.5, shared the miners' ambivalent attitude toward striking. While he told union members that there were "a number of strikes in our sub-district which should have been avoided" and that they had occurred "at a time when our country's need for coal was the greatest," he also reminded them that "strikes, at times are necessary to all trade unions, and especially is this true of weak organizations, whose existence depends entirely upon their economic power."[16]

The Hitchman coal mine, protected by federal injunction, impeded the Mine Workers' expansion into the panhandle of West Virginia. Defying the injunction, organizers signed up Hitchman employees. The general manager of the Hitchman mine described what happened next:

> On Thursday, June 28, 1917, I talked by telephone with a man with whom I was not acquainted, who told me he was William Roy, President of Sub-District 5, UMW.
>
> Mr. Roy said that he was placed in a peculiar position; that the employees of the Hitchman mine had been organized into a local of the UMW; that the charter had arrived on June 27, 1917, and was in McMechen, West Virginia; that he was ready now to talk with the Company about its running the mine union. He said he thought he could show me that the union would make a good contract, and anyway that for patriotic reasons we ought to be willing to get together.
>
> I told him I could not agree to meet him before some time on

Monday, July 2. He said that date would suit, and it was agreed between us that the meeting should take place in the lobby of the Windsor Hotel in Wheeling. Roy said that I would know him by his wearing a light ten dollar suit and a straw hat.

The members of the Board of Directors were unanimous in refusing to unionize, and instructed me to meet Roy, listen to what he had to say, and then tell him that we would not unionize.

I met Roy at 10 o'clock Monday morning, July 2. He explained to me that he realized all about the injunction. He said he had avoided organizing the men as long as he could, but that he couldn't get out of organizing the men and still retain his position and that he organized them on Sunday, June 10, 1917, in Bellaire, Ohio. He didn't want to come to the West Virginia side to organize then on account of the injunction.

I told Roy that the Company would not unionize the mine, but would wait for the decision of the Supreme Court. When I told him that, Roy said he was surprised at the Company taking such a position, and that he would publish us as unpatriotic, but that if we would unionize he would see to it that the public was made acquainted with the fact that we were patriotic and had signed up.

On July 12, 1917, the great body of our employees did not go to work. We had an average of 280 miners employed at the mine in the month of July up to the 12th and on the 12th we had only nine.

The Hitchman Company waited out the strike until November, 1917, when the Supreme Court upheld its individual employment contract. After the Supreme Court's decision, the union gave up its strike and the Hitchman mine resumed full production.[17]

The United Mine Workers tried to organize other panhandle mines. It was tough going. After a year's effort, Sub-District No. 5 increased its panhandle membership from 241 to 1,483, and these gains were at small mines only. In northern West Virginia exclusive of the panhandle, the Mine Workers achieved a breakthrough when the Consolidation Coal Company recognized it, adding 5,000 miners to its rolls. Political ambition and war patriotism induced Clarence W. Watson, who controlled Consolidation, to accept unionization. However, the coal fields in southern West Virginia remained solidly open-shop. By February, 1919, the UMW had approximately 40,000 members, representing about half the miners in West Virginia and an increase of 23,000 over its 1914 membership; but the crucial period of growth had been during the prewar years when Hatfield was governor.[18]

Simultaneously with his declaration of war on April 6, 1917, President Wilson ordered the activities and movement of alien enemies restricted. Under his orders, alien enemies could not display any enemy flag or insult the United States flag, nor could they live or travel within one-half mile of a military installation or a war industry. Enemy aliens who violated these orders were subject to summary arrest — the United States marshall was *not* to secure a warrant from the court.[19]

On May 22, 1917, the United States marshal for the northern district of West Virginia telegraphed the attorney general:

> The Hitchman Coal and Coke Co., with about 200 miners now at work, is supplying its entire output to the engine shops and for other fuel uses of the Baltimore and Ohio Railroad at Benwood West Virginia. It is threatened with a strike today of 140 of these men which number is made up of Germans, German Poles, and Austrians and Hungarians.
>
> These men are under the leadership of two men who are believed to be subjects of Austria Hungary but may be German Poles. They are not naturalized citizens of the United States. The effort to shut the mine down is confined to these Germans, German Poles, Austrians and Hungarians, and the company would like to have these two leaders arrested under summary process so as to prevent the shutting down of the mine before application can be made to the federal court for protection under civil process.
>
> The daily output of the mine is about 1500 tons and the

railroad depends soley upon the output for the operation of all its divisions which center in and near Wheeling.

What shall I do?

The Justice Department's special agents were not able to establish German citizenship, and the department dropped the case.[20]

Other miners were not so lucky. John Kowalezyk, "alien enemy trouble maker," was arrested by the local sheriff in Fayette County in the southern part of the state and delivered to the United States marshal, who detained him. The United States attorney reported the case to Washington:

> John Kowalezyk constantly incites feeling against mine operators as well as towards the government of this country. He apparently is the ringleader of a crowd of foreigners who are attempting to intimidate the loyal miners and to influence the negros in the district to rise up against the white man. The special agent reports that a couple of hours before his arrival in Scarbro a negro had been killed by a white man as a result of a disturbance. Reliable authorities at the coal mine state that unless the agitation is suppressed the mines will have to close.

The United States attorney recommended permanent internment (detention) for Kowalezyk.[21]

In another case, the president of the local union in Colliers informed on a fellow miner, John Mohorwick, accusing him of "fomenting trouble among the foreigners and of trying to start a strike." A month later the United States attorney discovered that the union president had used Mohorwick as a scapegoat for his troubles in the Colliers union. The Justice Department released Mohorwick on parole, requiring him to report weekly to federal officers, though never admitting its error to Mohorwick.[22]

In the first months of the war, the United States attorney for the southern district of West Virginia found himself so busy with "alien enemy" cases and failures to register for the draft that he set aside his normal casework. Later in the war, the Justice

Department tempered the zealousness of the United States attorney for the northern district in his prosecution of draft cases. To help determine the wilfulness of the defendants' failure to register, he had asked questions as to the defendants' affiliations with the Socialist party and the IWW. The Justice Department chided him and suggested that he "substitute questions which bear relevantly on the question of wilfulness, such as questions of absence from home, health or illness, enlistment or draft elsewhere, etc."[23]

Under this barrage many local unions demonstrated their patriotism by organizing flag raisings "to show the loyalty and the devotion which the foreign membership of the organization had for this country." Sub-District No. 5 of the Mine Workers went further. It ordered its alien members to legally declare their intention of becoming United States citizens within thirty days, on penalty of being dropped from the union. Frank Ledvinka, Sub-District No. 5 vice-president, declared:

> No alien should refuse at this time to declare his intention to become a citizen of the United States. The United States is at war and it is no more than right for any one who lives here to demonstrate that he is loyal to the United States government, and that, in my opinion, can only be done with each and every alien severing his connection with any foreign country and declaring his intention to become a citizen of the United States....
>
> I am asked if the declaration will change a man's draft classification. This leads me to believe that some of our boys are hiding behind the alienship in order to avoid military service. Anyone who wishes to live in America and receive all the advantages of America, and refuses to fight for America and for the maintenace of the American principles, I think very little of.[24]

Fearing that alien enemies would commit sabotage, on March 25, 1917, President Wilson federalized National Guard troops to protect strategic industrial and transportation sites. The regular army could not be spared as it was training for overseas duty. By

May, the War Department has assigned sixty thousand National Guardsmen on guard duty. This stripped the states of troops they depended on for suppressing civil disorder. The department commanders in the field, not the president, made the decisions as to where the troops should be stationed. This set a precedent for freedom of action on their part in suppressing civil disorders. These two events, the federalizing of the National Guard, which stripped the states of their own troops, and the Department Commanders' freedom to deploy these federal troops, occurred easily and naturally in the circumstances of a rapid, total mobilization for war.[25]

In his March 25, 1917, order Wilson acted under a clause of the Dick Act of 1903, empowering the president to call the National Guard into federal service when federal laws could not be enforced by the regular troops available. This clause of the Dick Act was designed to meet the direst emergencies, not typical civil disorders, and had never been used before. All other statutes involving the use of federal troops to suppress civil disorders, going back to the original statute of 1792, required a presidential preliminary proclamation commanding insurgents to disperse by a specified time before the deployment of federal troops. The preliminary proclamation was important because it publicly stated the gravity of the president's decision to impose military authority on citizens.[26]

Since the federal constitution reserved most policing responsibilities to the states, it had almost always been requests of state governments which had resulted in the deployment of federal troops to suppress civil disorder (the exceptions were when the federal government sought to enforce its laws). However, states must meet certain legal requirements before requesting assistance. They could request federal troops only if an insurrection (a rising of the people in arms against their government, its laws, or officers of the government) had occurred, and only it its own resources had been exhausted. In addition, the state legislature had to make the request, or the governor when the legislature could not reasonably be convened in time. The president remained the sole judge as to whether or not these requirements had been met. If he believed they had, then he issued his preliminary proclamation. Only if the insurgents failed to disperse could the president order federal troops into action. While presidents over the years have had somewhat differing interpretations as to the precise circumstances under which the preliminary proclamation should be issued, with few exceptions they have issued it. Wilson himself had carefully adhered to the requirement of issuing the preliminary proclamation during his first administration, when he ordered federal troops into Colorado and Arkansas.[27]

Very soon after the declaration of war, the procedure requiring the president's declaration of the preliminary proclamation was ignored. In April and May, 1917, the governors of Montana and Georgia used federal troops stationed in their states to suppress civil disorder without informing Washington. When the War Department found out, it did not reprimand the governors. Shortly thereafter, when the governor of Georgia informed Secretary of War Newton D. Baker that he would not be able to control anticipated draft riots, since the state's National Guard was no longer under his command, Baker established a system of direct contacts between all governors and department commanders.[28]

As of June, 1917, enemy agents had commited few acts of sabotage, the original reason for calling up the National Guard. At about the same time the War Department decided it needed more men for overseas duty. Therefore, it requested department commanders to submit a list of highly strategic sites at which guards should remain, leaving the remaining soldiers free for combat training. However, department commanders were slow to release their guards for combat training, and in a few instances, governors asked Secretary of War Baker to postpone reassignment of guards. Cornwell was one of them:

> In view of the fact that we are threatened with a strike of coal miners in this section of the State, I respectfully request that you allow the Second Regiment of the National Guard to

remain here until the miners' convention, which is to be held to consider the question of the strike, has adjourned.

Baker refused Cornwell's request:

I consider it impracticable to comply with this request. The troops referred to are now a part of the Federal Force, and their use in the suppression of disorder within any state is unauthorized, except in the manner provided in the Constitution.[29]

The secretary of war spared the United Mine Workers this time, but not the Industrial Workers of the World. In July, 1917, an IWW copper strike in Arizona prompted the department commander to request sweeping authority to arrest aliens and to restrain mobs led by aliens. In similar actions in Washington and Montana, the Army raided IWW halls, broke up camp meetings, and jailed dozens of union members. Although the army was forbidden by statute to act as a *posse comitatus*, the troops violated the law and made themselves available to federal, state, and local law officers for making arrests. The army continued to occupy IWW copper camps in Arizona and Montana until 1920 and 1921.[30]

At times the War Department questioned the wisdom of carrying out these police actions and curbed the zeal of its department commanders. However, the chaotic and seemingly ominous conditions following the armistice, November 11, 1918, removed all doubts. During the first half of 1919 an epidemic of strikes swept the country and race riots broke out in several cities. The immediate future looked bleak, with a police strike and a general strike expected in Boston. In addition, bituminous coal, steel, and railroad workers threatened nation-wide shutdowns. Fear generated during the war convinced many, including War Department officers, that radicals fomented these events. Meanwhile the states continued to be without National Guard units, since the units federalized during the war had been demobilized.

Believing disaster loomed ahead, on September 29, 1919, the War Department telegraphed department commanders that they were "authorized to take necessary action in cases of riot, serious disorder or other emergency, upon request of a state legislature, or of a proper executive when the legislature was not in session, without reference to the War Department." The War Department sent a similar telegram to all governors advising them of its action. In essence, the War Department made official its informal, illegal actions of the past two years. Secretary of War Baker announced the policy in a major address before the Ohio State Federation of Women Clubs:

> In our own country since the armistice there has been growing agitation and unrest manifesting itself sometimes in race riots and mob disorder, but for the most part evidenced by widespread industrial controversies. Our newspapers are daily filled with accounts of violent agitation by so-called Bolsheviks.
>
> The Administration in Washington is determined that every Federal agency shall be maintained in the full performance of its functions. We have an army of tried soldiers, of true Americans. They have seen too much disorder in the world to undervalue law and 'order in their own country.
>
> They will see to it that Federal laws are enforced and Federal agencies left unobstructed, and they will respond instantly to the call of any Governor to suppress riots and disorder in any part of the country.

President Wilson collapsed three days before Baker sent his September 29 telegrams to department commanders and governors, and he remained incapacitated for several weeks thereafter. Before his collapse Wilson had been preoccupied with trying to get his Versailles treaty passed in the Senate. It is unlikely that Wilson knew anything about what had transpired.[31]

The organized miners in West Virginia had become apprehensive in the months following the armistice. They had received no wage increase since the Washington agreement of October,

1917, and inflation had cut the earning power of pick miners to below the 1914 level. Meanwhile, operator profits mounted. In addition, the end to wartime-guaranteed production rekindled the organized miners' anxiety about competing against open-shop miners. In 1919, the most rapidly growing coal fields in West Virginia were the open-shop southern fields. Moreover, Logan County deputy sheriffs, illegal under the 1913 mine guard statute and paid for by the Operators Association, blocked UMW entry into the open-shop fields. When Cornwell had pushed for the establishment of the state police the previous spring, he had argued that the existence of the state police would make it possible to remove mine guards. However, he took no steps to remove them.[32]

Since January 1, 1917, District No. 17 of the UMW had a new president, C. Frank Keeney. Although in his early thirties, Keeney exhibited a deeply lined face and presented a tough demeanor. Fred Mooney, who had been elected secretary-treasurer along with Keeney, described him as "all fire and dynamite." Keeney had worked for nineteen years in the mines, and for most of his life in or out of the mines he had participated in labor struggles. A nondoctrinaire Socialist, he was dissatisfied with the conservative leadership of Thomas Cairns, who had led the district for several years. After the strikes on Paint and Cabin creeks, Keeney had formed a secessionist District No. 30, but in 1916 he agreed to dissolve District No. 30 and helped to organize a new District No. 17. Fred Mooney's election as secretary-treasurer was a boon for Keeney. Like Keeney, Mooney had grown up in the mines, considered himself a Socialist, since class struggle was an everyday fact of his life, and fought doggedly for the union. Somewhat more handsome than Keeney, he was just as tough.[33]

On August 29, 1919, Keeney mailed to local unions a letter reviewing the incidents in which Logan deputies had assaulted and jailed union sympathizers. Keeney promised his followers he would help them find a way "to organize these fields regardless of the opposition." On Labor Day, September 1, 1919, Keeney and other District No. 17 representatives tried to meet with miners just over the Logan County line from the Kanawha district.

> They made the attempt to meet us but were beaten back by the guards and operators. However, enough men met us to establish two local unions in that field. They began to arrest men and throw them in jail, discharged several, and evicted a few families; after which several pitiful appeals were made to this office. The miners of the Kanawha field immediately began to hold meetings all over the Kanawha district, and its adjacent territory, shut the mines down and armed themselves and started on the march to Guyan Valley in Logan County.
>
> The Governor met a body of 2,000 men a mile up Lens Creek on Friday night, September 5, gave them an address and insisted upon them to return to their homes and put the mines in operation, and promised to investigate the matter, stating that he could not permit violence to occur within the borders of the state.
>
> Then I addressed the miners, advising them to return to their homes and put the mines in operation. Numbers of the men called out to me: "Brother Keeney, your advice is good, but we are going to our unfortunate brothers in the Guyan field who are pleading for freedom and to resurrect the constitution of the state and nation and then we will return to the mines.
>
> They proceeded on with their march.[34]

Cornwell "took no chances" and telegraphed the department commander, General Leonard Wood, who put his troops on alert. Cornwell warned the marchers that unless they disbanded, the troops would be "thrown into the affected area on my request in a few hours." Cornwell's threat and further persuasion by Keeney finally stopped the march.[35]

As he had promised the marchers, Cornwell appointed a commission to investigate the conditions in Logan County. When Cornwell insisted on broadening the commission's inquiry to fix responsibility for the march, Keeney became suspicious. Shortly thereafter a few UMW supporters went to testify before the commission. On their way back to their homes in Logan

County assailants beat them up. After that, Keeney refused to cooperate with the commission. Instead, District No. 17 passed a resolution asking for a congressional investigation of Logan County on the ground that Cornwell's commission was biased and not interested in determining the truth.[36]

The miners' resolve to organize Logan County compelled Keeney to devise some kind of action. Under his instructions fifty organizers boarded a train and entered Logan County to set up a camp. A few hours beforehand Keeney had informed Cornwell and insisted that he protect them. When the train crossed over into Logan County, heavily armed Logan deputies climbed aboard. After spotting the deputies, the organizers decided setting up camp wasn't such a good idea after all, and they returned to union territory.[37]

Even before this incident Cornwell had become alarmed:

This statement, dictated to Miss Margaret I. Keller, and which will be preserved by her, is for my family and friends who are solicitous of my personal safety, and some of whom have warned me of rumors that I am marked by some members and officials of the United Mine Workers for assassination.

For some time I have felt that I am under sentence. I am trying not to let that influence me in what seems to be a plain public duty. I firmly believe we are in a crisis; that, unless people who believe in law and order and in the rights of all as against the privileges of classes assert themselves, not only our Government but civilization itself is doomed. If the sacrifice of my life will help stay the tide of Bolshevism and Anarchy, with which the country is threatened, I am not unwilling that the sacrifice, if necessary, be made. I want to record here that I have tried to be fair with and have at all times been courteous to the Mine Workers officials who have come to my office in numbers and often, both day and night. I have no personal hostility toward any of them. I have been frank with and never sought to deceive them. They know it. Their desire to get rid of me must be from a failure to use me and a fear that my influence is hurtful to their plans.

This statement is made in the face of a solemn conviction

that I will not be permitted to survive longer than some of the members and officials of the United Mine Workers in this section of the State become firmly convinced I will not stand aside and permit them to unionize the Guyan Coal Fields by force and in defiance of law.

Signed, this the 26th day of September, 1919.

John J. Cornwell

Governor[38]

The United Mine Workers' National strategy strengthened Keeney's hand. At its Cleveland Convention in September, 1919, the miners called for termination of the Washington Agreement and asked for new contracts increasing wages sixty percent, claiming that the armistice had ended the war and their obligation to abide by the Washington Agreement until April, 1920. The Wilson administration, in fact, had disbanded the Fuel Administration after the armistice. By the fall of 1919, the administration decided it must halt the rising wage-price spiral. It reinstituted the Fuel Administration and obtained a congressional amendment to the Lever Act giving the president the sole authority to determine the official end to the war, and thus the termination of the Lever Act.[39]

Garfield returned to his post as fuel administrator. He proposed a 14 percent wage increase, with none of the increase to be passed on to customers through higher prices. The Mine Workers rejected his proposal and threatened to strike on November 1, 1919, unless its demands were met. President Wilson countered by issuing a statement declaring that the strike was "not only unjustified but . . . unlawful. The law will be enforced and means found to protect the national interest in any emergency that may arise." He called Lewis a dictator, charging that the decision to walk out "has apparently been taken without any vote upon the specific proposition by the individual members of the United Mine Workers of America through the use of an almost unprecedented proceeding."[40]

Lewis refused to back down from the planned strike. He replied to Wilson:

I am an American, free born, with all the pride of my heritage. I love my country with its institutions and traditions. With Abraham Lincoln I thank God that we have a country where men may strike. May the power of my Government never be used to throttle or crush the efforts of the toilers to improve their material welfare and elevate the standard of their citizenship.

In the face of Lewis's obstinacy, the Justice Department sought a temporary injunction from Judge Albert B. Anderson, restraining Lewis and other Mine Workers' officials from putting the strike into effect. The injunction stunned Mine Workers' officials, since the administration had not invoked the Lever Act to block strikes during the war.[41]

After mid-October, undercover agents reported to Cornwell that the miners planned a second "invasion" of Logan County, either before or simultaneously with, the November 1 national strike. Reports of arms shipments to the miners increased Cornwell's apprehension. He telegraphed this information to Keeney, who was involved in UMW conferences in Washington, and Keeney returned to West Virginia on October 24 to calm his followers.[42]

Meanwhile, Cornwell took preliminary action. On October 22, 1919, he wrote Department Commander General Leonard Wood:

It is evident that I am going to be forced to call upon you for aid, and I may need very quick action. The talk among these people is revolutionary in the extreme, and I have every reason to believe that their efforts will be directed not only at the closing of the coal mines, but likewise at an attempt to usurp authority completely in the counties and in the State.

This letter is written after a very careful investigation of the situation in this district. I am not an alarmist and am merely trying to take time by the forelock to deal promptly and effectively with something that is inevitable.

General Wood replied that troops would be held in readiness and encouraged Cornwell to call him "in time to get the troops on the ground before the rioters could possibly reach the non-union district."[43]

Officers of the West Virginia Coal Association met with Cornwell on October 30, 1919, and asked him to bring in federal troops "so as to combat all radical influences in different sections of the State." The same day Cornwell officially requested federal troops and issued a proclamation prohibiting armed assemblages.[44]

At 4:00 A.M. the next morning, two battalions of infantry, about nine hundred men, departed on three special trains from Camp Taylor, Kentucky, for West Virginia. One company went to Clothier to block the anticipated route of the miners on their way to Logan County. Three hundred men went to Beckley in Raleigh County, a strategic location in the southern open-shop coal fields, and the balance of men went to Charleston to protect the capitol from miners who, according to Cornwell's sources, were "to come to the city 'prepared for any emergency' — armed." Later Cornwell and General Wood brought in seven hundred additional troops.[45]

Cornwell also wrote to sheriffs and mayors throughout the state on October 30, 1919:

> The strike of the United Mine Workers beginning November 1st will mean more than 50,000 idle coal miners in this State alone. Factories and mills will be compelled to close for want of fuel and railroad trains will cease to run if it continues very long. If that occurs the distribution of food will stop, bringing hunger and suffering in many places. Disorders may follow on a small or possibly, in some places, on a large scale. Indeed, the consequences of such a situation cannot be foreseen, for it will be utilized by the criminal and radical elements to ply their nefarious trades and to bring about a general social and industrial revolution. The number of persons, of native as well as of foreign birth, who will rejoice at an opportunity to plunge the country into Anarchy must not be underestimated.
>
> If such a situation arises in other States, which in my

judgment is most likely, we are bound to feel the effects of it in West Virginia. The vast majority of our people are not only liberty-loving and law-abiding but they are patriotic enough to make any sacrifice to protect and preserve public order. The only difficulty will lie in their failure to realize the dangers to which the State and organized society may be suddenly subjected. I am not an alarmist. I simply have information as to the accumulation of arms and ammunition, in this State, of which the public does not know.

Unfortunately there is no law on our Statute books to deal with such persons until and unless they commit some overt act . . . which leads me to make this suggestion:

There should be organized in each Municipality, under the leadership of the Mayor, and outside of the Municipality, in each county under the direction of the Sheriff, a COMMITTEE OF PUBLIC AID AND SAFETY, composed of patriotic, courageous and public spirited citizens, men who can be trusted and whose loyalty to the Government and its institutions is beyond question.

The first duty of these Committees will be to alleviate the inevitable suffering that will follow in the wake of a prolonged coal strike and any general industrial disturbance.

The second duty will be to aid the public officials, city, county and State, in preserving order and in protecting lives and property.

I realize that in the rural communities this suggestion will seem unnecessary and perhaps to some even absurd, but with hundreds of thousands of men out of employment in the State and the distribution of food stopped men will not stay in one place and starve while houses and barns are filled only a few miles away. Then it may be necessary to call the people from the peaceful communities to aid in preserving order in the industrial sections. In case of war or of insurrections the Governor is vested with rather wide authority and I intend to employ it to the limit, if necessary, to prevent any unseemly happenings in West Virginia. In doing that I shall expect and have a right to demand the cooperation not only of County and Municipal officers but of all law-abiding and Government-loving private citizens.

Will you kindly advise me whether you are willing to take steps, at once, to form such an organization within your Municipality, or County, as the case may be, for the purposes mentioned?[46]

Sheriff Howard Hastings of Ohio County, which included Wheeling, was not willing. He advised Cornwell:

> Conditions in Wheeling are quiet and we have no reason at this time to anticipate any change. A thorough investigation has disclosed no sign of Bolshevik or I.W.W. elements. We have, of course, strong union men, but none who are preaching the overthrow of the Government and none of whom could be classed as Anarchists or radicals.
>
> To create a committee of public aid and safety might possibly be misunderstood and bring about some unpleasant condition.

Hastings added that "the matter of preserving order, I feel, both within and without the city, is my responsibility." This was a slap at Cornwell's ordering state police into Ohio, and neighboring counties, to protect open-shop miners and to arrest agitators under his red flag law.[47]

Cornwell heatedly replied to Hastings:

> It was brought to my attention that there were several non-union mines in Brooke, Ohio and Marshall counties which could and would go on producing coal if the men were not interfered with but that threats were being made by union men and that unless protection was furnished promptly the men at the mines referred to would be intimidated, would leave, and after having once left could not be induced to return. I felt that there should be on hand some State officers whose jurisdiction extended to each and all of the several counties to meet any possible emergency.
>
> I note you say that after thorough investigation no signs of Bolshevik or I.W.W. elements have been disclosed. My investigations within the past few weeks have revealed the presence of such elements, which is another reason for my

action, and I have every reason to believe that there is in contemplation of these elements an active, open propaganda in the Wheeling district in the near future.

I might add that the situation with reference to the stopping of work by the coal miners is not, as I view it, an ordinary industrial disturbance. It has been declared by the President of the United States to be an unlawful act. Steps have been taken in the Federal courts, upon the theory that it is an unlawful conspiracy against the government and the people.

As the Chief Executive of the State it is therefore my duty to cooperate with the Federal government in an effort not only to see that law and order prevail, but to do everything properly within my power to facilitate the production of coal and to prevent the consummation of such a conspiracy. I am not therefore disposed to deal with this matter or handle it in the way strikes are ordinarily handled. It is unnecessary to say that I think the attitude of all public officials should be the same.

This letter is written in reply to yours in order that you may understand my attitude, as well as that I am not attempting to usurp the authority of the Sheriff of Ohio or of the Sheriff of Brooke or Marshall County; that according to my viewpoint conditions are unusual and extraordinary.[48]

Meanwhile Cornwell's state police had been busy.

STATE POLICE HAVE ARRIVED IN THE CITY; ENTER UP-RIVER MINING DISTRICT TODAY SEARCHING FOR ALLEGED I.W.W. AGITATORS.

Upon information that I.W.W.'s or some equally insidious band of men are secretly working in the Wheeling district to foment trouble among the striking coal miners, a squad of state police, under Captain John Esque, slipped into the city late last night, determined to run down the culprits. They came directly from Charleston under sealed orders, it was said.

They engaged an automobile at 4 o'clock this morning, and went out on the road to Wellsburg, where the agitators were last reported to have been seen distributing "Red" literature urging the strikers to blow up the mines. The circulars, it was said, were signed "Hayfard," in conspicuous red letters.

Incidently, persons several miles away, in or near Charleston, have been apparently the only persons to hear of these alleged agitators, Bolsheviks or I.W.W.'s who plan to bump Wheeling off the map. Even Sheriff Howard Hastings hadn't heard so much as a rumor about the gang said to be planning trouble for the local mines.

However, Governor Cornwell's 'gumshoe' squad hit the trail early this morning heading toward Wellsburg in search of the supposed gang of anarchists. If they have no more sleuthing fortune than they had on their last visit at the outbreak of the steel strike they will report to Charleston empty handed with the exception of a hotel bill.

[*The Wheeling Register* November 3, 1919.][49]

The bituminous miners struck on November 1, 1919, as they had threatened. In West Virginia none of the violence Cornwell anticipated materialized. However, the arrival of federal troops on the eve of the strike, October 31, made clear to the miners that the state government had sided with the operators and did not intend to respond to their grievances. Keeney wrote Cornwell:

We are both aware that the miners are law-abiding citizens; we are both aware that no class of people is likely to purchase arms and ammunition secretly, as you state you received information of, without being goaded to it by some powerful wrong. Hundreds of men do not commonly unite together, and despite the orders of the Chief Executive of the State, and of their District, proceed with the announced purpose of invading a certain section of the state. There must have been some powerful injustice that actuated them, which cannot be lightly dismissed by the statement that the five or ten percent of radicals and agitators in their midst stirred them up.

These men took this regretable step because they had come to the conclusion that the officials of their state would do nothing for them; that the miners' appeals were silently ignored; that the injustices and brutality with which their fellow miners in the Logan fields were treated would not be remedied by any state officials.

And, Mr. Governor, can we, in all fairness, denounce those men? Have they not, time and time again, through me as their accredited leader, produced evidence before you of a reign and system of brutality which is almost unbelievable in a country which professes democracy?

You appointed a commission to investigate into the conditions which were reported as existing in Logan county. Yet, while this commission was holding its session the men who testified before it were inhumanly beaten up when they returned to Logan county. Organizers whom we sent into Logan were met by hundreds of thugs armed with rifles and machine guns. All this, sir, has been presented to you. We have asked for protection for those miners who testified before your commission; that protection was not given. A sublime contempt for your authority was evidenced all along by the powerful system in control of the Guyan fields. And the miners in those unorganized fields are still being beaten up and not a state official's hand is raised in their behalf!

You say you brought troops here to protect the lives and properties of the citizens of the state of West Virginia. These troops are here to maintain order and to see that no unseemly attempts are made by the outraged miners to secure redress in an unlawful way for wrongs committed, and in this attempt, I shall co-operate with you to the best of my ability. But would it not be wiser, instead of preparing to suppress a possible uprising, to eradicate the wrongs which goad these men to take, or prepare to take, unlawful steps?[50]

On November 8, 1919, Judge Albert B. Anderson ruled that the Mine Workers' strike was illegal under the Lever Act. He added that under the then existing conditions the strike approached rebellion. He issued a mandatory injunction against the United Mine Workers and ordered its officers to recall the strike. The union capitulated. President John L. Lewis bitterly complained, "we cannot fight the government." Keeney ordered his men back to work and to accept the 14 percent wage increase.[51]

The miners refused to obey their leaders, and they did not return to work, either in West Virginia or elsewhere. In southern

West Virginia the army announced that it would protect miners from radicals, who presumably were preventing them from going to work. Intelligence officers prepared dossiers on these radicals and gave them to officials. But Keeney charged that the troops' presence interfered with the miners returning to work: "The men feel they are being regarded as outlaws as long as the troops remain on duty." Cornwell and General Leonard Wood came around to Keeney's view. On November 14, General Wood announced that he would withdraw the troops as soon as transportation could be arranged. Besides, he revealed, the troops were badly needed elsewhere.[52]

When Cornwell ordered the state police into the panhandle on November 1, 1919, one of their assignments was to guard Hitchman and other open-shop mines. The first response of the miners was anger, and they struck in support of the UMW; but later they gradually returned to work. Hitchman's manager credited their return to work to the continued presence of the state police. However, the unionized mines in the panhandle remained on strike into December.[53]

The mines in the northern section of West Virginia, exclusive of the panhandle, had neither state police nor federal troops to serve as guards. Open-shop operators in the northern Fairmont field had requested federal troops, and Attorney General A. Mitchell Palmer was receptive to their appeal. Cornwell advised against it since federal troops were in short supply; also, he feared their presence might needlessly antagonize the majority of miners who had been organized only for a year and a half. The same considerations applied to dispatching state police. The outcome was that the enforcement of the federal injunction in the Fairmont Field was left largely in the hands of the United States attorney, Stuart W. Walker:

> My own opinion is that unless some action is taken there will be bloodshed in the District within a very few days. Although the miners as a whole are quiet and inoffensive, there is among them a great number of rabid anarchists and Bolshevists, who

control the situation.

A very large per cent of the miners are anxious to work without change of conditions, and would be at work today despite the strike order, were it not for fear of bodily harm either to themselves or their families by a very few union associates of the worst character. In most of these instances I find that these associates are foreign born, have never been naturalized, and have no desire to be naturalized; that they are always criticizing the Government and making threats against it. They seem to fear no law. I think that these foreigners, unnaturalized, should be deported promptly. I believe by the deportation of a comparatively small number of persons of this character from this District labor troubles will be minimized.[54]

On November 12, 1919, organized miners in Star City in the Fairmont Field met to vote on returning to work. Many of the miners, of whom a large number were Russian, opposed returning to work and compelled the union leadership to postpone a vote on the issue until the next evening. Walker's version of what happened was that the Russians "took charge of the meeting, ousted the credited union officials, appointed committees to go immediately to arouse all Russians, passed resolutions condemnatory of the Government and openly threatened to march on Washington and forcibly take possession of the Government." Meanwhile, according to Walker, at another UMW local meeting in Grant Town, when the order was read that the miners should return to work, a known IWW member shouted, "To Hell with the President, and the United States Government. Tear the damn document up. We will not go to work, nor allow any one else to go to work." Walker reported these, and other events, to Attorney General Palmer and asked for instructions. Palmer, in turn, wired Cornwell for advice. Cornwell replied that these aliens "should have been deported long ago." Palmer ordered Walker to arrest them. In all, Walker took into custody thirty-seven radical aliens. Still the Fairmont miners would not go back to work.[55]

Some operators of organized mines seized the opportunity of

the Mine Workers' illegal strike to terminate the checkoff for union dues, or to revert completely to an open-shop status. This violated the Washington Agreement enforced under the Lever Act. Both Cornwell and Palmer opposed this blatant form of union-busting. Cornwell wrote to an operator in Moundsville who tried to institute the Hitchman individual employment contract that the federal government's objective, and his, was to maintain coal production but at the same time to be neutral in union versus nonunion struggles. When the New River Coal Operators Association tried to free itself from provisions of its contract with the UMW, Palmer insisted that the contract continue in force, provided the men returned to work.[56]

When December arrived and the miners stubbornly continued on strike throughout the nation, Attorney General Palmer made a tactical retreat. On December 6, 1919, he quietly met with John L. Lewis and offered to give a presidential bituminous coal commission the authority to consider an additional wage increase, provided the miners would return to work. Lewis accepted the compromise and the strike ended. Garfield resigned in protest on December 15, 1919, believing that the coal commission would sacrifice the principle of price and wage control. In fact, the Bituminous Coal Commission performed as Garfield predicted: it increased miners' wages 27 percent, which nearly equalled the inflationary loss in their real income during the war, and raised mining prices for mine-run coal 24¢ per ton.[57]

The wage increase alleviated the economic burden on the West Virginia miners. But the more serious problem of the rapidly growing open-shop coal fields in southern West Virginia continued unabated, threatening the future existence of the UMW. Moreover, in the name of state and national security, Governor Cornwell and federal officials had firmly established the precedent of using force to protect open-shop mines from union organizers.

Chapter Three

OF LAWS AND MEN

"I am not the law maker"

On May 8, 1920, William D. Ord, an executive of the Red
Jacket Consolidated Coal & Coke Company, informed Governor
John J. Cornwell that Fred Mooney and other union organizers
had arrived in Mingo County and had started agitating. He
continued:

> I posted at all our places yesterday a notice, to which I do not
> wish to give any publicity at this time outside of our own
> plants, but inclose for your personal information. I want to
> assure you that we will be as conservative as possible in
> handling this matter, but we must be firm. The maintenance of
> some unorganized mines is an absolute necessity to this
> country ....

> THE RED JACKET CONSOLIDATED COAL & COKE
> COMPANY BELIEVES:
> THAT each individual has an absolute and constitutional
> right to work for whom he pleases under such terms as may be

freely and mutually agreed upon.

THAT employers likewise have a right to employ whomsoever they please.

THAT any limitation or RESTRICTION OF THESE RIGHTS IS A DENIAL OF PERSONAL LIBERTY and of MANHOOD.

THAT the activities of any Union, Organization or persons not advocating and recognizing these principles can result only in TAXING the INDUSTRIOUS for the BENEFIT of the INDOLENT and in the restraint of PERSONAL and CONSTITUTIONAL LIBERTY, necessarily leading to decreased production and higher cost of living.

It has no desire to dictate to its employees what organizations they shall or shall not join but it states positively that it will not employ any one connected with an organization hostile to the above principles and hereby notifies any of its EMPLOYEES WHO AFFILIATE THEMSELVES WITH such a hostile organization to IMMEDIATELY sever their connection with the company and to MOVE OFF THE PREMISES.

It is sincerely hoped that the pleasant relationship which has existed between the company and its employees will not be interrupted and that each and every man in our employ appreciating the fairness and justice of the foregoing principles will continue with us.

RED JACKET CONS. COAL & COKE CO.[1]

On one point William D. Ord and the United Mine Workers agreed: that the organization of Mingo County by the UMW would open the way to unionizing all the open-shop counties in southern West Virginia. The UMW correctly recognized that it could not assure its members wage protection as long as southern West Virginia operators could undersell coal produced by operators in the unionized Central Competitive Field. The high quality of the southern West Virginia "smokeless" coal, the introduction of machinery into these relatively new fields, and chronic nationwide overproduction of coal made organizing these fields all the more compelling.

The largest coal operation in Mingo County, Red Jacket owned eleven thousand acres adjoining the Tug River, which flowed north to the Ohio River. Its mines remained isolated in the V-shaped mountain valleys in spite of the fact the town of Matewan was only three miles away. Red Jacket housed one thousand employees and their families in company residences and serviced them with company stores, a company theater, and two company schools — one for white and one for black children. Most of the miners were native-born citizens, but small numbers of Hungarians, Spaniards, and Italians worked in the mines as well. The company encouraged religion — "the more the better" — with a Mr. Harding from Cincinnati leading revival meetings.[2]

Red Jacket paid its miners by the amount of coal mined, as measured by the number of cars filled. The cars averaged two and one-half tons, but Red Jacket had no weigh scales to measure the exact weight. Were the miners unhappy about this? "There has never been any particular demand for it; in fact, I will say none," reported Red Jacket's director, Landon C. Bell. "Our people are perfectly willing to mine and load our coal and be paid on the basis that we pay them." The average miner earned $1,366 a year.[3]

Red Jacket belonged to the Operators Association of Williamson Field, which represented fifty-six operators on both sides of the Tug River in Mingo County, West Virginia, and Pike County, Kentucky. The operators assessed themselves ten cents a ton of produced coal to meet expenses. The headquarters for the Operators Association was in Williamson, the Mingo County seat, located nine miles down the Tug River from Red Jacket. There the operators planned their antiunion strategy. They agreed to have their men sign individual employment contracts.[4]

The mine superintendent for Red Jacket related the circumstances in which Red Jacket had its men sign the contracts:

About the 23rd of April, 1920, the union had a meeting there in Matewan. They advertised free jitneys down and got everybody from Mate Creek [Red Jacket] that they possibly could down there. I was down at Matewan myself. They had an open air meeting and spoke from a truck there and then they went into this little church, where they were supposed to sign up to the union.

After that meeting, the Company got up some contracts for all the men to sign that wished to stay with the Company and not join the union. Then I went to work to sign up all the men. It was along about the 10th of May, 1920.

Under the Red Jacket contract the employee agreed "that he will not belong to, or affiliate in any way with" any union and "will not knowingly work in or about any mine where a member of such organization is employed," on penalty of losing his job. Red Jacket, in turn, agreed not to employ union labor.[5]

Union organizers pleaded with the miners not to be intimidated into signing the individual employment contracts. Operative No. 24 of the Baldwin-Felts detective agency described a typical scene at a union meeting held in Matewan on May 14:

> There was a mass meeting of the miners here tonight, which was attended by about 500 men. The speaking was done in the open between the railroad depot and the street. Preacher Combs made a radical talk, in which he said that the operators bitterly opposed the union and had managed to keep most of the poor miners in ignorance of the benefits derived from the union by telling them that the union was composed of loafers and men who did not want to earn a living by work.
>
> "I am here to say that we do not want to work [for inadequate wages] but we want to earn."
>
> He said the superintendents were going to all the miners with a paper to be signed, which was an agreement that the miner would sign his birthright away for five years house rent. Combs said that no man should sign it; that those who did sign it were not as good as a yellow dog.
>
> He said the superintendent who would ask his fellow man to sign such a paper did not have a heart, that he carried a gizzard around in a heart's place. The men should all go home and tell

their wives that they had decided to make a change . . . tell her
that they were going to recognize the miners as human beings.
The Negroes were once in bondage and Abraham Lincoln gave
them their freedom, and the miners, both black and white,
were in bondage and the United Mine Workers were going to
give them their liberty.[6]

Claiming violation of its contract rights, Red Jacket sued for an
injunction against the United Mine Workers in September, 1920.
In November, 1920, the United States District Court issued a
preliminary injunction against the union. Later, 315 other
operators, virtually every open-shop mine in southern West
Virginia, joined in the suit to protect their individual employment contracts. In 1923, Judge George W. McClintic of the
United States District Court granted the operators a permanent
injunction against UMW organizing activities. The union
appealed to the United States Circuit Court of Appeals which, in
1927, upheld McClintic's injunction in a decision written by
Judge John J. Parker. The Supreme Court declined to hear the
case on a writ of certiorari, making Parker's decision law.

McClintic had found that the UMW had attempted "unlaw-
fully, maliciously, and unreasonably to induce, incite, and cause
the employees of the plaintiffs" to violate their contracts of
employment. Parker recognized the threat to the UMW in
McClintic's decision. He pointed out that the courts had
recognized the legality of trade unions, asserting the UMW "is
not to be condemned because it seeks to extend its membership
throughout the industry." But Parker also believed that the
union was bound by the *Hitchman* decision (1917) of the
Supreme Court, which held that the UMW could not cause
employees to violate individual employment contracts. Parker
concluded, in effect, that the UMW could attempt to extend its
membership into Mingo County, West Virginia, and elsewhere in
the nation, so long as it did not succeed in actually gaining new
members protected by the individual employment contract:

> To make a speech or to circulate an argument under ordinary circumstances dwelling upon the advantages of union membership, is one thing. To approach a company's employees, working under a contract not to join the union while remaining in the company's service, and induce them in violation of their contracts to join the union, ... is another and very different thing. What the decree forbids is this, "inciting, inducing, or persuading the employees of plaintiff to break their contracts of employment."

While Parker's decision effectively prevented the UMW from organizing nonunion miners presently under individual employment contracts, his decision gave the UMW some comfort in that it also affirmed the right of the UMW to strike. Parker emphasized that the individual employment contract was not binding after the expiration of the contract.[7]

Although the *Hitchman* decision provided the precedent the operators needed, Red Jacket alone could obtain a hearing in federal courts directly on the issue of individual employment contracts, because only it could claim diversity of citizenship between two states required for federal jurisdiction. The only way the other operators could benefit from the *Hitchman* decision was to claim jurisdiction under the laws of the United States. The Clayton Act (1914) permitted an individual corporation to sue for injunctive relief against a conspiracy to restrain interstate commerce, as outlawed by the Sherman Antitrust Act (1890). If the operators could persuade the federal courts that the UMW in its organizing drive had conspired to restrain interstate commerce, they could obtain an injunction against UMW's actions to induce the miners to break their individual employment contracts.

McClintic was easily persuaded. He ruled that the UMW had attempted to restrain interstate commerce by striking in Mingo County, and that therefore the union was an unlawful conspiracy under the Clayton Act. Parker disagreed, quoting section 6 of the Clayton Act which stated that unions shall not be "construed to be illegal combinations or conspiracies in restraint of trade, under the antitrust laws." He did not believe Congress wished to make unions per se unlawful, and he overruled McClintic on this point.[8]

But Parker still found the UMW guilty of conspiring to restrain interstate commerce. The Supreme Court's second *Coronado* ruling (1922), written by Chief Justice William Howard Taft, gave Parker his precedent. Taft wanted both to hold unions responsible for their excessive actions and to permit them to strike in furtherance of their legitimate goals of improving wages and working conditions. His solution was to require evidence of "clear intent" by the union to restrain interstate commerce before holding it in violation of the Sherman Antitrust Act. The facts in the second *Coronado* case, wrote Taft, revealed, first of all, that the strike had a substantial effect on interstate commerce and, secondly, that violence perpetrated by union members in support of the strike (according to the testimony of a dissident union officer) had as its purpose prevention of the nonunion coal from entering interstate commerce. The former evidence combined with the latter, ruled Taft, proved a "clear intent" to restrain interstate commerce. Following Taft's precedent, Parker held that the attempted organization of the Williamson field, and later strikes coming out of the organizational drive, proved that the UMW had prevented substantial production from entering interstate commerce. Parker found "other evidence as to intent" in the "campaign of violence and intimidation" incident to the organization drive.[9]

A vexing problem for the operators was the refusal of striking miners to leave their company homes promptly after they were evicted. In part this was because leaving their homes on short notice was a hardship. But also, many miners wanted to stay, because it gave them an opportunity to persuade, or dragoon, loyal employees into joining the union. In early May, 1920, Thomas L. Felts, manager of the Baldwin-Felts detective agency, met with the Operators Association to plan removal of union families from residences at the Stone Mountain Coal Company and other mining camps.[10]

At 11:47 A.M., on a rainy May 19, Albert C. Felts, Thomas L. Felts's brother, stepped down from train No. 29 onto the Matewan platform. Twelve big men, each carrying a Winchester rifle, accompanied him. The group made known their intention to remove union families from their residences at the Stone Mountain Camp. Sid Hatfield, the chief of police, and Mayor C. C. Testerman went up to the detectives and asked them what right they had to remove the union families. They replied that the operators had told them they had the right to do it. Hatfield asked them to show him the court orders. They said they didn't have anything to show and that two hours' notice was all they wanted. Hatfield retorted that "they could not throw those people out unless they had papers from the court."[11]

The detectives drove up to Stone Mountain camp and removed the miners, tossing their furniture and belongings into the muddy street. Meanwhile, the justice of the peace in Williamson wrote out a warrant charging the detectives with evicting the miners without cause and dispatched it to Hatfield in Matewan. The detectives returned to Matewan before the warrant arrived, but Hatfield was not without resource:

> We had an ordinance for nobody to have no gun unless he is an officer. I went up and told Mr. Felts — he was the boss of the gang — that I would have to arrest him. He said he would turn the compliment on me, that he had a warrant for me. He told me what the charges were and he said he would have to take me to Bluefield [Baldwin-Felts headquarters]. I told him that I would not go to Bluefield because I was chief of police. He told me that he would have to take me anyway. We walked down the street to where the Pullman stops for Bluefield. Some one told the mayor that the detectives had me arrested, and the mayor came out and asked what the charges were, and he told Felts that he would give bond for me.
>
> Felts told him that he could not take any bond, and the mayor asked him for the warrant, and the mayor read the warrant and said it was bogus. There was some argument about

their throwing out the people, and he shot the mayor. Then the
shooting started in general.

Fifty to seventy-five shots were fired. Ten men were killed, and
four others were wounded. Seven of the ten killed were Baldwin-
Felts detectives.[12]

The Operators Association charged that Sid Hatfield and
UMW sympathizers had conspired to kill their "law enforcement
officers." The favorable seven-to-three kill ratio for Hatfield's
side and the subsequent violent death of a major operator witness
did look suspicious. Hatfield complicated matters further by
marrying Mayor Testerman's young and pretty widow within ten
days of the battle, suggesting that more than one motive may
have been involved.[13]

Immediately after the battle, Thomas L. Felts dispatched C. E.
Lively to Matewan to obtain evidence against Hatfield and his
codefendants to be used in their trial. Twelve years of successful
union work (during which he was paid by both the UMW and
Baldwin-Felts) and a boyhood friendship with Fred Mooney made
him a superb undercover agent. He rented the first floor of the
UMW building and opened a restaurant. He served union
organizers meals (making a profit) and listened carefully. But he
failed to uncover any evidence that would persuade the jury to
convict the defendants.[14]

Lively pursued Hatfield after the trial. On August 1, 1921,
Hatfield and his wife, the former Mrs. Testerman, and another
couple went to Welch in McDowell County to appear in another
trial. As they climbed the courthouse steps, Lively and other
Baldwin-Felts detectives greeted them, drew their guns, and
pumped ten rounds into each of the two men, so perforating their
bodies that later they could not be embalmed. Mrs. Hatfield
buried her second husband beside her first, leaving enough space
between them for her own dead body to lie.[15]

The UMW tried to capitalize on the violent removal of the
miners and the resulting Matewan battle. C. Frank Keeney wired
the secretary of President Woodrow Wilson: "It is a case where

the Federal Government must take a hand.... Otherwise I fear that the outraged miners and other workers of the State may be driven to OTHER METHODS." Attorney General A. Mitchell Palmer, speaking for the ailing president, claimed that the president lacked authority to intervene, forcing the UMW back onto its own resources.[16]

The operators continued to remove miners from their homes, only now they adopted legal means. West Virginia law conveniently held that because the operator-owned residences were necessary to employment, the relationship of owner to renter was not that of landlord and tenant, which would protect the miner from abrupt eviction, but that of master and servant.[17]

As the operators removed the families, the union placed them in tent colonies near the mining operations. UMW relief workers put up the tents, passed out provisions, and kept up morale. When the operators brought in strikebreakers, the Mine Workers offered them free return tickets to get them to go back to their homes — in New York, Cleveland, Pittsburgh, and elsewhere. In one week Mooney returned two hundred strikebreakers. A mine operator described the scene:

> Always upon the arrival of a train carrying workmen into the field the railway station at Williamson was jammed with strikers, organizers, and agitators. Banners were paraded declaring the existence of the strike. Upon alighting the men would be surrounded by dozens and perhaps hundreds of the strikers, who would seek first to induce them to refuse to go further and to accept transportation back. Should this manner of persuasion fail, it was followed by a system of abuse, scathing denunciation, vilification, threats, and in frequent cases assaults.[18]

In mid-June District No. 17 held a convention in Williamson. The three thousand delegates demanded immediate union recognition from the operators. When the operators refused to meet with union representatives, District No. 17 called a strike for the Williamson field on July 1. The strike was not designed to pull more men out of the mines — most of them already had been locked out by the operators — but to hold union ranks intact. By late summer, Red Jacket experienced difficulty finding nonunion miners and raised its wages 25 percent.[19]

On July 17, 1920, a representative of the Operators Association informed Cornwell he had been approached by two men "claiming to be representatives of the Department of Labor." They handed the Operators Association's representative a written statement giving the United States Department of Labor's position:

> The Government has data and information that serious trouble is probable, constant agitation is on which might result in further loss of life and possible damage of property. The coal situation is such that the Government demands immediate settlement of this controversy in order to allow production to continue. The Government desiring to always deal justly with problems of this character has given this matter fair consideration from the standpoint of both employer and employee; therefore, as representatives of the Government we submit to you the following proposition:
>
> 1. The government is in favor of the policy of collective bargaining and advises that the policy be put in effect.
>
> There are two types of collective bargaining as thus defined: one in which the employees act as a group through the trade or labor union. The other in which a group of employees are represented by committees to confer with employers regarding conditions of employment.
>
> 2. There shall be no discrimination against employees in the exercise of their constitutional right to belong to any organization.
>
> 3. All employees evicted from homes shall be restored immediately and no discrimination whatsoever as to eligibility to employment shall be made against any one of said workmen on account of said strike or their participation therein.
>
> 4. We recommend the removal of the private agencies [detectives] now employed and that the regular constituted authority of county and State be invoked in the preservation of

law and order in this district, provided such becomes necessary.

The Operators Association was not interested. It would soon request federal assistance, but from the War Department not the Department of Labor.[20]

The operators first asked Sheriff G. T. Blankenship of Mingo County for assistance. If Blankenship would enforce law and order, as the operators envisioned it, the strikebreakers might make it through the jeering union crowds at the Williamson depot and past the hostile tent colonies into the mining camps. Blankenship had only two regular deputies for law enforcement, but he could deputize additional private citizens as needed. On May 25, 1920, Red Jacket mailed Blankenship a roster of its employees to be deputized and assigned to protect its property. When Blankenship refused to deputize them, claiming state law prohibited him from appointing mine guards, William D. Ord at Red Jacket complained to Cornwell. Cornwell approached Blankenship indirectly, asking him to report on the law and order situation in Mingo County — he knew Blankenship treated all operator requests for police protection suspiciously. Blankenship replied:

> My dear Governor:
> The situation remains very quiet in this section. In view of the fact that practically all of the mines in this field are organized we can not conceive any reason why there should be further disturbances.
> As to armed men parading the roads in mobs this is, as far as we can learn, untrue. Our attention has been called again and again to such rumors but upon investigation, after getting down to the facts, it develops that "so and so saw it and was telling me." We have asked that the names of such persons be divulged to us but we have never been able to ascertain a single person who recognized any member of the supposed mob.
> We assure you we will use every precaution in guarding against intrusions of this kind; and if the parties who are giving

you the information will only call our attention to these acts of
violence, we will endeavor to get at the facts; and if such
investigation develops an infraction of the law, those charged
shall be dealt with according to law.

We are having additional deputies sworn in at our session of
the county court tomorrow that we may be in position to
handle anything that might arise. It is quite true that we have
some radicals on both sides; but with the general impression
prevailing that it is a friendly contest, both will eventually
lessen their views to a more narrow channel.[21]

After finding Blankenship uncooperative, Red Jacket and
other operators asked Cornwell for state police intervention.
They assumed that the state police could order Blankenship to
halt UMW organizing activity. In fact, the state police were not
permitted by statute to interfere with Blankenship's law
enforcement policy. Accordingly, UMW organizing continued.
Exasperated, William D. Ord at Red Jacket badgered Cornwell:
"Is there no way by which the Constabulary [State Police] can
stop this verbal vilification to which our men are subjected when
ever their steps happen to cross the paths of the agitators or
malcontents?" Cornwell replied in the negative, only offering
hope that the law might be changed in the future. As far as Fred
Mooney was concerned, the state police at this time could not
have been fairer, and the United States Department of Labor
conciliator on the scene agreed.[22]

Not only did the state police tolerate union organizing, but
they also occasionally interfered with the actions of the
operators' private guards. The state police arrested two deputies
with Kentucky residence in June, 1920, for possessing unlicensed
revolvers and blackjacks. Their aggrieved employer asked
Cornwell to intervene, claiming that the deputies had immunity
from arrest in West Virginia. When informed of the operator's
complaint, the superintendent of the state police, Jackson
Arnold, ordered his men out of Mingo County, asserting: "So
long as I happen to be Superintendent I propose to conduct it as I
deem proper, regardless of attempts to dictate by letters of

innuendo or otherwise."[23]

The operators had a new idea in July, 1920. They persuaded Cornwell to order the state police back into Mingo County:

> What we would very much like to have now, and we believe our situation requires it — that you station about ten of these men at Borderland under the command of a captain or lieutenant, so that in case of any trouble, they will be on the ground, and we will not have to wait three or four hours to get them from Williamson.... Please do not infer that I am dictating to you.

The new tactic worked. The operators telegraphed Cornwell:

> PRESENCE OF SUFFICIENT STATE POLICE TO INSURE PROTECTION HAD THE EFFECT OF PEACE AND QUIET BEING MAINTAINED. WE ANTICIPATE THIS WILL BE THE RESULT AT MOST MINES WHEN SUFFICIENT PROTECTION IS APPARENT. WITH ENOUGH MEN PROPERLY PLACED BELIEVE THIS FIELD WOULD BE AT WORK ON NORMAL BASIS IN TWO WEEKS.

But Superintendent Jackson Arnold of the state police objected to the proposed expanded guard system:

> I do not believe more men should be sent to that county. In a conference with the ranking officers of the department it was agreed that the best way to handle the situation there was to keep twenty-five to thirty men in the county, distributed at advantageous points, and to be used as patrols radiating out from these points — this plan was fully explained to those whose investments in the county seemed to entitle them to consideration and was agreed to: but subsequently, it seems, these men have been used as stationary guards and it is desired to have more men for similar use, a policy, which if attempted to be carried out would call for five hundred men in that county alone.[24]

There was a practical problem in ordering five hundred state

policemen to guard the mines in Mingo County — West Virginia
only had seventy-five state policemen. An alternative police
force, the National Guard, had been federalized during the World
War. The only coercive force left was the U.S. Army. Because of
the wartime precedent eliminating the president's preliminary
proclamation, Cornwell on his own authority asked the
department commander to dispatch troops to West Virginia:

> Disorders and threatened disorders there are too numerous for
> the State police to deal with. I have seen more than a score of
> letters received by residents in the Williamson field in which
> the recipients were warned that they were to be killed. From
> these and from private information of plans that were in
> existence for the commission of other outrages I deemed
> prompt action imperative, if lives and property were to be
> protected.... We are not getting proper cooperation from
> some of the county authorities.

The first continent arrived by train from Camp Sherman,
Chillicothe, Ohio, on August 28, 1920. The next day squads
moved out to the mines located along a fifty-mile stretch of the
Tug River. The army headquarters camp in Sycamore Hollow,
near Williamson, provided trucks, mules, wagons, tents, and
other gear. The state police pulled out. Mooney observed that
Cornwell did *not* ask for troops to maintain law and order in the
operator-controlled counties, which were as disturbed by
violence as Mingo County.[25]

Cornwell's request for troops raised serious constitutional
issues. These did not bother the operators, but they concerned
Mingo County Circuit Judge James Damron. Damron jealously
guarded the law, believing it supreme over unions, operators,
governors, and judges. He was perhaps overly sensitive to
criticism of his own court, but considering his conviction that it
was the people who made the law he applied, his judicial
sensitivity happily was compatible with the people's interests.

After the Baldwin-Felts and Hatfield battle of May 19, 1920,
Damron went to Matewan to help maintain order. He asked gun

dealers to keep a record of firearms sold and the county clerk not
to grant new licenses to gun dealers. He impaneled a special grand
jury to investigate the violence. In his address to the jurors he
reviewed the events leading up to the shootings, including the
Mine Workers' effort to organize the coal field and the unlawful
eviction of miners from their homes by Baldwin-Felts detectives.
He added that there was evidence that bribes had been offered
county and municipal officers to permit the eviction of the
miners without warrant. He charged the jurors to investigate all
phases of the shootings, including the eviction of the miners, the
alleged offer of bribes, and murder and conspiracy to murder by
all parties. After the grand jury returned its indictments, Damron
prepared to try those charged.[26]

Cornwell had decided to bring the troops into Mingo County
while Damron was away on vacation in Ohio. Despite pressure
from operators to impose martial law as well, Cornwell decided
not to declare it, at least for the time being. In 1912-13, governors
Glasscock and Hatfield had declared martial law during the
strikes on Paint and Cabin creeks, with unfortunate conse-
quences for the governors' reputations, and Cornwell wished to
avoid this. When Damron heard that Cornwell had brought five
hundred troops into Mingo County, he feared martial law would
inevitably follow and wired Cornwell expressing his "surprise at
the thought of martial law in Mingo County." His immediate
concern was the Matewan trial, which was to begin shortly.
Martial law might necessitate a postponement of the trial for the
duration of the martial law period, and perhaps even the
replacement of civil by court-martial proceedings. Certainly, he
believed, a declaration of martial law would compromise the
principle of the supremacy of civil law in society:

> On the morning of August 30th I received a reply from you
> to the effect that I had been misinformed as to the
> contemplation of martial law and you quoted a telegram to
> Bronson, the Prosecuting Attorney: "There has been no
> proclamation of martial law in Mingo County and will not be if

public officials and private citizens cooperate in the enforcement of the law, the protection of life and property and the
punishment of crimes that have been or may be committed." While
this telegram was not to me, it was to the Prosecuting
Attorney, and if the words meant anything it certainly meant
that those who had committed offenses *must* be punished. You
evidently meant [I hope] that those who stood indicted should
have a fair and impartial trial, and, if guilty under the laws of
this State, they should be punished. I do not believe that you
intentionally meant to demand convictions or punishment of
crimes that had been committed, if it turned out that there was
justification.

On his return to Williamson, Damron's concern increased:

I was furnished with a copy of the Huntington Herald-
Dispatch, under date of September 1, 1920, which bore the
following headline: "Two hundred gunmen battle troops at
Chattaroy." This report was sent out to the associated press by
O. H. Booton, editor of the Mingo Republican, who told me
that the story was written from a report received over the
telephone from Chattaroy. I went to Chattaroy yesterday and
spent the afternoon discussing and gathering facts relative to
this shooting. I can assure you that this shooting, which is
mentioned in this Herald-Dispatch, was done by mine guards.
Electric lights along the front of the company's store had been
shot out; and I procured an admission from both the mine
superintendent and one of his guards that the guards shot them
out. The whole matter was not only disgusting, but it was plain
to any ordinary citizen that knew anything about conditions in
the county that this shooting was done merely to furnish some
excuse for martial law.

I also, the following day, made an investigation of the alleged
shooting at Thacker between the Federal troops and union
miners and found that the shooting was done by the Federal
troops alone; that this shooting was started by one of their own
men getting scared at a pig running around a box car and that
he fired on it and the other men, believing that the shot was
fired by some union miner, opened fire and kept it up

practically all night. A telephone message came to Williamson for help and Col. Burkhardt went to Thacker with a special train at 11 o'clock. In the meantime news was being sent out from Williamson by some one to the effect that battles were being had between Federal troops and union miners and that martial law was inevitable.[27]

To encourage the "inevitable" the operators met with Colonel Burkhardt and urged him to impress on Cornwell the need for martial law. Burkhardt obliged:

> These Gentlemen declare that conditions are, if anything, worse now than ever before. That none of the county officers are to be depended upon to make arrests or convictions. You have taken away all of your state forces, the only officials who could be depended upon to make arrests and cause convictions. You of course appreciate the peculiar status of U.S. Forces, and their handicap in making arrests unless Martial Law Exists. I request that you issue a proclamation declaring that the County of Mingo West Virginia is in a state of insurrection against the government of West Virginia and with which the State authorities are unable to cope and that you have asked the aid of the U.S. Government in restoring and maintaining order within the said county.[28]

Damron countered the operators' pressure on Cornwell by publicly lecturing his grand jury, and the governor, on constitutional government. He asserted that to declare martial law would amount to an admission that Mingo County was no longer capable of being ruled by civil law. Damron was not willing to concede this. He continued:

> The chief executive of our state, in whom the power to call for Federal aid is vested, has not only seen fit, but no doubt thought wise, to take the action he did. The Governor, among other things, offers the excuse that some of the county officials failed to co-operate with the state police in the enforcement of the law. Whatever grounds may have existed for this, I cannot

agree with him on the course taken by him. If a county officer
is charged with the enforcement of the law and fails or refuses
to discharge that duty, then he should be removed from office
by proper authorities without resorting to the extreme
measures that have been resorted to in this county.

I have said to the Governor of this state, and I say to every
man within the sound of my voice today, that this lawlessness,
to whatever extent it has been carried on, must stop and that, if
possible, without any intervention of military or martial law. I
shall and will exercise every power granted to me by the laws of
our state to put an end to it at once.

Damron followed up his address by ordering Sheriff Blankenship
to dismiss allegedly pro-UMW deputies and replace them with
professional and business men who presumably sided with
neither side in the controversy. He cancelled every pistol license
in the county. If shooting at mining camps continued, he
threatened to bring a posse of deputy sheriffs to the scene and
seize all weapons and ammunition.[29]

Damron's public attack angered Cornwell:

I have been, as you well know, trying to cooperate with you
in the enforcement of the law and the preservation of the
public peace. I was unable to confer with you about
substituting Federal troops for State Police as you were out of
the State just at the moment when witnesses [for the Matewan
trial] and citizens were being terrorized and driven from the
county.

I was shown more than a score of letters and affidavits of
reputable citizens of your county to the effect they were to be
killed, as was Anse Hatfield, prior to the assembly of your
court.

I have not sought to exceed my authority, but merely to
discharge a public duty. I shall continue that course.[30]

Replying, Damron insisted Cornwell's premise — that the
violence in Mingo County required the deployment of troops and

perhaps a declaration of martial law — was ill-founded:

> I did say, and I am forced to say now, that the facts did not justify the bringing in of Federal troops or of the declaration of martial law.
>
> As to the letters and affidavits of citizens of Mingo County to the effect that they were to be killed, as was Anse Hatfield, I know not from what source they came or for what purpose they were written. I do, however, know and knew at the time I left on my vacation that everything was being done to furnish grounds for not only bringing in the Federal troops but declaring martial law.
>
> I believe that if I had not taken the drastic steps that I did, and at the time I did, that martial law would have been declared.[31]

Cornwell earlier had cited violence at Willis Branch mining camp as an additional justification for his deployment of troops. But Damron placed full responsibility for the violence at Willis Branch on the Baldwin-Felts detectives hired by the company. Cornwell himself, on the day he requested the troops, asked the Willis-Branch company to remove the Baldwin-Felts men, commenting, "I believe that if it is understood up there that the Baldwin-Felts men are to leave, it will go a long way toward allaying the irritation."[32]

Damron agreed with Cornwell that violence in Mingo County was a problem. What they dissented about was whether the violence had reached the proportions of an insurrection justifying the deployment of federal troops and a declaration of martial law. Published figures for the nine months after the Matewan battle had placed the death tally as high as thirty-seven. In fact, there were twenty murders in Mingo County during this period, with ten accomplished in one grand spree during the Matewan battle. When these ten are subtracted, leaving ten, the figure is not greatly in excess of the normal murder rate for the county, and five of the remaining ten had nothing to do with the labor struggle.[33]

Moreover, this was Hatfield-McCoy country: many of the participants in the industrial struggle had seen their fathers and grandfathers take guns down off the wall and walk a hundred yards from the house to lie in wait for a family enemy. Incidentally, this tradition gave the miners an advantage, at least according to Keeney. When operators pointed out that more men were killed on the operator side than the union side, thereby attempting to prove that the UMW was the aggressor, Keeney patiently explained that the mountain men in the union ranks were expert shots and that the men the operators "imported in there to do the shooting could not equal them; that is all."[34]

In a long letter to Cornwell in September, 1920, Damron hammered out his final statement defending constitutional government. His theme was that the failings of democratic institutions should be corrected by the people according to law, not by authorities removed from the people:

The Jury System

We must recognize the known hostility of the American people (and Mingo has some of them) to any interference by the military with the regular administration of justice in the civil courts. You, I and a good many others who have watched the trials in inferiour courts may have lingering doubts whether the results in such courts were altogether consistent with the equal and impartial justice which the tribunals of the law are intended always to secure. It is impossible, as we all know and experience has taught us, in time of great popular excitement altogether to exclude prejudice and passion from the courts and jury box, but the correction for this is not for a [military] tribunal to attempt the exercise of authority not within its power and jurisdiction. Much must be left to the judgment and discretion of the inferior courts and jurors, and however in fact the powers of the inferiour court may have been exercised it must be presumed to have been exercised wisely.

Constitutional Protection of Life and Property

I have always favored and now favor, the state using such force as is at its command to guarantee protection of life and property, and whenever it has not such force at its command to guarantee such protection, then our laws should be amended so as to give the chief executive additional power to enforce the laws of the state without having to call for Federal military aid.

My own personal opinion is that we should have some legislation looking to the protection of corporate property and interests in time of strike. You well know that the sheriff of our county has refused to furnish coal operators with mine guards, claiming that under chapter 7, section 11, of the Code of West Virginia, that it is not lawful for him to do so. You further know that the department of public safety of this state, of which Col. Arnold is the head, has also refused to furnish the coal operators with mine guards, claiming that under section 15 and 20, respectively, of chapter 12 of the acts of the legislature of 1919, creating such department they are [*sic*, department of public safety is] prohibited from doing so. If these two departments of this state cannot, under the law, furnish protection to the property of the operators in time of strikes then the laws should be amended or authority delegated by Congress to the state to call upon the Federal Government for assistance.

"I am not the law maker"

You infer that I have not only made misrepresentations as to your acts or motives, but that I have had a change of heart. Governor, I want to assure you that during the eight years I have been on the bench I have, to the best of my ability, administered the laws of this state without showing any favors or partiality to any one or without bias or prejudice for any one.

I have had no change of heart; I have always felt, and feel now, that certain of the alleged principles for which the United Mine Workers stand are undemocratic and border closely upon an infringement of the constitutional rights of the individuals and corporations. Believing this, I have never been in sympathy with strikes made or called by union labor when there was nothing other than these undemocratic principles involved, but I am not the law maker and so long as I am on the bench I can only administer such laws as are on the statute books.[35]

The occupation of Mingo County by army troops shifted the balance of power to the operators. Keeney pleaded with the secretary of war to order the troops out. He described for the secretary, in lurid detail, the way in which the soldiers cleared pickets off the train platforms during the arrival of strikebreakers and intimidated union men in their tent colonies. Of greater significance was his quotation from the *Coal Mining Review*, an operator publication, that the "history of industrial conflicts has shown that when Federal troops were ordered into a strike zone the strike was lost. Federal troops are in the Williamson-Thacker district."[36]

Red Jacket's superintendent, William N. Cummins, agreed:

Dear Governor:

The troops maintenance here is at no cost to the county or state and if anything less than while in barracks at Camp Sherman. In case of emergency they are quite as convenient for mobilization, they are comfortably quartered and the experience is certainly excellent and broadening for the men.

Keeney's objection is the same that inspired the vicious fight against the State Constabulary. He may go as far as his lack of regard for truth will lead in his charges of partisanship but the merest surface inquiry will disprove it absolutely. Even were the men and their officers so inclined (and it is hard to be daily in touch with the situation without sympathy with the clean fight against tremendous odds which we and our loyal men have been making) the operators have been careful to insist that the attitude and action of the troops be strictly and consistently neutral.

As to how long this protection should continue, I will refer you to tabulated reports of our Committee with which you have been supplied. Since July 1st when the strike was formally declared, we have been constantly gaining in plants running, men at work and tonnage produced. Such improvement has been vastly accelerated since the troops came. Many men are still afraid to resume work owing to repeated rumors circulated by agitators that the troops are leaving; and the vicious activity of bands of thugs on trains, at Williamson, Matewan and other railroad points is still keeping out many old men who left to avoid trouble and desire to return.[37]

After Damron's public statement, early in September, that federal troops were not needed in Mingo County, the Wilson administration had asked Cornwell to consent to their withdrawal. Cornwell had agreed but stalled on setting the date. In October, Damron urged that the federal troops be gradually replaced by state police and sheriff deputies. But the operators sabotaged Damron's plan, wanting nothing short of full protection of their employees with mine guards — a condition which the union, and to a lesser extent Sheriff Blankenship and the superintendent of the state police, could not accept. William N. Cummins explained the operators' position to Cornwell:

> In his feeling that Mingo County should police her own territory and his objection to outside help, Judge Damron seems strangely blind to the fact that in this section of the county a condition has been brought about that is far beyond the normal local police ability of any community, just at a time when the police organization of Mingo has been so hopelessly undermined as to be entirely useless.
>
> The proposal to substitute one hundred Sheriff's Deputies for the troops now here is utterly impractical. Even supposing there were available sufficient men of the courage and civic devotion necessary, it is a service which should not be asked of any private citizen unless under conditions of such dire public need that no other course was possible. Strip these present soldiers of their uniforms and the back-bone of their value here is gone. A deputy sheriff is Sam Jones or Bill Smith so known before his service and so accountable afterward and it must be remembered that with the lawless, radical union agitators which the condition here has landed upon us, there is no such

animal as a neutral. There are but two attitudes, for and
against.[38]

Without explanation Damron resigned on October 31, 1920.
Cornwell appointed R. D. Bailey to complete his term. Damron
promptly accepted appointment as one of the operators'
attorneys for the Matewan trial, which he had presided over up
until this time.[39]

The army troops withdrew on November 20, 1920. Judge
Bailey tried to establish a combined force of sheriff's deputies and
state police to maintain order, but he had no more success than
Damron. Cornwell brought army troops back into Mingo County
on November 27. As before, the legal requirement for the
president to issue a preliminary proclamation was ignored. This
time Cornwell gave the troops the martial law authority the
operators desired; however, the authority was for qualified
martial law only. The civil courts remained open, and no
offenders were tried by a military commission, as had occurred
during the strikes on Cabin and Paint creeks in 1912-13.[40]

After a resolution was introduced in the Senate in February,
1921, to investigate the War Department for deploying soldiers
to police strikes, Secretary Newton D. Baker ordered the soldiers
back to Camp Sherman. Howard Sutherland, one of West
Virginia's senators, pleaded in vain with Baker on behalf of
Cornwell to keep them in Mingo County. When Baker volubly
quoted from the Constitution in defense of his decision,
Sutherland was unimpressed, writing Cornwell: "The Constitution, however, having been apparently violated for some weeks
already, it does not appear to me that his excuse is a valid one."[41]

For the nation as a whole, between July 1, 1918, and December
31, 1920, soldiers were deployed thirty times without the
president issuing the preliminary proclamation. The height of
war-conditioned thinking was reached in May, 1920, when the
War Department secretly prepared War Plan White, a complete
"war plan" for suppressing civil disorders. The Senate's criticism
of the War Department's use of soldiers in civil disorders led to a

general reappraisal of the policy and the reestablishment of the preliminary proclamation. By 1923, the prewar policy of requiring the preliminary proclamation had become standard operating procedure.[42]

In September, 1920, — in the midst of the political maneuvering in West Virginia on the deployment of federal troops — Red Jacket officially sued for its injunction against the UMW. On November 3, 1920, Judge Edmund Wadill, Jr. awarded Red Jacket a preliminary injunction. It enjoined Keeney, Mooney, and all the members of the UMW "from in any way or manner interfering with the said contracts of employment" between Red Jacket and its employees. Superintendent Cummins at Red Jacket mailed copies of the injunction to Mayor E. K. Beckner of Matewan:

> You are doubtless fully aware of the conditions existing in your town under which the activity of certain vicious and disorderly characters have rendered it unsafe for our men to pass through the town in normal procedure to and from trains. Any interference with these men in our employ will be a direct violation of the order of injunction, and I would suggest that you so inform your Police Chief and any Deputies on duty and have them so inform all others in order to avoid the sure consequences of such contempt of Federal Court.

On November 29, 1920, three UMW members assaulted two Red Jacket employees. The federal court convicted them for violating the injunction and sentenced them to sixty days in jail. Conviction was easily and quickly obtained, since the accused were charged with violating the injunction instead of a criminal statute and were tried before a judge instead of jury. Red Jacket's management undoubtedly was pleased.[43]

The injunction proceedings, and accompanying contempt of court trials, also had attrition value for Red Jacket, since Keeney, Mooney, and District No. 17 lawyers dissipated much energy and spent large sums defending the union and its members.[44]

But the injunction had an additional benefit for Red Jacket. When in May, 1920, William D. Ord tipped off Cornwell about Red Jacket adopting individual employment contracts, Red Jacket gave Cornwell the ideological underpinning he probably needed to enable him to stand up to Sheriff Blankenship's and Judge Damron's criticism about his employing force against the miners. Indeed, this political value may have been more important to Red Jacket than the injunction suit itself, which grew out of its adopting individual employment contracts. Of course, Blankenship and Damron were right to oppose Cornwell's actions — statutory law did not support West Virginia using force aginst the union. State Police Superintendent Jackson Arnold best summed up the situtation: "If you had regular officers of the law that would live absolutely up to the law, why, then organizers could go into these unorganized fields with impunity, and it would simply result in the entire county being organized."[45]

The miners' embittered experience with Cornwell impelled them to run their own candidate, Samuel B. Montgomery, in the Republican gubernatorial primary of 1920. The operators' candidate, Ephraim F. Morgan, narrowly defeated Montgomery in a three-way race. Montgomery then ran in the election as a non-partisan candidate. Morgan won the election, receiving 150,000 votes. But Montgomery, as a third-party candidate, received a surprising 81,000 votes. The Democratic candidate received only 42,500 votes. Montgomery supporters claimed that their candidate ran even better than the official tally indicated. They charged that in open-shop counties deputy sheriffs, who supervised the counting of ballots, invalidated and destroyed thousands of ballots marked for Montgomery.[46]

The operators believed victory was at hand during the spring of 1921. The recession of that year helped, shifting the economic burden from the operators to the union. Miners began to abandon the union and return to the open-shop mines. Superintendent Cummins at Red Jacket discovered he could reduce his wages to the prestrike level and still find men willing to work.[47]

The newly inaugurated governor, Ephraim F. Morgan, yielded to operator demands in May, 1921, and requested federal troops. The War Department denied his request in keeping with the restoration of the preliminary proclamation and admonished him to exert more effort on his own to maintain order. Shortly thereafter, Morgan declared martial law in Mingo County and organized a volunteer state police force made up of "respectable" Mingo citizens. Under the command of Captain J. R. Brockus of the state police, the volunteers entered their first engagement on June 14, 1921, at the Lick Creek tent colony, between Williamson and Matewan. Brockus had stopped at the tent colony to investigate a shooting:

> As we were getting out of the car on the hillside on the public road a shot was fired. We discussed the matter there a little, and finally the major ordered Sergt. Taylor, who was carrying one of these machine guns, to sprinkle the hillside. He was rather slow doing it and he told him a second time. These guns fire a clip of 20. He opened fire and fired about half that number and stopped. Another shot or two was fired from the hill, and he finished the clip, firing 20 shots altogether, and the firing ceased.
>
> We went back to Williamson and had our signal sounded, which is four blasts of the fire whistle repeated three times, and in about 10 minutes approximately 70 men responded with rifles and ammunition. They were loaded in cars and drove out.
>
> We took the main force and formed a line and struck down that rough, rugged country — a line a mile long. We came right down through the colony. It was rather hot for a time, and I should say there was between 50 and 75 shots fired. We marched on to the county road and then went over to the bridge; and about the time I got to the bridge somebody called from the hillside, and he called me by name, and I answered, "What is the matter?" He answered, "It is Bowles; I am shot; come and help me." I sent a man up and had him brought out.
>
> At that point they stated that a miner had been killed up there. We did not have any particular time right then to hunt

up the dead, so we proceeded to gather up what men were in the colony. Now, on that round-up I think we got 47 men and formed them on the railroad track and then took them into Williamson. They were locked up in the city jail.[48]

At about the same time as the Lick Creek operation, the state supreme court of appeals ruled that Governor Morgan's declaration of martial law was invalid because it was enforced by civil agencies. Accordingly, miners detained in jail were released. This decision was surprising in light of the court's earlier unequivocal endorsement of governors Glasscock's and Hatfield's use of martial law in the strikes on Cabin and Paint creeks. Morgan issued a new proclamation of martial law on June 27, 1921, which conformed to the Supreme Court's requirements. Under it he enrolled 130 Mingo County citizens into the state militia and assigned it the task of maintaining peace. Offenses against martial law were nonbailable and beyond the pale of the civil courts. Offending miners were detained in jail without charges or forced to leave the state at the whim of Major Thomas B. Davis, acting adjutant general.[49]

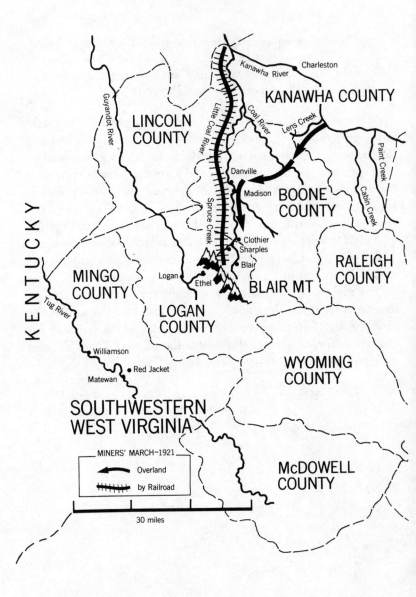

Chapter Four

THE MARCH

"The thugs are coming!"

On the evening of August 26, 1921, a locomotive engineer for the C. & O. began an after-supper game of pool in Clothier, West Virginia. Armed coal miners entered the pool hall and ordered him to run the C. & O. train to Danville.

> I held off as long as I dared. I tried to get word to the dispatcher, but the wires were down and I could not get anyone. Then it was my suggestion that they send a man ahead on a motor car to flag for us.[1]

In Danville later that same evening, Jack Brinkman, a musician in The Old Kentucky Show, walked over to the train depot after his performance to see what the commotion was about. A union miner asked: "Was he for them?"

> "Certainly I am with you and for you, if that will do you any good," and they told me to get on the train "or else," and the man who was doing the talking had a 38 special pistol, and I got on the train, and I judge that was the best thing to do.

The train moved up the Little Coal River and Spruce Fork to Blair, nestled beneath the mountain that gave the town its name. It stopped frequently, picking up seven hundred men in all before it reached Blair. Blair Mountain geographically separates Boone and Kanawha counties, largely organized by the UMW, from Logan, Mingo, and McDowell counties, in which open-shop operations predominated.[2]

Logan County directly abutted the union-controlled counties and served as the gateway for the UMW to reach the more distant Mingo and McDowell counties. The sheriff of Logan County, Don Chafin, ruled with an iron hand, enforcing the open-shop for the operators. Although under West Virginia law a sheriff cannot succeed himself, Chafin had been either sheriff or deputy sheriff for a number of terms. He had also been assessor and county clerk. The operators supplied Chafin all the money he needed to run his political organization and to hire deputy sheriffs. For the first nine months of 1921 the operators paid him $61,517. No stranger entered Logan County without Chafin first establishing his identity and business. If he did not pass scrutiny, Chafin and his deputies slugged him and sent him out of the county on the first train. Over the years Chafin acquired several battle scars, including one earned by losing a pistol draw to William Petry, vice president of District No. 17 of UMW. Along with his backwoods prowess, Don Chafin possessed the trim look, handsome dress, and assurance of the college man he was — the perfect model of a corporation representative.[3]

Since July 1, 1920, the Mine Workers had struck the Mingo County coal fields located immediately to the west of Logan County. Both miners and operators had resorted to violence. Unidentified but undoubtedly prounion assailants entered into a drunken brawl with State Policeman Private Kackley, who was on strike duty, and killed him; similarly unidentified but undoubtedly prooperator assailants lynched Frank Ingram, a black union member, beat him, and left him dying on railroad tracks. After Governor Ephraim F. Morgan imposed martial law, the Mingo County jail overflowed with union organizers and strikers, necessitating a transfer of prisoners to McDowell County.[4]

As the Mingo strike went into its second year on July 1, 1921, the miners became disheartened and demanded that their president, C. Frank Keeney, bear down upon the Mingo operators. Keeney assured them:

> We are going to organize that coal field down there if it takes all the United Mine Workers of America to do it. All of Don Chafin's hired gunmen, and all of the companies' thugs and all of Governor Morgan's Cossacks couldn't prevent us.

Keeney called on liberals throughout the nation to organize constitutional leagues to support the civil liberties of West Virginia miners.[5]

Events took a critical turn when on August 1, 1921, District No. 17 threatened to march several hundred citizens into Mingo County to protest against the jailing of strikers. The mine operators equated "march" with "invasion," and using an analogy to the world war, talked with foreboding of Logan County becoming another "Belgium" for their enemy to cross on its way into Mingo County.[6]

Governor Ephraim F. Morgan was a tall, heavy-set man, with gray hair parted in the middle and a full, strongly lined face. He did not understand the miners. On his way to Sunday School on August 7, 1921, three weeks before the miners hijacked the Danville train, Morgan observed miners gathering for a mass meeting across the street.

> When I came back, some were speaking. I could hear them very plainly on the porch from the house, but I couldn't distinguish what they were saying, and after dinner, about 2 o'clock, I drove out into the country.[7]

On his return, he courteously met with miners waiting to present to him resolutions adopted by the mass meeting. The miners viewed their situation as increasingly serious, and their adoption of the resolutions reflected this. In the midst of a nationwide recession and operator demands for wage cuts, the union had held firm, only to discover that coal production soared in open-shop West Virginia counties. Meanwhile, coal production dropped to 40 percent in union fields. Some union miners had worked only thirty days since January 1, 1921. In their resolutions they asked Morgan to bring the Mingo miners and operators together to establish a joint commission for adjusting wages and other disputes. In his reply of August 17, 1921, Morgan said he would not establish the joint commission because to establish it would imply official recognition of UMW miners and the Mingo operators had stated categorically that they would not recognize the UMW. It was a matter of law. In the *Hitchman* decision (1917), continued Morgan, the United States Supreme Court had declared: "An employer is acting within his lawful rights in making non-membership in a union a condition of employment. . . . [This] is a part of the constitutional rights of personal liberty and private property."[8]

Since the dispute had no status in law, Morgan reasoned it did not exist:

> There is no fight in West Virginia between the operator and union miner. In the three large coal mining counties in West Virginia, that are unorganized, the feeling between the operator and the miners is as amicable, if not more so than in the organized fields. In the counties operated by nonunion labor in order to secure employment the employees have accepted voluntary reductions in wages.
>
> All the trouble that has arisen is the result of some agitators and organizers representing the United Mine Workers, not resident in the unorganized fields, desiring to organize same.[9]

In the middle of August, Don Chafin received information that union men in Kanawha and Boone counties had left the mines and taken to the roads. They reportedly had bought or looted weapons, ammunition, and food and had posted armed guards on the highways to turn back intruders hostile to their movement. He telephoned this intelligence to Governor Morgan, and Morgan empowered him to protect his county. Chafin mustered an army from deputies and volunteer citizens and ordered it into a defensive position along Blair Mountain.[10]

Although Morgan refused to acknowledge the existence of the labor dispute, he could not deny the fact that armed miners were taking to the roads. On August 24, he attempted to persuade the miners to disband. He asked Mother Jones, who in her nineties had reached the end of her long organizing career with the UMW, to turn back the miners then assembling on Lens Creek. Mother agreed and read the miners a telegram purporting to be from President Warren G. Harding asking the men to return peacefully to their homes. The miners asked Keeney and Mooney to verify the telegram. Mooney called Harding's secretary and discovered that Mother had faked the telegram. When challenged, Mother evaded the issue and charged Keeney and Mooney with urging the miners on while she had been trying to turn them back. Betrayed and angered, the miners did not return to their homes; they continued up Lens Creek, over to Danville, and on to Blair.[11]

After the Mother Jones debacle the crisis assumed dimensions Morgan could understand — he knew how to deal with law breakers:

> Radical leaders of the United Mine Workers with criminal intent have sought to place themselves above the law. This is a time when the people of West Virginia who believe in the maintenance of law and order must stand united.

Morgan telegraphed President Harding a request for troops. Harding refused. Instead, he dispatched General Bandholtz to Charleston.[12]

At 3:05 A.M. on August 26, 1921, the same day the miners hijacked the train from Danville to Blair, Brigadier General H. H. Bandholtz arrived in Charleston, only thirty miles east of

Danville. He immediately met with Keeney and Mooney. Mooney gave the following account:

> Bandholtz said, "You two are the officers of this organiza-
> tion, and these are your people. I am going to give you a chance
> to save them, and if you cannot turn them back we are going to
> snuff this out just like that," and he snapped his fingers under
> our noses. He further said: "This will never do, there are
> several million unemployed in this country now and this thing
> might assume proportions that would be difficult to handle."
>
> "Would you arm us with a statement signed by you telling
> the miners what the consequences will be if they do not turn
> back?" Keeney and Mooney asked.
>
> "No," said Bandholtz.
>
> "Then I believe our trip will be fruitless," Mooney replied.
>
> "Yes, I will give you a note," and immediately he dictated
> one.
>
> Securing a taxi we started out to intercept the advance
> columns. While en route up Lens Creek, we passed several
> small groups of miners encamped or moving on to join the
> main body.
>
> We moved up Droddy Creek, thence across the mountain
> into Danville. Marchers were strung out along this creek from
> mouth to head. Each company was under the direction of an
> ex-soldier. Seven hundred of these boys were in both the
> Spanish-American War and the World War. In charge of one
> of these companies was Harvey Dillon of Winifrede and
> veteran of both wars. When he saw who was in the cab he split
> his company, forming an aisle through which we passed. He
> stopped at the advance end and blocked the way.
>
> "Boys, what are you fellows doing here?" he asked. After
> reading General Bandholtz' note to him, we explained the
> situation.
>
> "Boys, are you telling us straight?" he asked.
>
> "Read the ultimatum," I said, handing him the note.
>
> "That's his signature all right for I was an orderly under him
> in the Philippines and I would know his signature anywhere."
> Turning to his company, he said: "Salute! damn you salute."
> Following the salute he turned to his men. "Boys, we can't

fight Uncle Sam, you know that as well as I do." Turning to us he inquired, "What shall we do, turn back from here?"

"No. Take your men on into Danville and wait until we can arrange for special trains to take you out," we replied.

During the entire conversation just recorded, Dillon was crying as were many of his men. Tears of defeat coursed their way down many cheeks. The majority of his men were dressed in regulation army clothing, including helmets, and several of them were carrying gas masks.

We overtook the advance columns as they were leaving Madison, pushing on in the direction of Blair in Logan County. We prevailed upon them to turn back and congregate in the ball park at Danville until we could talk to them. "We are going on," they insisted.

"Boys, you better listen to reason, for you are all going to be slaughtered if you proceed," we warned.

When they were convinced that we were really telling the truth, they agreed to return to the ball park and go into camp with those with whom we had conferred along the route.

After securing a room and some food at a hotel we followed the remaining marchers to the ball park at Danville. During the meeting, many of the miners and their friends were bitter and denunciative toward us because we had intercepted them; but after we read the message from General Bandholtz they quieted down and became more reasonable. However, even then we were skeptical about permitting them to take a vote. "We are not going to call for a vote, we are just going to ask you to take our advice and let us take you out of here," Keeney admonished. Many grumbles and threats were heard, some cried, some cursed, while others acted as though they appreciated the effort we made to get the message to them on time.

We returned to the hotel and I tried to arrange for special trains to transport them out of the territory.

Sundown brought Lewis White from Blair. He was riding a velocipede, was coatless, and carried two Smith and Wesson revolvers of the latest type. When he stopped at the depot where Keeney and I were standing he said, "What the hell you fellows mean by stopping these marchers."

"To prevent them being slaughtered," we informed him.

"Oh, hell! What you two need is a bullet between each of your eyes," he said. Being worn out and not in very good mental or physical condition, it was "nip and tuck" which one of us took the lead in extending him an invitation to try his hand.

From Lewis White had come many of the reports that the gunmen were firing on and had killed women and children at Blair. I believed then and believe now that White was an undercover operative for the gunmen.

Fifteen or twenty minutes after Lewis White arrived at Madison the commandeered train came down, and after he boarded the coach it went on to the ball park at Danville. Speeches were made to the miners by White and several of his colleagues in an effort to get them to board the train and go on to Blair.

It was several hours before any promise of a special train could be secured and eventually it appeared that we were being thwarted through the governor's office. There was an Associated Press representative along with us and he said, "Let me get on that phone and see what I can do." He went through to Pittsburgh, contacting his superiors by telephone, and soon afterward we were notified that the train was on its way and would arrive about 3:00 A.M. We were very apprehensive while the commandeered train was in Danville that a part of the men would leave Danville before we could get the special train in there to take them out.

The special train arrived at 5:00 A.M. and the miners crowded aboard. There were 786 men on the special train. I know that because I helped to check the men up to get the fares correct. It was continued from St. Albans to Fayetteville and way points. Several extra street cars were run to Cabin Creek Junction.

The next day, August 27, unaware that the Danville train had been hijacked during the night, General Bandholtz returned to Washington, satisfied with the results he had obtained.[13]

When Don Chafin learned that Keeney and Mooney had turned the miners back at Danville on the afternoon of August 26, he recalled his army from Blair Mountain. But when at 11:30

P.M. he received word that the hijacked train was on its way to Blair, he sounded the fire whistle in the town of Logan, sending his men back up Blair Mountain.[14]

Governor Morgan had specifically instructed Chafin to hold the line on Blair Mountain and not to advance. However, the governor had also granted him permission to arrest miners who on August 12 had disarmed two state policemen and two of his deputies. Chafin called the commander of the state police on duty in Mingo County and asked for assistance, which he provided. At 5:00 P.M. on August 27, Captain Brockus, accompanied by ninety men, met Chafin at Ethel, a mining camp four miles west of the intended objective, Sharples. Chafin turned over to Brockus two hundred deputies and the warrants for arrest. The posse moved up Dingess Run, over Blair Mountain and, at nightfall, started down Beech Creek. Captain Brockus recounted what happened:

> We moved out about dark down past the creek near the railroad and we were challenged by a detachment of five men who commanded us to halt. We stopped and they asked us who we were. We told them and we ordered them to surrender which they did without resistance, we simply walked up, took their rifles away from them. There were five men in the party, three high-power rifles and two shot guns. Two of the men were Russians and could not speak English and admitted they were not citizens of the United States. We placed them under arrest and put them at the head of the column and explained to them if we were challenged again for them to answer and tell the men who they were so they would not fire into the column. We marched down I suppose some 300 yards and met a car, it was a Ford car, I think, and it had three men in it, they were all armed. We disarmed them and placed them in with the other prisoners.
>
> We marched on to what is known as Sharples. We met another detachment of armed men. We had already stopped when we saw them coming up. I answered their challenge commanding us to halt and they asked who we were. I told them state police, they wanted to know what we were doing there and I stated we were patrolling the road, it was the first

thought that come to my mind. I asked what they were doing out there armed at that time of night. One man replied, "By God, that is our business." He had no more than gotten the words out of his mouth when one of the men fired on our party. They were pretty well lined up in front of us. At that instant our men returned the fire. All five of them hit the ground. I heard afterwards two were killed and three wounded. The firing became general, they were shooting from the houses, from doorways and windows, they turned all the lights on in this little mining camp and it lighted up the public road. Our men slid off the side of the road, it is graded four or five feet through the camp. We passed word back to all our men to cease firing which they did. We decided the best thing to do was to move back, get in the dark and assemble our men and check up to see if we had lost any. We found the police were all there and the deputies pretty well together in the rear of us.[15]

Brockus did not try to serve the warrants again. His troops suffered no casualties — surprisingly, considering Brockus's assertion that the miners had fired first. But in the confusion five prisoners escaped; one deputy got lost and the miners captured him; several men lost miscellaneous hats, revolvers, ammunition, and musette bags; and at Ethel the next morning a Logan Mining Company employee accidentally shot Private George Duling in the head and killed him.[16]

After the Sharples engagement, women and children began fleeing Sharples and Blair. Armed miners streamed in to take their places. Governor Morgan sent the adjutant general of West Virginia and UMW leaders to Sharples to try to cool union tempers. The delegation read the miners a letter from Keeney advising them to lay down their arms and return to their homes. The miners replied that lack of protection made returning home unthinkable. In the past, they said, the Logan deputies had not beaten up their people unless their families had crossed over the mountain to the town of Logan on innocent business, such as recording deeds at the courthouse. But now the deputies had deliberately crossed over into their district and disturbed their peaceful lives, and they intended to defend themselves to the last. The governor's delegation reported their response to the miners:

> They were admonished of the direful effect that always resulted to the community when men attempted to take the law into their own hands and attempt to administer so called justice, and did not allow the regularly constituted authorities to function; that the individual could not supercede the commonwealth and while they might for a few days accomplish their purpose that very soon they must expect a force superior to their own to come in and restore the regular established government and that those concerned might expect to be punished for their illegal acts.[17]

When Morgan received word that the hijacked train had reached Blair and that Captain Brockus had encountered armed resistance at Sharples, he again appealed to the president. In his request he embellished his description of what he now termed an "insurrection" with an unsubstantiated report that a thousand miners led by Bolshevists from Indiana, Ohio, and Illinois had joined the West Virginia miners. He also sent to Washington a delegation of distinguished West Virginians to present his request to the president.[18]

Initially, the secretary of war telegraphed Morgan that United States troops could be ordered to West Virginia only after all efforts of the local law enforcement agencies had failed to suppress the insurrection. General Bandholtz had advised the secretary of war that Morgan had not used all the resources at his command to halt the miners' march. Former Governor Henry D. Hatfield had told the attorney general much the same thing. Since it increasingly appeared that Morgan was losing control of the situation, the administration reversed course and Harding issued a preliminary proclamation ordering the insurrectionaries to disband. He sent Bandholtz back to West Virginia to find out whether or not the miners would obey his proclamation. If they did not obey it, the president would send in the troops.[19]

By August 31 events began to outpace Keeney's and Mooney's

ability to control them: the miners resented the two leaders'
efforts to turn them back, and even threatened to harm them.
Keeney and Mooney also learned that the Mingo County grand
jury was about to return indictments against them on five counts
ranging from misdemeanor to murder. Although convinced of
their own innocence, they remembered the gunning down of Sid
Hatfield and Ed Chambers on August 1, when they appeared for
trial in McDowell County. They decided, as Mooney described
the occasion, "to 'clear out' for a few days." They left Charleston
at 12:15 A.M. of September 1 and crossed the Ohio River to Point
Pleasant. R.M. Williams, a district field worker, met them at
Point Pleasant and transported them to Columbus where,
continued Mooney, "with the assistance of John 'Jock' Moore we
found suitable headquarters."[20]

General Bandholtz arrived in Charleston the same day Keeney
and Mooney left. He sent staff officers accompanied by Philip
Murray, vice president of the UMW, and David Fowler, a UMW
organizer, to Sharples to find out if the miners had obeyed the
president's proclamation. The investigating party also carried
with them a letter from Governor Morgan assuring the miners
that they "would not be molested by state or county authorities
while making a sincere effort to return to their homes in
compliance with the proclamation of the President." They found
the residents of Sharples unrepentant and sullen.

> The women seemed to say more than the men. They did not
> want the men to go back unless the United States troops were
> there to see that they were protected.
> "My God, Mr. Fowler, it would be all right if it were the
> union's affair, and we would say nothing; but it is not the
> union's affair, and the people of West Virginia are here to
> protect their honor."

The investigating party recommended that troops be sent in, and
Bandholtz telegraphed Washington for them. He observed that
they would not have been necessary had the evacuation train
arrived promptly in Danville on August 26, and had Chafin not

sent over his "ill-advised and ill-timed advance movement of state constabulary on the night of August 27 resulting in bloodshed. . . . Many persons seem to think that they will disperse as soon as troops appear. I am taking no chances."[21]

Although the trains had been spotted and units alerted for embarkment, the first troops would not arrive until September 2, and they would not reach the combatants on Blair Mountain until September 4.

Meanwhile the miners and their opponents could play the war game. Jack Brinkman, the reader will recall, was the musician from the Old Kentucky Show whom the union miners had forced to board the hijacked train destined for Blair on the evening of August 26. At 2:00 the following morning, Brinkman stepped off the hijack train at Spruce Valley Tipple, a few minutes' walk from Blair. Someone gave him a sandwich and coffee and billeted him in a home. There wasn't much going on around there for a few days, Brinkman reported. However, he added:

> Everyone seemed to be excited, — there was no one working. There seemed to be fear on the part of some of them that they could expect an attack from the Logan side. Every one appeared to have an arm, a pistol or a high-power rifle. As near as I could judge, it was like a man walking around with a chip on his shoulder.

Henry Cole came out of the mines when the trouble started and earned five dollars a day boiling beef in the yard for Mrs. Riggs at the Spruce Valley Hotel. Sam Marlowe spent most of his time up in a grove, just back of the schoolhouse, having a little card game. A few stray shots fell into Blair. When Mrs. Ike Wilburn set down the feed bucket on her back porch on her way in from milking her cow, a bullet struck it and knocked it over. [22]

After news of the Sharples engagement reached Blair, the mood became apprehensive. Patrols scouted Blair Mountain for the enemy. Knowing the password, "I come creeping," could make the difference between life or death. On the afternoon of August 30, Jack Brinkman joined a hundred other men at the schoolhouse to hear Reverend John Wilburn instruct them on their patrol assignments for the next day. Reverend Wilburn, a round-shouldered, tired little man, had been pastor of the Baptist Church in Blair for five years. He supported his family by working in the mines. At the military briefing he harangued the men, suggesting they plan on eating dinner in Logan the next day and *not* to bring back any prisoners.[23]

Before evening a patrol climbed a mile and a half to the ridge of the mountain, set out guards to warn against surprise attacks by the Logan deputies, and camped for the night. In the morning they awakened to shots coming from the gap. Wilburn sent out scouts and ordered the rest of the body to follow. Brinkman recalled what happened next:

> The Rev. Wilburn was leading the party, and when we got up to where Gore, Muncy and Cafalgo [Logan deputies] were standing we were asked by Gore who we were, and the Rev. Wilburn asked who they were and demanded the password. Then Gore demanded the password from us, and he was again asked the password by Rev. Wilburn, and in unison Gore, Cafalgo and Muncy said, "Amen," and when they said "Amen," the firing started. It did not last long, but it was long enough to down these three men. There had been a negro standing along side of me and he was hit by a high power ball, and he fell. I looked to see how badly he was injured, and noticed that he was wounded, and I went to the head of the column where they were bunched up and looking at the men who fell. One man who had been shot was Muncy and he was lying in the trail in a twisted position. He made some remarks about their having shot the wrong fellow, and for us not to shoot again; and Kitchen said he would kill the God damned son of a bitch and thug, and he raised his rifle — it was a 401 caliber, I know because it was the only one in the party, and he shot him over the left eye. When the ball pierced his head, and then through it, his head jumped up off the ground and the blood welled out like water would out of a hose where you turn

it on and the pressure is light.

There was some remarks made about we ought not to have done it, and I got out of there after that as quick as I could. I started off the hill with Jess Wilburn and two others, and we were carrying the body of this negro who had been shot. He was shot in the small of the back and the bullet came out up here between the collar bone and the clavicle, and his lungs must have been torn because every few yards we had to stop and turn him over and let the blood run out of his wound. It was too much for this boy and he fainted. We took him to Dr. Milliken's office and placed him on the table and he died.[24]

On August 30, the day before the miners killed Gore, Muncy, and Calfago, Governor Morgan relieved Don Chafin as commander of the Logan army and appointed Colonel William E. Eubanks, a National Guard officer — presumably to clothe the Logan army with state authority. Eubanks brought 250 American Legion Volunteers with him from Welch in McDowell County, making a total of 2,500 men under his command. Governor Morgan obtained 40,000 rounds of ammunition, 400 rifles, and two machine guns from the governor of Kentucky to supplement the personal arms of Eubank's army. Eubanks also had three airplanes which flew missions on September 1:

I had reports that a number of men, from three to five hundred, were coming up certain roads to attack my position, and as I wished to stop them, and as I could not advance by order of the Governor, I dropped those bombs. When they hit if anyone got in the cloud or the gas they would be made very sick, — they would vomit, — it would cause extreme nausea; the other bombs, if any part of it hit them it would hurt them very badly. They were made out of six inch pipe nipples with union joints, filled with black powder and nuts and bolts and any kind of scraps like that.[25]

Every day of the war Eubanks reported engagements with the enemy. His troops maintained continuous fire "driving back repeated attempts by the miners to advance." Occasionally the

Logan militia suffered casualties and nearby doctors and nurses treated them. When the Logan militia captured enemy miners, they imprisioned them in the Logan County jail.[26]

On the miners' side, Jack Brinkman and a few miners drove down to Clothier and again ordered a railroad engineer to take out a train for transporting supporters to Blair. The miners cut the wires on the C.&O. line to secure their operation, and when a railroad repair crew went out to correct the damage, they were prevented from doing so by the presence of armed men. Altogether, the miners made three more train trips, bringing in a total of two thousand more supporters. During this hijacking operation the C.&O. was forced to suspend its normal traffic.[27]

To care for their casualties the miners turned one of the Blair Schoolhouse rooms into an aid station. Nurses in uniform with UMW insignia treated the wounded until doctors could be called in. In all, the miners' army suffered perhaps fifteen casualties (The Logan army had half the number). Part of the schoolhouse also served as a makeshift command post. From there the leaders sent out fresh men to the firing line to relieve worn-out militia. Firing was continuous, reported a participant: "It would echo and roll around so much — sometimes you would think they was right down in Blair. Machine guns cracked up there, you would think the whole place was coming down on you.[28]

War correspondents rushed to West Virginia. Mildred Morris of International News Service attempted to cross through the lines at Sharples. Accompanied by miners and two male reporters, she hiked from the miners' position toward the Logan forces. After sighting them, the Logan forces opened fire, slightly wounding one male reporter, and took the correspondents prisoner. When they discovered they had a woman captive, Mildred Morris, they reviled her with epithets, driving her to hysteria before she reached the town of Logan and the safety of a hotel room.[29].

The spokesmen for the two armies reveled in the glory of the event. Governor Morgan spoke of the "volunteer army of defenders who, with patriotic motive, offered themselves to the

State to be used in crushing the insurrection and restoring law and order." Philip Murray visited the miners' front. He boasted that the way the battle was going there would be little cause for further complaint about Chafin's deputies: "it was self-evident to any casual observer that the outcome was inevitable, as the citizens' army was making steady advance into the camp of its enemy."[30]

But if the events on Blair Mountain seemed like war to the participants, to Captain John J. Wilson arriving on the scene it lacked credibility:

> It was a comic opera war of the miners going up after breakfast, staying up an hour or two, and coming down for a confab or a little airing and going up again and wasting thousands and thousands of rounds of ammunition and hitting no one.
>
> They were under the impression the thugs from Logan were after them. "The thugs are coming! The thugs this, or the thugs that." As they came from the firing line they all said: "Three more days and we would have been in Logan." It would have been about three years before they advanced a foot from the way they looked.

When U.S. Army Major Thompson talked with Colonel Eubanks about arrangements for relieving the Logan army, Eubanks conversation impressed him as muddled. Upon arrival in Logan, Thompson discovered why: he found Eubanks and his staff so intoxicated as to render them unfit — they had been on a drunk for at least twenty-four hours. Leaders were divided among themselves. There was no organized plan of defense. Many persons joined the defenders in search of adventure, and after tasting it, disappeared. Boys fourteen and fifteen years old manned positions with high-powered rifles. Frequently men fired off cartridges for no apparent reason.[31]

Late at night on September 2, the 19th Infantry Company, the first detachment of the United States Army to arrive on the scene, detrained in Danville. The next day it moved up the Little Coal River and Spruce Fork to Sharples. With the help of UMW officials, Major Charles T. Smart persuaded the miners to surrender their weapons and return to their homes. Many of them boarded the same train the troops had come in on for the return trip down the river. Early the following morning, September 4, the 19th Infantry moved on to Blair. Again the miners cooperated with the army's request to disband and go home. In all, during the next four days 4,000 miners left the battle zone on roads and trails and another 1,400 left by rail. They turned over four hundred firearms to the troops, but they hid many hundreds more in the hills. The army did not fire a shot during the entire operation. Women and children refugees returned to their homes.[32]

The army brought to the operation a practiced efficiency acquired in putting down thirty domestic disturbances since the World War. General Bandholtz commanded 2,320 soldiers brought in from Kentucky, Ohio, and New Jersey. Besides the rifle and machine gun companies, the War Department ordered a chemical warfare detachment to West Virginia. It was equipped with tear gas designed to penetrate any mask used outside the Chemical Warfare Service — it was only "slightly poisonous," causing headaches, vomiting, and severe coughing. The chemical detachment did not employ its gas except during a demonstration for newsmen.[33]

Military intelligence officers investigated the marchers. They found little IWW and Bolshevist literature in their hands and only one radical newspaper, the *West Virginia Federationist*, "a vile, lying and colorful sheet." They estimated 10 percent of the marchers were Italians, Russians, and Hungarian Poles, some of whom might be subject to deportation. In general, they described the marchers as "poor, ignorant creatures who will believe anything that they are told"; who eagerly join in mob rule; and have "little appreciation for right and wrong."[34]

For the first — and last — time, the Army Air Force participated in quelling a civil disturbance. Brigadier General

William (Billy) Mitchell flew into Charleston from Washington on August 26, shortly after General Bandholtz arrived by train. Mitchell met with newspersons and briefed them on how he would handle the marchers:

> All this could be left to the air service. If I get orders I can move in necessary forces in three hours.
>
> Question: How would you handle masses of men under cover in gullies?
>
> Gas. You understand we wouldn't try to kill people at first. We'd drop tear gas all over the place. If they refused to disperse then we'd open up with artillery preparation and everything.

When Keeney turned back the miners at Danville, Mitchell returned to Washington. However, Mitchell ordered the 88th Squadron at Langley Field, Virginia, to prepare for deployment in the event the miners resumed their march. On September 1, the War Department ordered the squadron to West Virginia. Fifteen DeHavillands equipped with machine guns and ammunition and two Martin bombers without bombs (the bombs went by railway express) took off for Roanoke, Virginia, where the pilots spent the night.[35] The next morning the ground was soft from rain. The pilots jacked up their planes and pulled them out of the mud. At 6:30 A.M. the first plane got away. When Lieutenant Valentine S. Miner's turn came, he took off and crashed into an adjacent field. The air service later dismantled his plane and shipped it to an Ohio depot for repair. Captain John J. Devery, Jr. made it to Beckley, West Virginia, when engine trouble forced him down. On landing, he broke the plane's axle, shock absorber, and one wheel. Lieutenant Leslie Arnold, who had taken off from Aberdeen, Maryland, was blown off course and missed Charleston completely. He put down near Fairmont, West Virginia, and hit a fence on landing. Meanwhile, Lieutenants Goodrich and Liebhauser lost themselves in fog and spent the night of September 2 in Mooresburg, Tennessee. The next day, they flew into a storm and made forced landings. Goodrich hit a ditch, slicing off his landing gear; Liebhauser hit a fence, and his plane burst into flames. Miraculously, all the pilots escaped serious injury.[36]

The remaining pilots who reached Charleston safely flew reconnaissance missions. General Bandholtz instructed them not to drop any bombs, fire any machine guns, or do anything that would excite the miners. It soon became apparent that Bandholtz did not need the planes at all, and he ordered the pilots to return to their bases. Shortly after takeoff, one of the planes rolled into a nose dive and crashed. It took three days for residents of Twentymile Creek to find the strewn remains on a mountainside. Hearing cries and groans from the brush, they discovered one survivor who had crawled away from the cockpit. The air service crated up the remains of the four other airmen and shipped them home.[37]

The central issue was not the efficiency with which the U.S. Army suppressed civil disorder, but the legitimacy of its deployment within a state. Governor Morgan's position was clear: the miners' march amounted to insurrection, therefore it had to be suppressed. Since he lacked sufficient force at his command, he expected the federal government to supply promptly the necessary force.

Morgan became annoyed when the federal government refused to send in the army promptly. But as previously discussed, the president can employ the awesome power of military rule only under procedural restrictions that are designed to prevent abuse. In due course, President Harding signed the preliminary proclamation of August 30 commanding all persons to disperse and return to their homes. Bandholtz carried with him a martial law proclamation signed by the president, but since the miners dispersed he did not use it.[38]

Bandholtz properly limited his duty to disarming the miners and sending them home. When Morgan asked him to arrest miners on behalf of Logan County authorities, Bandholtz refused, stating that federal troops cannot arrest persons for crimes committed against the state. State officials have never had the legal authority to use federal troops as posse comitatus.[39]

If Morgan could not appreciate the need for constitutional restraints on the power of the president, he could take comfort in the spontaneous action of the citizens of Logan County:

> Had federal troops arrived earlier the lives of several of our citizens would have been saved, but it might be that it were better that this lawless mob should have been convinced, as it was, that the loyal citizenship of Logan County, with the assistance of its neighbors, was able to prevent the forcible entry of its members into that county for the purpose of destroying property and murdering its citizens.[40]

When Morgan requested federal legal action against the miners, he received a more sympathetic hearing. He found an ally in Colonel Walter A. Bethel, a judge advocate on Bandholtz's staff in Charleston. Morgan carried his plea to Attorney General Harry Daugherty and won his support, while Bethel pressed the War Department. In his brief, Bethel stated that the president's proclamation specified the hour by which the miners were to disband. Therefore, he contended, if the miners remained engaged in prohibited activity after that hour, they were guilty of insurrection against the United States. He conceded that the law might not support prosecution, but nonetheless, he argued, the attempt should be made — if the law needs to be changed, "the sooner it is known the better." He added:

> The insurgents wilfully and deliberately defied the President's proclamation and the power and authority of the United States until they were confronted by a force that made resistance dangerous and useless. They were not ordinary lawbreakers. They had become public enemies whom the Army of the United States was authorized by law to shoot and kill. The laws of the United States expressly authorize that extreme remedy, not as a punishment, but as a necessary preventive

measure. Do such laws imply that those who are not killed shall escape punishment for one of the most serious crimes known to the law?

The West Virginia insurrection is over but there will no doubt be others. I do not recommend the trial of all or of many of the insurgents. The trial of one or two or, at the most a few, is sufficient. It is only necessary that the law be vindicated.[41]

Bethel recalled the 1894 railroad strike during which the United States employed both troops and a court injunction against Eugene Debs and other union leaders. The courts, not the army, according to Debs's own testimony, broke the strike. To Bethel the lesson was that the authority of the law must be inposed in order for force to be effective. Bethel had no difficulty persuading Acting Secretary of War James W. Wainwright to recommend prosecution of the miners who had disobeyed the president's proclamation. Both Wainwright and Daugherty importuned the president, but Harding "was not inclined to favor it."[42]

In the end it did not really matter if the federal government prosecuted the miners or not. The marchers returned to the mines in Kanawha and Boone Counties; and the Mingo County strikers became disheartened and drifted back to their mines, or moved on to other coal fields for work. The operators found the presence of the federal troops so beneficial that they urged Washington to assign them indefinitely to West Virginia. Secretary of War John Wingate Weeks did not like the idea. He did not wish to be placed in the position of using federal troops to undertake police duty for the state; besides, their deployment in West Virginia made a shambles of his austere budget. But the need for coercion won out over economy. Bandholtz retained seven hundreed troops in West Virginia, pending full reorganization of West Virginia's National Guard which had been authorized by the legislature in July. All federal troops on the Logan (open-shop) side of Blair Mountain moved out, leaving only the union counties under military occupation. The FBI agent in Mingo reported "better conditions have been restored," with the miners in their tent colonies "suffering deprivation." Inclement weather further discouraged them. And the state police arrested two UMW organizers for holding public meetings without permission in violation of state martial law.[43]

Governor Morgan and Logan County officials began prosecution of the miners under state law in a "righteous endeavor to punish the guilty."

> While it will be impossible to punish all those who participated in this rebellion against the State, for many were forced to engage in the insurrection against their will, every effort will be made to punish the guilty leaders, who, after inciting their followers to take up arms, sought to escape just punishment and the danger of conflict by remaining a safe distance from the actual scene of warfare.[44]

On September 18, Keeney and Mooney voluntarily returned to face prosecution for alleged crimes commited both in Mingo and Logan counties. John L. Lewis wired Morgan, asking him to assure the safety of Keeney and Mooney. Morgan fired back a telegram charging Lewis with complicity in the rebellion:

> Your silent encouragement of unlawful acts would indicate that Lenin and Trotzsky are not without sincere followers in your organization. It is a matter of record that you have not lifted your voice in protest against this violence and that you have sought to hinder rather than help the constituted authorities punish those who have been indicated for the gravest offenses in our statute books.[45]

When the grand juries returned their indictments in September and October (and more were to follow), Morgan felt assured that law and order would be vindicated. But Thomas C. Townsend, a UMW lawyer intimately involved in the West Virginia labor conflict, did not share Morgan's satisfaction.

> We all favor, or should favor, law and order based on justice. I desire, however, to register my protest against the use of term

'law and order' as a smoke screen behind which to hide oppression, lawlessness and the invasion of personal rights guaranteed by the Constitution.

The situation in Logan County to-day is maintained in the name of 'law and order.' I have found no one outside of Logan County who favors that kind of law and order.

Herod saw fit to put to death all the children under 2 years of age, to preserve law and order.

Nero accused Peter and Paul of spreading a pestilential supersititon which they called the Gospel. He killed them in the name of law and order.

King George III stationed soldiers in the homes of the Colonists to eat out their substance and destroy their liberty in the name of law and order.

There can be no law and order in West Virginia or any place else, until there is a restoration of those rights of mankind guaranteed by the Constitution, and no power has ever been strong enough, or ever will be strong enough to stifle the voice of the freeman.[46]

Chapter Five

REFORM

"I know, and you know, and God knows,
that there is only one escape."

The Wilson administration's wartime suppression of civil rights spurred Roger N. Baldwin and others to found the American Civil Liberties Union (originally the Civil Liberties Bureau and later the National Civil Liberties Bureau). The ACLU fought many legal battles on behalf of pacifists, socialists, and trade unionists who ran afoul of Washington officialdom for impeding the war effort. After the war, the West Virginia miners' struggle captured the ACLU's attention. On March 31, 1920, Roger Baldwin wrote C. Frank Keeney:

> Jack Spivak, recently of the New York Call, suggests that I write you directly in regard to the plan we have for being of some service to you in your fight for free speech and the right to organize in south West Virginia.
>
> You will note by the enclosed what this organization is trying to do is to establish civil liberty in the United States. We want to get into the fight in every industrial district where the autocrats of industry challenge the workers' right to organize.

> We hope to make West Virginia conditions an issue which
> will be known all over the United States. We are prepared to
> fight the thing through in the courts and in the field.

Keeney accepted Baldwin's offer of assistance, and Spivak, who
had been working for District No. 17 for several months, became
the ACLU's field representative.[1]

Shortly after the ACLU made its commitment to assist Keeney,
the Matewan street battle (related in chapter 3) took place on
May 21, 1920. After the battle, Sid Hatfield, the chief of police in
Matewan, and his associates were charged with murdering Albert
C. Felts of the Baldwin-Felts detective agency. Roger Baldwin
immediately approached the defense counsel, Harold W.
Houston, about providing legal assistance. Houston turned him
down, believing that outside legal talent would alienate the jury.
Besides, Houston expected to win an acquittal easily, since the
citizens of Mingo County sided with the miners.

Baldwin shrewdly recognized that there was potentially more
to the trial than simply the defendants' innocence or guilt. It
could also serve as a vehicle for publicizing the miners' cause, and
he offered the ACLU's assistance in this capacity. "The trial,"
wrote Baldwin to Houston, "ought to be not a defense of those
indicted but a prosecution of the coal operators, introducing in
evidence the entire record of their conspiracy to deprive the
citizens of West Virginia of their legal rights." Houston accepted
Baldwin's offer to publicize the miners' cause.[2]

Baldwin then asked W. Jett Lauck, an economist for the UMW
as well as for the Commission on Industrial Relations and the
National War Labor Board, to do research for Houston. Baldwin
also asked Neil Burkinshaw, a news reporter and public relations
man, to handle publicity. The ACLU supplemented Burkinshaw's
publicity efforts by persuading several journalists to cover the
trial and the miners' story in general. These included the *New
York Evening Post* and *Survey Graphic*. Houston won his expected
acquittal on March 21, 1921. The jury accepted the defendants'
argument that they had shot and killed Albert C. Felts in self-
defense.[3]

As related above, in September, 1920, the Red Jacket Consolidation Coal and Coke Company sought a federal injunction against the United Mine Workers. Simultaneously, forty-six companies of the Pocahontas Coal Operators' Association and the Algonquin Coal Company of Mercer County, along with the Algoma Coal Company in McDowell County, sought similar injunctions from state courts. All these cases based their arguments on the Supreme Court's *Hitchman* decision of 1917. Houston advised Baldwin: "That case, I am very much afraid, practically forecloses all the questions of law involved. It really, in my opinion, is now merely a matter of proof."[4]

Baldwin asked Felix Frankfurter for advise. Frankfurter recommended his former assistant on the National War Labor Board, Max Lowenthal. Lowenthal believed that the *Hitchman* decision could be reversed in a new test case because it was "bad law." Others were much less optimistic. The counsel for the AFL, Jackson H. Ralston, believed that the only remedy lay with congressional legislation, and he so advised Albert DeSilver, a ACLU director. But, DeSilver wanted immediate action. He proposed civil disobedience:

> Let the miners in West Virginia violate the injunction and go to jail in such numbers that practical consideration will force the abandonment of the enforcement of the injunction.
>
> Have the very highest officials of the American Federation of Labor and such other prominent and distinguished citizens as can be secured, acting on behalf of the United Mine Workers, violate the injunction and be sentenced to jail for contempt. This is a rather heroic alternative to put up to the officials, but it has certain advantages in addition to its disadvantages.

DeSilver did not find any eager volunteers.[5]

A committee of ACLU personnel familiar with the West Virginia situation decided on December 4, 1920, that the most effective course left open to District No. 17 was to appeal to Congress. Houston agreed and arranged to have the miners petition for a congressional investigation. Congress did not respond until after violence flared up anew and Governor Ephraim F. Morgan declared martial law in Mingo County. Finally, on June 21, 1921, the Senate directed its Education and Labor Committee, under the chairmanship of William S. Kenyon of Iowa, to investigate the conditions and "recent acts of violence" in the coal fields of West Virginia. The first phase of the hearings opened in Washington on July 14, 1921, and lasted two weeks. The Mine Workers did not receive a favorable press. Baldwin blamed his public relations man, Neil Burkinshaw, and fired him.[6]

After the committee had recessed, C. E. Lively shot and killed Sid Hatfield and an associate on the courthouse steps in McDowell County. The miners began their march from Kanawha County toward Logan County on August 21, 1921. In the wake of these events, Kenyon hoped to resume committee hearings on the scene in West Virginia during September. A majority of the committee objected, and Kenyon substituted an informal, personal investigation by himself and two other committee members who were sympathetic toward the miners.[7]

Baldwin traveled to West Virginia to organize the publicity in connection with the presentation of the miners' case. J. Charles Laue, a reporter for the *New York Call*, accompanied him as a publicity agent. Baldwin was pleased with his results:

> We endeavored particularly to put the operators on the defensive, since they had succeeded in getting the miners in that position as a result of the Washington hearing.
>
> The means for doing this was to reach the press associations (Associated, United, International and Universal) with copy which would carry on the wires. Our campaign was prepared only with wire service in view and our releases were timed for them.
>
> All of these releases were carried in one way or another, particularly in the West Virginia papers and by the Hearst and Scripps papers. Newspaper correspondents who accompanied the Senate committee were all friendly and all of them sent out

extensive dispatches based upon the material we gave them or
to which we tipped them off.[8]

District No. 17 and the American Civil Liberties Union had
hoped the Senate investigation would lead to collective
bargaining between the Mine Workers and the operators. In
September, President Harding encouraged these hopes by
suggesting, in response to an inquiry from John L. Lewis, that the
Senate committee might bring about a settlement between the
miners and the operators. Lauck sounded out Kenyon about
having the committee follow up on Harding's suggestion. Kenyon
readily agreed. Lauck's plan was to have the president write
Kenyon a letter urging him to adjust the dispute between the
miners and the operators. Kenyon then would call representatives of both parties for a hearing and receive their points of view,
after which he would draw up an agreement and urge each side to
accept it. Lauck reported to Philip Murray, vice president of the
Mine Workers, that:

> You will be able to do so. The operators, on the other hand, will
> not sign anything unless they are coerced, and the plan is to
> have Kenyon and the President coerce them. I have worked
> out the matter with Kenyon and he is to take dinner with
> President Harding tomorrow evening, and hopes to start the
> ball rolling at once.
> Of course, there may be a snag at the White House, but I am
> confidentially informed that the President is very anxious to
> settle the matter and has written twice to Kenyon to this effect.

Unfortunately for Lauck there was a snag. The operator
associations from Logan and Mingo counties had met with
Harding and declared their opposition to presidential intervention supporting, however indirectly, collective bargaining.
Caught in the middle, Harding decided to do nothing.[9]

Hearings before the full Senate committee in Washington
resumed in October. Baldwin asked Frank P. Walsh, chairman of
the Commission on Industrial Relations and co-chairman with

William Howard Taft on the National War Labor Board, to present the miners' position. Walsh eagerly accepted the assignment:

> In West Virginia the operators have the most archaic way of treating the miners in the nonunion field. However, it is all one part of a great big fight. The oppressed in West Virginia are no different from those in Dublin or Limerick, and they have their counterpart not only through this country but all over the world. Sometimes it would look as though it was hardly worthwhile fighting it, but I suppose some of us were born with that feeling of revolt in our souls, and just cannot help keeping up the struggle.

Following a strategy developed by Lauck, Walsh told the committee: "We expect to prove that what is going on in West Virginia is the result of a general conspiracy; that in the coal fields the operations being performed there are being carried out by the direct command of the United States Steel Corporation."[10]

Philip Murray followed Walsh and explained in more detail to the senators how United States Steel controlled coal operations in southern West Virginia. Murray revealed that the largest coal producer in the state, the United States Coal & Coke Company, was a subsidiary company of United States Steel. The United States Coal & Coke Company operated eleven plants at different points in the Pocahontas field (McDowell County) in 1918 and employed 3,888 men, or nearly twice as many men as the next largest company. The second largest producer in the field was the Pocahontas Fuel Company. The president of this company, Isaac T. Mann, was associated with Judge Elbert H. Gary of United States Steel in a syndicate purchase in 1901 of the largest portion of the Pocahontas field. Mann also controlled the Red Jacket Consolidated Coal & Coke Company, located in Mingo County. It was the largest producing company in that county and employed the largest number of men.[11]

While Lauck never doubted that United States Steel was behind the operators' militant antiunion policy in Mingo and

Logan counties, he was unable to discover *direct* United States Steel Corporation ties with operations in those counties. In his testimony, Samuel Untermyer, attorney and counsel for the Pujo "money trust" committee, pushed Lauck's argument as far as he could:

> Taking the whole situation together, from my knowledge of the United States Steel Corporation and its interlocking direc-torates, and knowing its attitude on the labor question and the fight it is making, and taking into account the fact that it is the largest operator in West Virginia, I should say that the United States Steel Corporation could dominate this situation. If they said tomorrow, "let the unions be recognized," they would be recognized.[12]

The Senate committee remained unmoved by Lauck's argu-ment. This was not surprising; the committee never gave Kenyon more than nominal support for carrying out the Senate-mandated West Virginia investigation. In the end the committee did not even write a report.

Kenyon, however, wrote a personal report. In it he condemned both sides for perpetrating violence and taking extreme positions. The central issue, he concluded, was whether or not there existed a right of collective bargaining for employees. The employers had argued that it was one of their fundamental rights to be able to discharge any employee for any reason they saw fit, including membership in a union; and they cited the Supreme Court's *Hitchman* decision in support of their position:

> This court repeatedly has held that the employer is as free to make nonmembership in a union a condition of employment as the workingman is free to join the union, and that his is a part of the constitutional rights of personal liberty and private property, not to be taken away even by legislation, *unless through some proper exercise of the paramount police power.* [Italics added]

Kenyon believed that the modifying clause, "unless through

some proper exercise of the paramount police power," provided an opening for congressional legislation to restrict the right of employers to make nonmembership in a union a contractual matter:

> The Constitution is a live, not a dead instrument. Modern industrial organization has brought problems which require new laws and new interpretations of the Constitution. It is recognized that in the world as it exists to-day, certain restrictions upon personal liberty, however regrettable in theory, must be imposed in practice in order that greater damage may not otherwise be done to the body politic. Factory inspection laws, child labor laws, 8-hour legislation for women, 10-hour legislation for men — these and innumerable other forms of legislation, all of which restrict in greater or less degree the rights of persons and property — have been passed, have been approved by the courts.[13]

Specifically, Kenyon proposed that Congress legislate an industrial code for coal, similar to that already existing for the railroads, which would require collective bargaining between employers and employees. But, Kenyon opposed industry-wide collective bargaining, which was the major goal of the UMW, and would allow each mining operation to negotiate with its own employees. Moreover, Kenyon's code would require compulsory arbitration of labor disputes, despite UMW objection to it, if the employer and employees could not agree on a contract. Kenyon's opposition to industry-wide collective bargaining and his advocacy of compulsory arbitration earned him the enmity of the UMW (he already had earned that of the coal operators for advocating collective bargaining) and assured congressional inaction on his report.[14]

As the ACLU and the UMW were preparing for the last Senate hearings in October, 1921, the Borderland Coal Corporation, and sixty-two other unnamed companies in Mingo County and across the Tug River in Pike County, Kentucky, sought to enjoin the UMW from organizing their employees in violation of their individual employment contracts. Already burdened by other injunction suits, Houston despaired: "I think there is little doubt that back of this suit is arrayed, either openly or covertly, the entire forces of the coal interests."[15]

In private notes Lauck analyzed Borderland's argument:

The intention of Borderland Coal Co., et. al. is really a selfish movement to maintain an advantage in labor costs and competitive conditions.... Because an effort is being made to have them accept conditions and relations which the overwhelming opinion of the industry has declared to be just and reasonable, and which 75% of the [nation's bituminous] operators have put into practical operation, and which further, have been sanctioned by impartial tribunals such as the Bituminous Coal Commission, Borderland et. al. make the absurd contention that they are the victims of an unlawful conspiracy.

Looking back to his time working for the War Labor Board, Lauck told Kenyon's committee:

We were taught there that the Hitchman decision was constitutionally right, but morally wrong.... We cannot have a proper measure of industrial democracy until ... by simple legislation of Congress there will be certain rights, like to the civil and personal rights in the Constitution, which will be extended to industrial life.

Eventually the *Borderland* case was consolidated with the *Red Jacket* case and appealed to the United States Circuit Court of Appeals which, as related in chapter 3, upheld the injunctions. By the time litigation in all the *Red Jacket* cases fruitlessly came to an end, the United Mine Workers had spent more than $8,000,000.[16]

The American Civil Liberties Union's original strategy in 1920 called for a "free speech fight" in southern West Virginia. After many delays, on March 4, 1923, the ACLU arranged to have the Reverend John A. Ryan, the Reverend Henry S. Huntington, and Arthur Garfield Hays speak to a public meeting on the courthouse steps in Logan, Logan County. The Civil Liberties Union hoped Sheriff Don Chafin would arrest the speakers, enabling the speakers to challenge Chafin in the courts. Chafin, who attended the meeting, chose not to interfere. Nonetheless, the Civil Liberties Union considered the meeting successful, since it asserted the principle of free speech in Logan County. The meeting stimulated a counterprotest meeting in Logan County against the ACLU's "invasion of Logan" and much adverse criticism of the civil rights organization in West Virginia newspapers.[17]

The Logan free speech fight in March, 1923, turned out to be the ACLU's last effort in West Virginia. District No. 17 officials were overwhelmed by problems resulting from the Mingo strike, the miners' march of 1921, as well as a nationwide coal strike in 1922. An ACLU official, who was on an inspection trip in West Virginia in the summer of 1922, wrote Baldwin that the union was "submitting to the conditions in these counties ... the reason being that all their resources, financial and physical, are being exhausted by the matters that arise out of the strike. ... Mr. Houston and his assistants are occupied to almost the limit of their physical and mental resources by eviction suits and injunction suits and criminal proceedings." Tired and defeated, Houston wrote Baldwin that the union no longer had faith in the ACLU's ability to help the miners organize the mines. On that note the ACLU decided that it, too, should admit defeat, and it quietly terminated its West Virginia effort.[18]

Although the American Civil Liberties Union had not been able to help the miners win union recognition, it had not been without influence. When federal troops occupied Mingo County in the late summer and fall of 1920, the ACLU helped pressure Washington to remove them. As discussed above, Secretary of War Newton D. Baker finally ordered the troops out of West Virginia in February, 1921.[19]

The Civil Liberties Union and the Mine Workers attempted to obtain an injunction limiting the mine-guard system in Logan County in 1923. It failed; but in 1925 Governor Howard M. Gore secured a similar injunction which restrained the sheriff from using public funds to guard private property. If the Logan operators wanted guards in the future, they would have to hire their own, and none of them could be employees of the county or have authority to arrest offenders. This legal victory produced only limited results, as Logan County deputies continued to harass union members as a part of their regular duty.[20]

On January 30, 1922, the ACLU Executive Committee authorized its representatives to ask federal district attorneys in West Virginia to bring proceedings against officials who denied miners their constitutional rights. The following October and November, in what appears to have been a related action, Elliott Northcott, federal district attorney for southern West Virginia, investigated Logan County's election procedure. He discovered that Sheriff Don Chafin totally controlled Logan County:

> Early in the development of this coal field an arrangement was seemingly entered into between the operators on the one hand and the local officials on the other to prevent the unionizing of the field. One, Don Chafin, who is an extremely able and shrewd native and who developed the political leadership necessary to carry out the arrangements entered into, took charge of the County from a political standpoint.
>
> In return for his handling of the situation with regard to the unions, the operators have turned over to Chafin as his share of the arrangements complete political control of the County, the operators furnishing the necessary money to keep the organization going.
>
> Enormous sums of money have been furnished Chafin for this purpose and he has in his employ a number of Deputies Sheriff who are controlled by him or under his direction. No stranger can go into Logan County and do business without first satisfying Chafin as to his identity and the nature of his business, and a number of instances have occurred where strangers have been beaten up and ordered out of the County on the first train because they did not satisfactorily pass Chafin's scrutiny....
>
> The situation is that elections, both primary and general, in

Logan County are in no wise representative of the sentiment of the County; nor are the citizens there allowed in any way to express their preferences in these elections. Chafin with his Deputies absolutely dominates practically all of the polling places. Only such voters are allowed to vote as suit the organization. Election results are figured up and given out in advance as to what the County will do.

As United States Attorney, I am convinced that a condition exists in Logan County that is not compatible with the principles upon which the Government rests and that there exists a conspiracy to suppress and intimidate citizens of the United States in the free exercise of privileges secured to them by the constitution and laws of the United States, and that some action should be taken to punish the conspirators and put an end to the conspiracy.[21]

Eighteen months later, in September, 1924, Attorney General Harlan F. Stone ordered Northcott to prosecute Chafin. However, Northcott decided not to seek an indictment against Chafin on the charge of violating election laws because the fall election campaign already was underway. Instead, since Chafin was a partner in a speakeasy, Northcott sought an indictment against him for violating the Volstead Act. Chafin was convicted by a jury in October, 1924, and given the maximum sentence of two years in prison and fine of $10,000.[22]

The operators' strong position in West Virginia was bolstered by the American Plan movement to end collective bargaining. This movement was a successor to the Anti-Boycott Association of prewar years and the League for Industrial Rights founded in 1919. After Judge Elbert H. Gary's defeat of the steelworkers' attempt in 1919 to organize United States Steel, numerous antiunion organizations sprang up throughout the nation. These local groups came together at a conference of twenty-two state manufacturers' associations in Chicago in January, 1921. Here the name "American Plan" was officially adopted. The new antiunion offensive enabled corporations to break national strikes among seamen, packing-house workers, and railway workers. In 1923, the AFL reported a drop in membership of 1,052,000, or 24 percent, from its 1920 high figure of 4,676,000 members.[23]

The American Plan affiliated group in West Virginia was the American Constitutional Association. Governor John J. Cornwell founded it:

> After the Armistice I began making a series of public speeches trying to arouse the people of the State to an understanding of the trend of the radical element inside of organized labor as well as the efforts of the communistic and radical socialists who were outside of organized labor. I felt that it was going to bring a great deal of trouble and that if a healthy public sentiment could be created it would aid me to deal with the situation. After I had made several of these speeches some business men in the southern end of the State who understood my motive got together and discussed the question of forming an organization to carry on this work and to broaden the scope of it. I was asked to take the Chairmanship and did so reluctantly.[24]

Cornwell's foremost example of "the radical element" influence in unions was the United Mine Workers. Especially galling to him was a statement in the Mine Workers' constitution of 1913 that the miners should receive the "full social value of their product," and Cornwell interpreted this to mean that operators should receive nothing. But the phrase could be interpreted differently; C. Frank Keeney interpreted it to mean that there should be a fair return to the operators who own the tools of production, as well as to the miners who labor.[25]

By May, 1921, the American Constitutional Association had a thousand members and the endorsement of the West Virginia Manufacturers' Association and the leading coal operators' associations. Judge Elbert H. Gary contributed $5,000 to the association after first requiring subsidiary companies of United States Steel doing business in the state to endorse it.[26]

The American Constitutional Association was basically a propaganda organization. It bombarded employees with anti-union literature, won the right to teach civics in the public schools, distributed America First posters, and prepared patriotic advertisements for newspapers.[27]

Much of the American Constitutional Association's propaganda countered propaganda that the ACLU had generated:

> West Virginia has been maligned, vilified, misrepresented, wilfully and malaciously lied about by unscrupulous newspaper correspondents and propagandists. Scurrilous articles and ludicrous cartoons have appeared in the large metropolitan newspapers.
>
> We have been held up to ridicule and made to appear as a state composed of the most lawless people to be found in the world. We have become the Ireland of America in the eyes of the entire nation.
>
> We have been investigated times without number. So-called social and relief committees from New York, Philadelphia and Baltimore; newspaper reporters from practically every state in the Union; and even an investigating committee from the senate — all these and more, too, have spent one, two and three days investigating us. Then elaborate reports have been made in which are pictured the horrible conditions which their imaginations have conjured up.
>
> Some of the best people in the world are to be found right here in West Virginia. The best blood of the nation, the purest Anglo-Saxon descendants live in the mountain regions of the state.
>
> It is time for every 100 per cent West Virginian to show his colors. Our enemies have been at work hurling shrapnel into our midst. We have turned the other cheek too long. Wake up, West Virginia![28]

Not unrelated to the American Constitutional Association's propaganda effort was the operators' attempt to try the participants in the miners' march of 1921. Shortly after the march, grand-juries in Mingo, Logan, and Kanawha counties indicted 1,276 men altogether for various crimes, including murder, insurrection, and carrying weapons. The most serious indictments charged Keeney and Mooney, and twenty-two other men, with treason. Keeney and Mooney spent 109 days in jail before they were released on bail. From his jail cell Mooney denounced the indictments:

> We are caught between the nether millstones of a gigantic conspircy hatched between the law and unlawful violence. Those who are trusted with the enforcement of existing law know and admit that the gunman system against which we have been fighting for 20 years is wrong and the workers along with their trade union representatives are victimized in order to cover up and camouflage official cowardice.[29]

The prosecution bypassed Keeney and Mooney for the first treason trial, and instead selected William Blizzard, a young District No. 17 organizer. The defense won a change of venue for Blizzard from Logan County to Charles Town in Jefferson County. Charles Town was a quiet village in the Shenandoah Valley. The courthouse in which Blizzard was tried was the same one in which John Brown was convicted for treason and sentenced to hang, in 1859, for attempting an armed insurrection to free slaves.[30]

While the state officially prosecuted Blizzard and his associates, attorneys for the coal operators actually conducted the prosecutions. They billed the state later for $125,000. Neither the county prosecuting attorney nor the state attorney general participated in the trials. United Mine Workers attorneys defended the miners. District No. 17 created the Mingo County Defense League, which raised $46,000 nationwide to defray legal expenses. John L. Lewis represented the international union at Blizzard's trial, sitting at the defense counsel's table.[31]

The treason provision in the West Virginia constitution adhered to the language of the federal constitution: "Treason against the State shall consist only in levying war against it, or in adhering to its enemies, giving them aid and comfort." The prosecution contended that the miners' march was a war levied against the state. Specifically, the prosecution sought to show that Blizzard, along with the other participating miners:

> marched in military or battle array from Marmet in Kanawha County into and through Boone County and thence into Logan County, and that on reaching Logan County they there engaged in a series of battles with the military forces of the State, and that the purpose these conspirators had was to go through Logan County and while traversing it, they were to kill the high sheriff of Logan County and his deputies, and then march into Mingo County where martial law had been declared by the Governor of the State, and there release a large number of prisoners who had been incarcerated in the jail of Mingo County for violation of the martial law proclamation of the Governor and for violation of the law, and to nullify martial law then existing in that county.[32]

The defense maintained that the miners had intended to make a peaceful demonstration — that no assault upon the Logan jail or the sheriff had been planned; that the men were moved by a desire to protect their homes against thugs whom they understood to have been employed by their opponents; and that without the aggression of the state police at Sharples on the night of August 27, 1921, which resulted in the killing of two miners, the men would have returned peacefully to their homes.[33]

To support its claim that the march was a peaceful demonstration, the defense pointed to the miners' mass meeting on August 7, 1921, in Charleston, at which they presented Governor Morgan with a list of grievances, among them that the governor call the state legislature into special session to carry out the Republican party pledge in its 1920 platform to correct "the abuses that have grown up under the so-called private guard or DETECTIVE SYSTEM in the State." Morgan testified at the trial that the state had no national guard and that its Department of Public Safety, the state police, was inadequate. Therefore, he believed it would have been useless for him to have reconvened the legislature, as the miners had requested, as he was certain it would refuse to abolish the private guard system until the state was prepared to guard lives and property by some other means.[34]

Judge John Mitchell Woods's most difficult task was instructing the jury on the difference between treasonous and felonious intent:

> Every violent opposition to the execution of the laws of the state, every resistance by force and violence to the officers of the state in the performance of their duties is not treason. Rioters may assemble together in an unlawful assembly, they may conspire to do an unlawful act, or a series of unlawful acts. Their purpose may be to commit a felony, or to commit a misdeameanor, and they may proceed with arms and with the intent to use violence to accomplish their designs, and yet it wouldn't be a treason.
>
> It would not be a treasonous reason for an unlawful assemblage of individuals to come together unless their purpose is by force and violence to commit some act or some acts, which, if successful, will subvert the government in whole or part.[35]

Moreover, the state constitution, as did the federal, required that the same overt treasonous act must be testified to by at least two witnesses. However, the doctrine that "in treason all are principals," said Judge Woods, broadly defined the overt act to include any act, accessory or principal. This doctrine went back to John Marshall's decision in the *Bollman* case, in which he had ruled:

> If war be actually levied, that is, if a body of men be actually assembled for the purpose of effecting by force a treasonable purpose, all those persons who perform any part, however minute, or however remote from the scene of action, and who are actually leagued in the general conspiracy, are to be considered as traitors.

After considering the evidence in the context of Judge Woods's instructions, on May 25, 1922, the jury acquitted William Blizzard.[36]

In August, 1922, the state tried Walter Allen for treason and won a conviction. Two witnesses testified that they saw Allen with the "armed forces in Logan County." Therefore, the jury concluded that he was leagued in the treasonous conspiracy with them and sentenced him to ten years in prison. The defense moved to set aside the verdict and for a new trial on the grounds that during the trial, or shortly thereafter, three of the state's witnesses were appointed deputy sheriffs of Logan County and were paid from funds contributed to the sheriff by the coal operators. Woods denied the defense's motion, but agreed to release Allen on bail pending an appeal. Allen jumped bail and disappeared. The state dropped charges against the other twenty-two men charged with treason.[37]

The operators' attempt to take vengeance on the miners by means of the treason trials essentially failed, and this failure is consistent with the history of treason trials in the United States. There have been few convictions for treason; and when persons have been convicted, they frequently were pardoned later, as for example, were the leaders of the Whiskey Rebellion in 1794. Probably, therefore, even if the higher courts had upheld Allen's conviction, he would have been pardoned.[38]

After the treason trials, the state prosecuted C. Frank Keeney for murder. He was acquitted. The state did win murder convictions for the Reverend John Wilburn, his son John Wilburn, and Edgar Combs for killing John Gore. But in due course all three received pardons from the governor.[39]

The Mine Workers began a nationwide bituminous strike on April 1, 1922. The union had failed to bring the operators of the Central Competitive Field into a common conference, with western Pennsylvania and the two largest Ohio districts holding out. The UMW forbade other unionized district organizations, such as in West Virginia, to negotiate agreements until the basic wage scale in the Central Competitive Field had been agreed upon.

Both sides prepared themselves for a long struggle. The stakes were high, with the Mine Workers believing that a successful strike would achieve its final goal of organizing the entire bituminous coal industry, and the operators believing that a victory over the UMW would permit the widespread development of open-shop mines. From his perspective, Secretary of Commerce Herbert Hoover analyzed the struggle:

> The conviction I get from conferences with unionized operators and miners is that we are faced with a greater battle between them than ever before — a battle that may prostrate the entire country. The men will have had only about 165 days employment in 1921 and even at high daily and per ton rates are suffering greatly in many districts and will resist any scale reduction. We are in fact in a most vicious circle of trying to support an overplus of mines and miners.
>
> The miners believe they control sufficient production of coal to paralyze industry in the country and in the final analysis other great trade organizations will support them and that being able to paralyze the entire nation to a degree that will bring to them some favorable solution at the hand of the Government. They seem to consider that it is necessary to make this demonstration before they enter upon the process of conciliation of any kind.[40]

The UMW's strike call affected open-shop as well as organized miners. In the panhandle of West Virginia, William Roy and Frank Ledvinka, who had tried to organize the Hitchman mine in 1917, renewed their efforts. Hitchman countered by seeking a contempt of court order against them and their associates for violating the original court injunction issued in 1917. Hitchman charged, among many other accusations, that Roy and Ledvinka had dragged three of its employees, Lawrence Stewart, George Clark, and Isaac Wilson, to the Miners Temple in Bellaire, Ohio, across the Ohio River from the Hitchman mine. After their arrival, Roy and Ledvinka hung placards on them "on which were printed the words 'I'm a dirty scab.'" A large crowd in the temple jeered at the hapless trio. Following this ritual, Roy and Ledvinka made speeches encouraging Hitchman's employees to join the union and to go out on strike.[41]

Roy and Ledvinka and their associates were successful. Two hundred and thirty Hitchman employees, including Stewart, Clark, and Wilson, joined the UMW and supported the strike, reducing the Hitchman work-force to fifty-nine men. W. E. Baker, Dayton's successor as United States district judge, found the defendants (sixteen altogether) guilty. He fined some of them $100 to $250, but others he required to post a bond of $2,000, which would be forfeited if they disobeyed the injunction in the future. In addition, he made Roy, Ledvinka, and higher UMW officers, "promise the court that they will, from this day forth, strictly obey the injunction in spirit, and in every respect." Finally, Baker ordered the *United Mine Workers Journal* to publish a statement:

> calling special attention to the fact that the Hitchman mine is not to be unionized ... as well as to the fact the injunction forbids any effort to induce the Hitchman employees to leave their employment or to break their contract of service to join the United Mine Workers of America, even by peaceful argument or persuasion.[42]

The bituminous strike did not go well for the Mine Workers, and after two and a half bitter months, on August 15, 1922, it signed a contract with a minority of the operators in the Central Competitive Field which continued the old wage scale and working conditions until March 31, 1923. Gradually the remaining operators in the old union fields accepted the settlement. In January, 1923, the UMW made a one-year contract with operators in a Tri-State Competitive Field consisting of Ohio, Indiana, and Illinois, eliminating western Pennsylvania. This agreement left the former wage scale and working conditions unchanged.

One of the provisions of the bituminous settlement ending the 1922 strike called for a special government coal investigating body. Coincidentally, Senator William E. Borah, an advocate for nationalizing the coal industry, urged a congressional investigation of the industry. Congress responded to both requests by creating the United States Coal Commission, its members to be appointed by the president. The commission was handicapped by not having a clearly defined purpose and by not receiving full congressional and presidential support. Consequently, its report of 1923, though it included invaluable detailed information, failed to come up with a viable national coal policy. For example, the report recognized that overproduction should be restricted, but limited its recommendation to the platitudinous statement that the operators and the public jointly should stabilize the industry in terms of market potential.[43]

Buried within the commission's special report on civil liberties in the coal fields was a strong objection to the Supreme Court's *Hitchman* decision. The commission recognized that under the Supreme Court's decision the "'yellow-dog' contract is legal," but went on to declare that it was "a source of economic irritation, and is no more justifiable than any other form of contract which debars the individual from employment solely because of membership or nonmembership in any organization."[44]

The failure of the 1922 bituminous strike was felt quickly in West Virginia. District No. 17 admitted defeat in Mingo County in October, 1922, and terminated the strike that had been going on in that county since July, 1920. Most operators in the organized fields in West Virginia demanded a wage reduction from the settlement the Central Competitive Field had agreed to in August, 1922. The New River operators refused to sign a new contract at all and immediately began open-shop operations.[45]

Keeney and Mooney were willing to adjust to the operators' demands for wage reductions in order to preserve the union, but John L. Lewis was bent on a "no backward step" strategy. He ordered Keeney and Mooney to appear before the executive board of the union at Indianapolis. Mooney recalled the meeting:

> John L. Lewis was bitter in his denunciation of the miners' union officials in West Virginia. He berated us for trying to

shoot the organization into the state and for the indebtedness
incurred while trying to secure working agreements, despite
the fact that the economic condition was a direct result of
pursuance of policies forced upon the outlying territories by
him.

Keeney and Mooney resigned, or more likely, were forced out of
office by Lewis. Lewis then suspended the district's autonomy
and placed Percy Tetlow, a trustworthy lieutenant, in charge.
This was a typical Lewis tactic (including his charge against
Keeney and Mooney of radicalism — "trying to shoot the
organization into the state"), which he repeated many times in
other districts. By this method he built a powerful monolithic
organization obedient to his command.[46]

The Mine Workers signed the Jacksonville agreement in
February, 1924, with the operators in the Central Competitive
Field — Ohio, Indiana, Illinois, and western Pennsylvania. The
agreement renewed the old pay scale and working conditions.
Operators in the Kanawha field in West Virginia refused to
adhere to the pattern set by the Central Competitive Field and
would not sign a new contract. They evicted union miners from
company houses and hired mine guards to enforce the evictions.
Between 1922 and 1925 the Kanawha operators evicted 10,000
miners, or 50,000 people, including the miners' families.
Strikebreakers taking the union miners' jobs accepted a 35
percent cut in wages under the 1917 union scale.[47]

The northern West Virginia operators gazed enviously on the
newly established open-shop mines in the Kanawha Field. Since
the northern operators already had signed contracts with the
UMW, they had to abrogate their contracts before they could run
open-shop. After doing so, they obtained *Hitchman* injunctions to
prevent the UMW from organizing their mines again. From 1926
to 1928 state courts in West Virginia issued over two hundred
Hitchman injunctions on behalf of operators in northern West
Virginia. Among other things, these injunctions prohibited
parades on public highways, meetings in miners' halls located on

their own property, and meetings in churches.[48]

West Virginia's coal production steadily increased as the number of its open-shop mines grew. At the same time, coal production in the organized Central Competitive Field dropped. For example, West Virginia produced 71,254,000 tons of coal in 1913 as compared to 151,680,000 tons in 1927. But Ohio produced 36,000,000 tons of coal in 1913 as compared to 14,000,000 tons in 1927, and Illinois produced 61,000,000 tons of coal in 1913 as compared to 45,000,000 tons in 1927. Meanwhile, in West Virginia, in 1926, miners worked 225 days a year, averaged $3.75 per day and earned a yearly wage of $843.75. But in Illinois, in 1926, miners worked 162 days a year, averaged $7.50 per day and earned a yearly wage of $1,215.00.[49]

During 1925-26 many operators in the organized Central Competitive Field followed the example of the West Virginia operators (and other leaders in union busting such as the Pittsburgh Coal Company of western Pennsylvania) and switched to open-shop mining. By March, 1927, when the Jacksonville Agreement ended, the UMW, which once had been a powerful organization of 500,000 miners, was reduced to 50,000 members. When the remaining operators in the Central Competitive Field insisted on regional and local contracts in the new agreement, the Mine Workers struck in protest. After fifteen months, in July, 1928, the UMW capitulated. It agreed to the dismantling of the Central Competitive Field bargaining unit and authorized union districts to negotiate their own contracts.[50].

The disastrous 1927-1928 bituminous strike impelled the Senate Committee on Interstate Commerce to investigate the conditions in the coal fields of Ohio, Pennsylvania, and West Virginia. Testifying before the committee, John L. Lewis attacked the *Hitchman* decision:

> The Federal courts hold that the employer through the yellow dog contract acquires a property right in the nonunion status of his workman that entitles him to an injunction

against our efforts to peaceably persuade his employee to quit
work and join the union.

I here denounce the doctrine that the employer can
covenant with his employee to rob him of the opportunity of
hearing us preach the gospel of unionism to him, or to preclude
us from appealing to him by fair argument and peaceable
persuasion.

He appealed to Congress to act "to the end that the oppressive
instrumentalities of government may be kept from interfering
with us in our struggle for an American standard of wages and
citizenship."[51]

The chairman of the Committee on Interstate Commerce,
James E. Watson, prepared a bill to meet Lewis's objective.
Watson's bill would have established a code for the bituminous
industry guaranteeing the right to collective bargaining and
would have regulated wages, prices, and profits. Watson hoped to
win the support of operators by including a provision setting
aside the antimonopoly provisions of the Sherman Antitrust Act,
thereby encouraging operators to produce less competitively and
more efficiently. Although he was a Republican, Watson
received no support either from President Coolidge or President
Hoover, and his bill died.[52]

At about the same time that the Senate Committee on
Interstate Commerce began its investigation of the bituminous
coal industry, the Senate Judiciary Committee began investigating the use of injunctions in labor disputes. Hearings started
on February 8, 1928, before a subcommittee consisting of George
W. Norris, chairman of the Judiciary Committee, and Thomas
Walsh, and John J. Blaine. All three members were progressives
and sympathetic to limiting the use of injunctions in labor
disputes. The Senate hearings coincided with a national
conference on injunctions called by the AFL.[53]

The bill before the subcommittee was introduced by Henrik
Shipstead of Minnesota. It would deny equity courts any
jurisdiction to protect property that was not "tangible and
transferable." Shipstead had introduced his anti-injunction bill

as a favor to his friend, Andrew Furuseth, who was president of the International Seamen's Union. Furuseth espoused the theory prevalent in organized labor that injunctions were issued in labor disputes on a strained definition of property. Historically, courts issued injunctions primarily to prevent irreparable injury to property. The "property" involved in most labor injunction cases was not the tangible property of the employer, but the intangible rights (market opportunities) which arose from relationships established with employers and customers. These rights, organized labor argued, were really personal, not property rights, and it was only by treating them as property that injunctions could be issued in most labor cases. Samuel Gompers endorsed this view, and the proposed Pearre Anti-Injunction Bill of 1908 was based on it. Belief in it led organized labor to insist on Congress including a statement in the Clayton Act that "the labor of the human being is not a commodity." Unfortunately for this theory, it went against precedent, based on many legal decisions, which upheld the assertion that property consists of rights, duties, and relationships, as well as tangible things.[54]

Shipstead's bill received little support in subcommittee testimony. Indeed, the AFL could find only one attorney who would endorse it, since most attorneys believed it was futile to try to attack labor injunctions that way. Notwithstanding, the subcommittee heard much testimony on the evils of labor injunctions. Morris L. Ernst, testifying for the ACLU, charged that labor injunctions denied organized labor the rights of free speech and free association. An UMW representative cited Senator George Wharton Pepper's address to the American Bar Association on July 8, 1924, in which he warned that near revolutionary sentiment was building up in the unions against the federal courts. Pepper's address was all the more startling because he was a conservative.[55]

After the completion of the hearings on March 22, 1928, Norris invited five labor experts to Washington to draw up a sound bill: Edwin E. Witte, an economist educated by John R. Commons who had worked for the Commission on Industrial

Relations in 1914; Felix Frankfurter, a Harvard law professor who had worked for the National War Labor Board; Herman Oliphant from Columbia University Law School; and Francis B. Sayre from Harvard Law School. From May 1 to 3 four of the five, with Sayre absent, locked themselves in a Senate committee room and prepared a bill. They knew it would be difficult to undo the Supreme Court's *Hitchman* decision upholding the individual employment contract. Their strategy was to have Congress declare the individual employment contract unenforceable in the courts. Witte advised the Senate subcommittee: "that even this involves a reconsideration of the doctrine announced in the *Hitchman Coal & Coke Co.* case, but this does not seem an insurmountable obstacle, particularly in view of the fact that the grossly inequitable character of these contracts was not brought to the court's attention." Witte had in mind the New York Court of Appeals decision in *Interborough Rapid Transit Co.*, where the court refused to sanction injunctions to enforce yellow dog contracts because of their inequitable character.[56]

Oliphant is credited with being the chief author of the union brief in the *Interborough Rapid Transit Company* case. He argued that the individual employment contract used by the company was not valid since, relatively speaking, the workers had no bargaining power when dealt with separately. He quoted from Williston on *Contracts*, volume 3, section 1627:

> A relationship between parties to a transaction which tends to give dominance to one over the other may be an important element in determining whether duress was exercised. And courts of equity have established the principle that when such a relation exists, the burden is thrown upon the dominant party to establish the fairness of the transaction and that it was a free act of the other party.[57]

Oliphant argued that the disparity in bargaining power between the employer and the worker in making the individual employment contract arose in part from the size of the modern business organization:

When one party to the contract is an employer of many men and the other party is an individual among these men, there is nothing approaching equality between the two parties. In modern large scale business, the work contract is a take-it-or-leave-it offer on the part of the employer.

There was also disparity in bargaining power between the employer and the worker in the stake in the contract:

For the employer it is no life and death matter, only his profits are concerned. The worker has everything at stake. His life and his family welfare depend upon the work contract.

One of the most important elements of disparity in bargaining power was in the technique of bargaining:

The employer is a trained, educated and experienced bargainer. He can hire expert counsel and secure market-wide information. The average workman is seldom capable of driving as good a bargain as a skilled and shrewd negotiator. He has neither the time nor the opportunity to become a skilled bargainer himself, nor has he the means to employ high priced counsel to negotiate and to draft his work contract. "Moreover, the employer as a negotiator has the moral ascendancy of class and tradition. Economically he is still a 'master' dealing with his 'men.'"[58]

Privately, Witte was not confident that a congressional declaration that individual employment contracts were unenforceable in the courts would stand federal judicial review, even with the precedent of the New York Court of Appeals decision in the *Interborough Rapid Transit Co.* case, but he thought it was "worth trying."[59]

In May, 1928, the Senate Judiciary Subcommittee recommended to the full committee a new Norris bill drawn up by the labor experts as a replacement for the Shipstead bill. The subcommittee conducted hearings on this bill during December, 1928. Because the AFL failed to endorse this bill at its next convention, Norris took no further action. The next year the federation changed its attitude and came out strongly for the Norris bill. The committee reported out the Norris bill in the spring of 1930, but with an adverse (10 to 7) majority report, and it got no further.[60]

The Senate's apparent lack of interest in the Norris bill during the spring of 1930 only partially revealed the Senate's political temper. For the Senate also reacted with unusual hostility toward President Hoover's nomination, on April 10, 1930, of Judge John J. Parker to the Supreme Court. Hoover nominated Parker to replace Associate Justice Edward Terry Sanford, who had died on March 8, 1930. Parker, forty-four years old, had been a judge of the United States Fourth Circuit Court since 1925. Before then he had been an unsuccessful Republican candidate for several North Carolina offices, including the governorship. Hoover wanted a Republican and a southerner — partly because Sanford had been a southerner and partly because his advisers hoped the Republican party might be able to make inroads into the Democratic South.[61]

While Parker was an able jurist, he had had the misfortune, as discussed above, to have written the United States Circuit Court of Appeals' *Red Jacket* decision (1927). The *Red Jacket* injunction, which affected 40,000 miners in southern West Virginia, became perhaps the most hated injunction of the 1920s. William Green, president of AFL, vehemently opposed Parker's nomination in testifying before the Judiciary Subcommittee. The effect of Parker's *Red Jacket* decision, said Green, "was to make criminals out of law-abiding, honest, loyal American citizens if they requested, in the exercise of peaceful and law-abiding methods, working men to join with them in labor organization." Parker, in a letter to the subcommittee, asserted that he had no choice but to uphold the individual employment contract because he was bound by the Supreme Court's *Hitchman* decision. William Green retorted that "a judge must be able to do more than merely seek the easiest way in rendering decisions."

However, Thomas C. Townsend, one of the UMW attorneys who worked on the *Red Jacket* case, defended Parker, testifying that Parker was in fact bound by the Supreme Court's *Hitchman* decision.[62]

By the time Parker's nomination reached the floor, senators found themselves besieged by mail from labor's supporters. During the debate, Senator Norris became labor's chief spokesman:

> I have here a cartoon taken from a newspaper. It is the picture of a man applying for a job. He is standing before the rich manufacturer. He is out of work. He wants to be able to support himself and his family, and as he presents himself before the mahogony-top table of the employer he is presented with a yellow-dog contract. In substance, that contract says, "I agree not to organize for my own protection."
>
> What does he do? In the mists that seem to surround him and that pervade the atmosphere of the room he sees a picture. He sees the wife of his bosom standing there, holding to her shriveled breasts her babe, his child, and beside the pleading mother stands at her feet a little boy, the image of his father, his son, grasping the tattered fragments of the torn skirt of the mother and looking up into her face through blinding tears, pleading with that mother for bread. When he sees that picture, what does he do? What would you do, brothers? What would I do?
>
> I know, and you know, and God knows, that there is only one escape. We must sign on the dotted line, and so this man signs. He goes, perhaps, down into the bowels of the earth. The coal king's slave he is, digging there the coal. He has signed a contract by which he has agreed not to join a union. He has signed a contract that says that the employer can change the hours of labor, the conditions of labor, and the price of labor without his consent. He has agreed to it all in advance to save the wife and babe and boy. He has to work longer. He has to commence earlier. The wages, perhaps, are cut down; and after a while he realizes that he is losing his physical strength. He sees that he is being ruined; that he can not live and keep up

the pace.

So he consults his fellow workmen — men in the same condition, with the same kind of a family. He violates his contract when he does it, and he does it stealthily. He is afraid he will be caught. So they organize, so that combined they may demand better working conditions and better wages. But when they do it they violate this sacred "yellow-dog" contract, and they know it. They must do something to save their own lives and to protect their wives and families, and yet the very thing they are doing they have agreed not to do.

In similar debates in past sessions conservative senators had scorned Norris's speeches, but not this time. Senator William E. Borah noted with satisfaction, "Not a single Senator has soiled his lips with an endorsement of the yellow dog contract."[63]

The National Association for the Advancement of Colored People likewise opposed Parker's nomination. When Parker was a gubernatorial candidate on the Republican ticket in North Carolina in 1920, the *Greensboro Daily News* quoted him as endorsing a 1900 amendment to the North Carolina constitution which had virtually disenfranchised black voters. The amendment had provided for a poll tax, literacy tests, and moreover, a grandfather clause which the United States Supreme Court had declared unconstitutional in 1915. In addition, the newspaper quoted Parker as saying: "The participation of the Negro in politics is a source of evil and danger to both races and is not desired by the wise men in either race or by the Republican Party of North Carolina." Parker unsuccessfully tried to explain away his statement. Yet, his record on black-white relations also had a positive mark. He wrote a decision in January, 1930, declaring unconstitutional a residential segregation ordinance in Richmond, Virginia.[64]

The NAACP's opposition to Parker was based on more than just his racist campaign statement. After the stock market crash in October, 1929, blacks tried to meet with President Hoover to discuss their worsening conditions. In the onslaught of depression, blacks were rapidly losing jobs they had gained only with difficulty during and after the world war. The ensuing depression also led to increased racial tensions. Hoover refused to receive black petitioners at that time or to consider any ameliorative governmental action. Thus Hoover's appointment of Parker provided blacks a chance to retaliate.[65]

The NAACP asked Hoover to withdraw Parker's nomination. After Hoover refused, Walter White, the acting secretary of the NAACP, appeared before the Judiciary Subcommittee to oppose Parker's confirmation. Neither the subcommittee nor the AFL representatives welcomed White. Undetered, however, the NAACP went back to its constituency to rally support. It sponsored mass meetings in border and northern states and urged black churches, fraternal, labor, and civic organizations to telegraph senators their opposition to Parker and to threaten them with retaliation at the polls if they voted for Parker. The Parker fight marked the political arrival of previously ignored black voters.[66]

On May 7, 1930, the Senate denied confirmation to Parker by a vote of 41 to 39. For the first time in thirty-six years the Senate had rejected the president's nominee to the Supreme Court. The coalition that defeated Parker included Republican progressives, regular Republicans who feared reprisals in the fall election, and northern and southern Democrats. A few months earlier, only twenty-six senators had voted against the confirmation of Charles Evans Hughes's nomination to the Supreme Court.[67]

While the AFL credited itself with defeating Parker, the evidence indicates that a much more powerful social force was operating — one that affected blacks as well as organized labor. The depression had shaken most Americans' confidence in their government, and they wanted their senators to register their disapproval. Parker's nomination presented a convenient opportunity for the senators to do that.[68]

Prior to the congressional election of 1930, the AFL Nonpartisan Political Campaign Committee urged state federations to make candidates' support of the Norris Anti-Injunction

Bill the single issue determining labor's political support. Twenty-two state federations actually sent questionnaires on the Norris bill to candidates. In the 1930 election the AFL claimed it defeated six senators and forced the voluntary retirement of four others before the election. But since nationwide AFL political activity was in fact minimal, the election results instead indicated a spontaneous repudiation of Herbert Hoover's policies. Overall, the Democrats won control of the House by five votes in contrast to the previous Republican majority of 100, and reduced the Republican majority in the Senate from eleven votes to one.[69]

The AFL's modest political activity on behalf of the Norris bill signaled a new direction for the federation. Throughout the 1920s the AFL had adopted a policy of union-management cooperation, deliberately avoiding confrontation with business. This was due in part to the Republican administrations' notable lack of zeal on behalf of labor, in part to the success of the American Plan and the open-shop movement, and in part to the relatively high wages that workers earned in some key industries. Until late 1930, the federation was willing to follow business's lead, even in solving the depression that came after the stock market crash in October, 1929. The extent of the federation's conservatism was seen in its squabbles with the American Civil Liberties Union. In 1923, it attacked the ACLU for undertaking a study of injunctions, since it had already begun a similar study. And Samuel Gompers repeatedly charged that the ACLU was a pro-Soviet organization.[70]

The major exception to the AFL's conservative stance was its endorsement of the Progressive presidential candidate, Robert M. La Follette, in 1924. La Follette campaigned on a platform attacking the antilabor decisions of the Supreme Court and calling for a congressional review of Supreme Court rulings. After La Follette's defeat, the AFL lost hope for the passage of remedial legislation.[71]

Hoover did not call the newly elected Congress of 1930 into session until December, 1931, the latest possible time under the law. Accordingly, Norris postponed efforts to obtain Senate approval of his anti-injunction bill until after December, 1931. But AFL members in two states did not have to wait for Senate action. Ohio outlawed the *Hitchman* individual employment contract in the spring of 1931, and Wisconsin passed a state version of the complete Norris bill in July, 1931, using as its model a bill prepared by the ACLU.[72]

Early in 1931 Frank Keeney returned to organize West Virginia's increasingly desperate miners. By 1931, one-third of West Virginia's 112,000 miners were unemployed and another third worked only one or two days a week. Since Lewis had forced Keeney out of District No. 17 in 1924, Keeney had tried a couple of business ventures; but he found he could not stay away from his real mission in life, which was to try to improve the lot of miners.[73]

Keeney had been a delegate in 1930 at the anti-Lewis Reorganized United Mine Workers of America convention in Indianapolis led by Alex Howit, Oscar Ameringer, Adolph Germer, and John Brophy, among others. Keeney intended to form a branch of the reorganized union; but when it collapsed (to be revived later as the Progressive Miners of America), Keeney went ahead on his own and founded the West Virginia Mine Workers Union. Northern liberals supplied Keeney with money, and organizers from A. J. Muste's Brookwood Labor College volunteered their time. Fred Mooney also joined up again with Keeney.[74]

The Mine Workers fought the WVMWU by breaking up their meetings and other strong-arm methods. Mooney was appalled:

> It was hard for me to understand the tactics being used by the United Mine Workers' officials for I had been a member of that organization almost continuously for 19 years. I had always understood it to be founded upon democratic principles. I had heard its leaders boast of its high ideals, prate of its tolerance, and express pride in the fact that it was the only institution of any kind on the American continent that had solved the

melting pot. I had never known it to be guilty of suppressing free speech or breaking up public gatherings, no matter by whom or for what purpose they were being held. I had always regarded it as a shrine into which men entered and were then freed from the restrictions so often practiced by intolerant public officials, thug-ridden coal communities, and communities governed by fanatics.[75]

Keeney led 150 miners and their families on a march from the Kanawha Field to Charleston in June, 1931, to petition Governor William G. Conley for help. The miners told the governor that they had had no work for weeks and had nothing to eat. Governor Conley replied that he could do nothing for them, explaining that, "the government was a business institution and its business had to be conducted along lines that safeguarded the interests of all citizens." The governor did deign to contribute ten dollars of his own money to the miners for food. The union struck in support of its demand for recognition in July. Operators immediately evicted union miners from company houses and replaced them with strikebreakers. The Red Cross soon cut off its assistance to the strikers. Compounding Keeney's difficulties was competition from the National Miners' Union, which was closely tied to the Communist party. It also began organizing West Virginia miners. By August, the WVMWU's meager resources were exhausted. Keeney terminated the strike and the union disintegrated.[76]

As soon as the new Congress convened in December, 1931, Norris reintroduced his anti-injunction bill. The Judiciary Committee reported it to the floor, this time favorably 11 to 5. Two committee members who had opposed the bill in 1930 had been defeated for reelection. In addition, there were more Democrats and fewer Republicans on the reorganized committee, and the Democrats tended to support the bill.[77]

Andrew Furuseth continued his opposition to the Norris bill throughout 1930 and 1931. While Norris respected Furuseth personally, he feared that his continued opposition might lead to the defeat of effective anti-injunction reform. He wrote Frankfurter:

> Mr. Furuseth's attitude on the labor question stands as an obstacle in the way of any accomplishment. Those who oppose us are going to utilize to the very limit the objections of Mr. Furuseth. There were some people, perhaps, who advocated his objections in good faith, but the powerful ones and those whom we have to fear will not be good-faith objectors. They will take advantage of the division in the labor ranks and get under the banner of Andrew Furuseth, not because they believe in him or would follow him, but because in this particular instance it would serve their purposes best.

Under Furuseth's influence the AFL tried to make another attempt to change the Norris bill in December, 1931. Frankfurter read the proposed changes and gasped: "the AFL recital is not only not helpful; it is harmful." Norris finally stopped the federation from interfering any further by making clear that its continued support of Furuseth's outmoded ideas would risk scuttling this opportunity for reform of labor injunctions.[78]

The ACLU created a Committee on Labor Injunctions to rally nonlabor support for the Norris bill. It was chaired by Charles F. Amidon, a former federal judge, and was made up of academicians, writers, and churchmen. The National Civic Federation, a conservative organization traditionally concerned with creating good will between labor and business, declared itself for the bill in January, 1931. Opposition came mainly from employers' associations, the United States Chamber of Commerce, and the American Bar Association. The Senate passed the Norris bill 75 to 5 on March 1, 1932. Meanwhile, Representative Fiorello H. LaGuardia, who had no earlier connection with the legislation, introduced the same bill in the House, where it passed 363 to 14. Considering past opposition to the bill, the final vote was stunning.[79]

Hoover reluctantly signed the bill on March 23, 1932 (a veto would have been meaningless in face of the strongly affirmative congressional vote), but he also stated that the bill's constitutionality would have to be settled in the courts. He released an opinion by Attorney General William D. Mitchell in which Mitchell declared that the act did not prevent federal suits to enjoin unlawful conspiracies under the antitrust laws. Norris retorted:

> The statement of the Attorney General does not add much credit to the great office which he holds. It is an argument which would be more suitable if made before a Justice of the Peace. It will be used as a peg upon which great corporations and trusts will hang their arguments when they follow the covert attack in an attempt to invalidate the law in the courts. This statement, in connection with President Hoover's oft repeated policy of elevating Judges who have become famous for their inhuman and unjust injunctions, discloses the real feeling of both the President and the Attorney General.

But the Supreme Court refused to invalidate the law. Justice Owen J. Roberts wrote for the majority in Lauf v. E. G. Shinner & Co. (1938) that, "there can be no question of the power of Congress thus to limit the jurisdiction of the inferior courts of the United States."[80]

The Norris-LaGuardia Act undid the Supreme Court's *Hitchman* decision of 1917, achieving what Justice Brandeis had advocated in dissent fifteen years earlier. The act declared that individual employment contracts cannot serve as a basis for any equitable (or legal) relief; and its corollary, that no injunction shall forbid any workman to become or remain a member of a labor organization nor forbid any other person to persuade workmen to join a labor organization. In addition, the act set forth eight other courses of conduct in labor disputes that were not to be enjoined. This list was similar to section 20 of the Clayton Act, but it avoided the frequent use of the qualifying "lawfully" or "in a lawful manner," which made that section meaningless. Another provision of the act stated a public policy that workmen shall have full freedom of association and the right to designate representatives of their own choosing and that no restraining order or injunction can be issued in violation of that public policy. Finally, the act introduced many procedural requirements for the issuing of injunctions which substantially limits their use.[81]

The passage of the Norris-LaGuardia Act did not result in unionization of the coal mines in West Virginia. Unionization came only after the passage of the National Industrial Recovery Act on June 16, 1933, which in section 7(a) implemented the employees' right to organize and bargain collectively that the Norris-LaGuardia Act had protected. The NIRA also provided that industries and the federal government draw up codes regulating production, competition, and wages. In this respect, it was similar to the measure Senator James E. Watson proposed for the bituminous coal industry in 1928. The incorporation of section 7(a) and industrial codes into the act was due in no small part to W. Jett Lauck, who helped Senator Robert F. Wagner draft the NIRA bill. Under the NIRA, the president enforced the terms of the codes, and this meant that corporations had to comply with section 7(a) and bargain collectively.[82]

When the National Industrial Recovery Act became law in June, 1933, Lewis risked the whole Mine Workers' treasury on a massive organizing drive. Mine Workers' organizers moved into every coal field, shouting, "The President wants you to join the union!" They didn't bother to explain which president they meant, F.D.R. or Lewis. The miners responded by the thousands. In West Virginia it took only two days to organize Logan County and a week more to organize the remaining counties. On September 21, 1933, the Mine Workers and bituminous operators signed the Appalachian Agreement for 314,000 men, covering Pennsylvania, Ohio, West Virginia, Virginia, eastern Kentucky, and Tennessee. Indiana and Illinois of the old Competitive Field were left to later supplemental agreements. At the Mine Workers' Indianapolis convention in January, 1934, John L. Lewis proudly reported the union "has substantially accomplished the task to which it has been dedicated through the forty-four years of its history. It has at last succeeded in bringing into the fold practically all the mine workers in our great North American continent."[83]

Bibliography

This bibliography includes all items cited in the Notes and other materials pertinent to this study which the author found helpful. For more complete bibliographies on related topics one should turn elsewhere. *Struggle in the Coal Fields: the Autobiography of Fred Mooney*, ed. J. W. Hess (Morgantown: West Virginia University Library, 1967), includes a very good bibliography. Robert F. Munn, *The Coal Industry in America, a Bibliography and Guide to Studies* (Morgantown: West Virginia University Library, 1965) provides an exhaustive listing of works relating to all aspects of the coal industry. Manuscript holdings in the West Virginia University Library are listed and indexed in *Guide to Manuscripts and Archives in the West Virginia Collection* (Morgantown: West Virginia University Library, 1974) by James W. Hess. The National Archives in Washington proved to be an extremely valuable source for documentary material relating to the role of the Justice Department, the army, and other federal agencies.

UNPUBLISHED MATERIAL

Adjutant General File, War Department, Modern Military Records. National Archives.

American Civil Liberties Union Archives. New York Public Library.

Bittner, Van Amberg. Papers. West Virginia Collection, West Virginia University Library.

Coal Strikes, Records 1912-1913. West Virginia Collection, West Virginia University Library.

Cornwell, John Jacob. Papers. West Virginia Collection, West Virginia University Library.

Dayton, Alston G. Papers. West Virginia Collection, West Virginia University Library.

Department of Labor Records. National Archives.

Frankfurter, Felix. Papers. Library of Congress.

Fuel Administration Records. National Archives.

Garfield, Harry A. Papers. Library of Congress.

Glasscock, William E. Papers. West Virginia Collection, West Virginia University Library.

Justice Department Records. National Archives.

Lauck, W. Jett. Papers. University of Virginia Library.

Miners' Treason Trial Papers, 1921-1923. West Virginia Collection, West Virginia University Library.

Morgan, Ephraim F. Papers. West Virginia Collection, West Virginia University Library.

Norris, George W. Papers. Library of Congress.

Papers Relating to the Nomination of John J. Parker to be an Associate Justice of the United States Supreme Court, 71st Congress. National Archives.

Pardon Attorney Records. National Archives.

Walsh, Frank P. Papers. New York Public Library.

Witte, Edwin E. Unpublished Private Papers Gathered for the Commission on Industrial Relations. New York State School of Industrial and Labor Relations, Cornell University.

PUBLIC DOCUMENTS

Biennial Report, Bureau of Labor of West Virginia 1913-1914. Charleston: Tribune Printing Co., 1914.

Biennial Report of the Bureau of Labor of West Virginia 1919-1920. Charleston: Tribune Printing Co., 1920.

Federal Aid in Domestic Disturbances 1903-1922. Senate Doc. no. 263, 67th Cong., 2d sess., 1922.

Garfield, Harry. *Final Report of the United States Fuel Administrator 1917-1919,* 1921.

Mining Investigation Commission. *Report of West Virginia Mining Investigation Commission, Appointed by Governor Glasscock on the 28th Day of August, 1912.* Charleston: Tribune Printing Co., 1912.

Report and Digest of Evidence Taken by Commission Appointed by the Governor of West Virginia in Connection with the Logan County Situation. Charleston: Tribune Printing Co., 1919.

Report of the Secretary of Labor 1914, 1915.

Reports of the Department of Labor 1918, Reports of the Secretary of Labor and Reports of Bureaus, House Doc. no. 1449, 65th Cong., 3d sess., 1919.

U.S. Bureau of Labor Statistics. *Labor Relations in the Fairmont, West Virginia Bituminous Coal Field,* Bulletin no. 361, prepared by Boris Emmet, 1924.

U.S. Coal Commission. *Report of the United States Coal Commission,* Senate Doc. no. 195, 68th Cong., 2d sess., 1925. 5 vols.

U.S. *Congressional Record.* Vol. 72.

U.S. House of Representatives, Committee on the Judiciary. *Official Conduct of Judge Alston G. Dayton,* Report no. 1490, 63d Cong., 3d sess., 1915.

U.S. Immigration Commission. *Reports of the Immigration Commission: Immigrants in Industries,* vol. 6, part 5, Senate Doc. no. 633, 61st Cong., 2d sess., 1911.

U.S. Senate, Committee on Education and Labor. *Hearings Pursuant to S. 37, Conditions in the Paint Creek District, West Virginia,* 63d Cong., 1st sess., 1913. 3 vols.

U.S. Senate, Committee on Education and Labor. *Hearings Pursuant to S. 80, to Investigate the Recent Acts of Violence in the Coal Fields of West Virginia and Adjacent Territory and the Causes which Led to the Conditions which Now Exist Said Territory,* 67th Cong., 1st sess., 1921-22. 2 vols.

U.S. Senate, Committee on Education and Labor, *Report, Investigation of Paint Creek Coal Fields of West Virginia,* 63d Cong., 2d sess., 1914.

U.S. Senate, Committee on Interstate Commerce. *Hearings Pursuant to*

S. 105, Conditions in the Coal Fields of Pennsylvania, West Virginia, and Ohio, 70th Cong., 1st sess., 1928. 2 vols.

U.S. Senate, Committee on the Judiciary. *Hearings on S. 1482, Limiting Scope of Injunctions in Labor Disputes,* 70th Cong., 1st sess., 1928.

U.S. Senate. *Final Report and Testimony Submitted to Congress by the United States Commission on Industrial Relations,* Senate Doc. no. 415, 64th Cong., 1st sess., 1916.

U.S. Senate, Subcommittee of the Committee of the Judiciary. *Hearing on the Confirmation of Honorable John J. Parker to be an Associate Justice of the Supreme Court of the United States,* 71st Cong., 2d sess., 1930.

U.S. Senate. *West Virginia Coal Fields, Personal Views of Senator Kenyon and Views of Senators Sterling, Phipps, and Warren,* Report no. 457, 67th Cong., 2d sess., 1922.

COURT CASES

Bittner et al, v. West Virginia-Pittsburgh Coal Co., 214 Fed. 719 (1914).

Hitchman Coal & Coke Co. v. Mitchell et al., 245 U.S. 229 (1917).

Hitchman Coal & Coke Co. v. Mitchell et al., 245 U.S. 229 (1917), Cases and Points.

International Organization U.M.W. v. Red Jacket Consolidated Coal & Coke Co., 18 Fed. 2d 839 (1927).

Lauf v. E. G. Shinner & Co., 303 U.S. 323 (1938).

Mitchell v. Hitchman Coal & Coke. 214 Fed. 685 (1914).

Oates v. U.S., 223 Fed. 1013 (1915).

Red Jacket Consolidated Coal and Coke Company, et al. v. John L. Lewis et al. Transcript of the Record, District Court of the United States for the Southern District of West Virginia. Charleston, 1923. 3 vols.

    Additional papers on the case are filed in the District Court of the United States for the Southern District of West Virginia in Charleston, West Virginia. This was a consolidation of twelve cases. A final decree was entered on each case, the effective provisions of which are those approved by the District Court in the *Carbon Fuel* case, 288 F. 1020. The consolidated cases were finally decided by the Circuit Court of Appeals in International Organization U.M.W. v. Red Jacket Consolidated Coal & Coke Co., 18F 2d 839 (1927).

Schwartz v. U.S., 217 Fed. 866 (1915).
Scoric v. U.S., 217 Fed. 871 (1915).
Younge v. U.S., 223 Fed. 941 (1915).

BOOKS

Adams, Graham, Jr. *Age of Industrial Violence 1910-1915: The Activities and Findings of the United States Commission on Industrial Relations.* New York: Columbia University Press, 1966.

Alinsky, Saul. *John L. Lewis: An Unauthorized Biography.* New York: G. P. Putnam's Sons, 1949.

Ambler, Charles Henry, and Summer, Festus P. *West Virginia, the Mountain State.* 2d ed. Englewood Cliffs, N.J.: Prentice-Hall, 1958.

American Federation of Labor and Congress of Industrial Organizations. *American Federation of Labor: History, Encyclopedia, and Reference Book*, vols. 1, 2 (1881-1923). Washington: The AFL-CIO, 1960.

Bernstein, Irving. *A History of the American Worker 1920-1933: The Lean Years.* Boston: Houghton Mifflin Co., 1960.

———. *A History of the American Worker 1933-1941: Turbulent Years.* Boston: Houghton Mifflin Co., 1970.

Bing, Alexander M. *Wartime Strikes and Their Adjustment.* New York: E. P. Dutton & Co., 1921.

Coben, Stanley *A Mitchell Palmer: Politician.* New York: Columbia University Press, 1963.

Corbin, David A. "Frank Keeney Is Our Leader, and We Shall Not Be Moved: Rank-and-File Leadership in the West Virginia Coal Fields." *Essays in Southern Labor History: Selected Papers, Southern Labor History Conference, 1976*, edited by Gary M. Fink and Merl E. Reed. Contributions in *Economics and Economic History*, no. 16. Westport, Conn.: Greenwood Press, 1977.

Cummings, Homer, and McFarland, Carl. *Federal Justice: Chapters in the History of Justice and the Federal Executive.* New York: The Macmillan Co., 1937.

Douglas, Paul H. *Real Wages in the United States, 1890-1926.* Boston: Houghton Mifflin Company, 1930.

Dubofsky, Melvyn, and Van Tine, Warren. *John L. Lewis: A Biography.* New York: Quadrangle/The New York Times Book Co., 1977.

Fetherling, Dale. *Mother Jones the Miners' Angel: A Portrait*. Carbondale: Southern Illinois University Press, 1974.

Finley, Joseph E. *The Corrupt Kingdom: The Rise and Fall of the United Mine Workers*. New York: Simon and Schuster, 1972.

Frankfurter, Felix, and Greene, Nathan. *The Labor Injunction*. New York: The Macmillan Co., 1930.

Frey, John P. *The Labor Injunction: An Exposition of Government by Judicial Conscience and Its Menace*. N.P., 1923.

Ginzberg, Elik, and Berman, Hyman. *The American Workers in the Twentieth Century; A History through Autobiographies*. New York: Free Press of Glencoe, 1963.

Green, Marguerite. *The National Civic Federation and the American Labor Movement 1900-1925*. Washington: Catholic University of America Press, 1956.

Hart, H. L. A. *The Concept of Law*. Oxford: Clarendon Press, 1961.

Hinrichs, Albert Ford. *The United Mine Workers of America and the Non-Union Fields*. Studies in History, Economics and Public Law, vol. 110, no. 1. New York: Columbia University Press, 1923.

Hoover, Herbert. *The Memoirs of Herbert Hoover*. Vol. 2; *The Cabinet and the Presidency, 1920-1933*. New York: The Macmillan Co., 1952.

Interborough Rapid Transit Company Against William Green et al., Brief for Defendants. New York: The Workers Education Bureau Press, 1928.

Johnson, Donald Oscar. *The Challenge to American Freedoms: World War I and the Rise of the American Civil Liberties Union*. Lexington: University of Kentucky Press, 1963.

Jones, Mrs. Mary. *Autobiography of Mother Jones*. Chicago: Charles H. Kerr & Co., 1925.

Jordan, Daniel P. "The Mingo War: Labor Violence in the Southern West Virginia Coal Fields, 1919-1922." *Essays in Southern Labor History; Selected Papers, Southern Labor History Conference, 1976*, edited by Gary M. Fink and Merl E. Reed. *Contributions in Economics and Economic History*, no. 16. Westport, Conn.: Greenwood Press, 1977.

Lambie, Joseph T. *From Mine to Market; The History of Coal Transportation on the Norfolk and Western Railroad*. New York: New York University Press, 1954.

Lane, Winthrop D. *Civil War in West Virginia: A Story of the Industrial Conflict in the Coal Mines*. New York: B. W. Huebsch, 1921.

Laslett, John H. M. *Labor and the Left: A Study of Socialist and Radical Influences in the American Labor Movement*, 1881-1924. New York: Basic Books, 1970.

Lauck, William Jett, and Watts, Claude S. *The Industrial Code: A Survey of the Postwar Industrial Situation, a Review of Wartime Developments in Industrial Relations, and a Proposal Looking to Permanent Industrial Peace*. New York: Funk and Wagnalls Co., 1922.

Lee, Howard B. *Bloodletting in Appalachia: The Story of West Virginia's Four Major Mine Wars and Other Thrilling Incidents of Its Coal Fields*. Morgantown: West Virginia University, 1969.

Lewis, John L. *The Miners' Fight for American Standards*. Indianapolis: Bell Publishing Co., 1925.

McCormick, Kyle. *The New-Kanawha River and the Mine War of West Virginia*. Charleston: Matthews Printing Co., 1959.

Murphy, Paul L. *The Meaning of Freedom of Speech: First Amendment Freedoms from Wilson to FDR*. Westport, Conn.: Greenwood Publishing Company, 1972.

Norris, George W. *Fighting Liberal: The Autobiography of George W. Norris*. New York: Macmillan, 1945.

Perlman, Selig, and Taft, Philip. *History of Labor in the United States, 1896-1932*. Vol. 4: Labor Movements. New York: Macmillan Company, 1935.

Post, Louis F. *The Deportations Delirium of Nineteen-Twenty*. Chicago: Charles H. Kerr & Company, 1923.

Preston, William, Jr. *Aliens and Dissenters: Federal Suppression of Radicals, 1903-1933*. New York: Harper Torchbooks, 1963.

Rankin, Robert S. *When Civil Law Fails: Martial Law and Its Legal Basis in the United States*. Durham, S.C.: Duke University Press, 1939.

Rich, Milton. *The Presidents and Civil Disorder*. Washington, D.C.: The Brookings Institution, 1941.

Segal, Melvin James. *The Norris-LaGuardia Act and the Courts*. Washington, D.C.: American Council on Public Affairs, 1941.

Spivak, John L. *A Man in His Time*. New York: Horizon Press, 1967.

Struggle in the Coal Fields: The Autobiography of Fred Mooney, edited by J. W. Hess. Morgantown: West Virginia University Library, 1967.

Swain, George T. *Facts About the Two Armed Marches on Logan*. Charleston: George T. Swain, 1962.

_____. *The Incomparable Don Chafin: Review of the Life of Logan's Dauntless and Indomitable Sheriff, Who Prevented the Invasion of*

Logan County on Two Occasions by Armed Miners from the Kanawha Valley Coal Fields. Charleston: George T. Swain, 1962.

What the Coal Commission Found; An Authoritative Summary by the Staff, edited by Edward Eyre Hunt. Baltimore: The Williams and Wilkins Company, 1925.

White, Walter. *A Man Called White: the Autobiography of Walter White.* New York: Viking Press, 1948.

Witte, Edwin E. *The Government in Labor Disputes.* New York: McGraw-Hill, 1932.

Zieger, Robert H. *Republicans and Labor 1919-1929.* Lexington: University of Kentucky Press, 1969.

Zucker, Norman L. *George W. Norris: Gentle Knight of American Democracy.* Urbana: University of Illinois Press, 1966.

ARTICLES

American Citizen (American Constitutional Association, Charleston, W. Va.), vols. 1-4, no. 3 (1921-1924).

Corbin, David A. "Betrayal in the West Virginia Coal Fields: Eugene V. Debs and the Socialist Party of America, 1912-1914." *The Journal of American History* 64, no. 4 (March, 1978): 987-1009.

["Editorial"]. *Coal Mining Review,* (September 15, 1920): p. 10

Johnson, James P. "Drafting the NRA Code of Fair Competition for the Bituminous Coal Industry." Journal of American History, 53, no. 3 (December, 1966): 521-41.

Kutler, Stanley I. "Chief Justice Taft, Judicial Unanimity, and Labor: The Coronado Case." The Historian, 24, no. 1 (November, 1961): 68-83.

————. "Labor, the Clayton Act, and the Supreme Court." *Labor History,* 3, no. 1 (Winter, 1962): 19-37.

Lynch, Lawrence R. "West Virginia Coal Strike." *Political Science Quarterly* 29 (December, 1914): 626-63.

McCormick, Kyle. "The National Guard of West Virginia during the Strike Period of 1912-1913." *West Virginia History* 22 (1960): 34-35.

Maurer, Maurer, and Senning, Calvin F. "Billy Mitchell, the Air Service and the Mingo War." *Airpower Historian* 12 (1965): 37-43.

Quenzel, C. H. "A Fight to Establish the State Police." *Journal of Criminal Law and Criminology* 34 (May-June, 1943): 61-67.

Randall, James G. "Miners and the Law of Treason." *North American Review* 216 (1922): 313-21.

Raushenbush, Carl. "The Use of Injunctions in Labor Disputes." *Editorial Research Reports* 1 (February 4, 1928): 113-33.

Sayre, Francis B. "Inducing Breach of Contract." *Harvard Law Review* 36 (1923): 663-703.

Watson, Richard L., Jr. "The Defeat of Judge Parker: A Study in Pressure Groups and Politics." *The Mississippi Valley Historical Review* 50, no. 2 (September, 1963): 213-34.

Wilson, Edmund. "Frank Keeney's Coal Diggers." *The New Republic* 67 (July 8, 1931): 195-99.

Witte, Edwin E. "The Federal Anti-injunction Act." *Minnesota Law Review* 16 (May, 1932): 638-58.

_____. "'Yellow Dog' Contracts." *Wisconsin Law Review* 6 (1931): 21-32..

Newspapers

Baltimore Sun, May 16, 1922.

The Charleston Gazette (W. Va.), 1908-22.

Clarksburg Telegram (W. Va.), September 21, 1912.

The Fayette Journal (Fayetteville, W. Va.), May 15, 1913.

New York Call, May 4, 1922.

New York Evening Post, March 3, 1921.

New York Post, February 24, and 25, 1921.

The New York Times, 1907-32.

Pick and Shovel (Fayetteville, W. Va.): September 7, 1921; February 21, 1923; September 19, 1923.

The Pittsburgh Dispatch, May 16 (or 17), 1914.

United Mine Workers Journal, 1917-31.

Washington Post (Washington, D.C.), April 29, 1922.

West Virginia Federationist, September 15, 1921.

The Wheeling Intelligencer (W. Va.), 1907-21.

The Wheeling Majority (W. Va.), 1908-20.

The Wheeling Register (W. Va.), November 3, 1919.

DISSERTATIONS, THESES

Anson, Charles P. "A History of the Labor Movement in West Virginia." Ph.D. dissertation, University of North Carolina, 1940.

Barb, John M. "Strikes in the Southern West Virginia Coal Fields, 1912-1922." Master's thesis, West Virginia University, 1949.

Barkey, Frederick Allan. "The Socialist Party in West Virginia from 1898 to 1920: A Study in Working Class Radicalism." Ph.D. dissertation, University of Pittsburgh, 1971.

Crawford, Charles B. "The Mine War on Cabin Creek and Paint Creek, West Virginia in 1912-1913." Master's thesis, University of Kentucky, 1939.

Farber, Milton Lewis, Jr. "Changing Attitudes of the American Federation of Labor Toward Business and Government, 1929-1933." Ph.D. dissertation, Ohio State University, 1959.

Fox, Harry Donald, Jr. "Thomas T. Haggerty and the Formative Years of the United Mine Workers of America." Ph.D. dissertation, West Virginia University, 1975.

Johnson, Donald Oscar. "The American Civil Liberties Union: Origins, 1914-1924." Ph.D. dissertation, Columbia University, 1960.

Posey, Thomas E. "The Labor Movement in West Virginia: Cautious Reformer." Ph.D. dissertation, University of Wisconsin, 1948.

Schlaback, Theron Frederick. "Edwin E. Witte: Cautious Reformer." Ph.D. dissertation, University of Wisconsin, 1966.

Notes

* *designates source for quotes.*

Introduction

1. *T.C. Townsend, *Martinsburg West Virginia Evening Journal*, September 15, 1923. Reprinted in U.S. Congress, Senate, Committee on Interstate Commerce, *Hearings pursuant to S. 105, Conditions in the Coal Fields of Pennsylvania, West Virginia, and Ohio*, 70th Cong., 1st sess., 1928, 2 vols., p. 1183. Cited hereafter as *Conditions in the Coal Fields*.
2. *Quoted by Joseph E. Finley, *The Corrupt Kingdom: the Rise and Fall of the United Mine Workers* (New York: Simon and Schuster, 1972), p. 24.
3. Ibid., p. 225.
4. Ibid., pp. 206-07.
5. Saul Alinsky, *John L. Lewis: An Unauthorized Biography* (New York: G. P. Putnam's Sons, 1949), p. 4.
6. Hitchman Coal and Coke Co. v., Mitchell et al., 245 U.S. 229 (1917), *Cases and Points*, Certiorari to Circuit Court of Appeals for Fourth Circuit, Brief for Petitioner (October term, 1916), 24: 13. Cited hereafter as 245 U.S. 229, *Cases and Points*; Harry Donald Fox, Jr., "Thomas T. Haggerty and the Formative Years of the United Mine Workers of America" (Ph.D. diss., West Virginia University, 1975), p. 184.
7. Ibid., pp. 188, 191, 225.

Chapter One: **ORGANIZE**

1. Restraining Order, entered January 14, 1908, Alston G. Dayton Papers, West Virginia Collection, West Virginia University Library; cited hereafter as Dayton Papers; *The Wheeling Intelligencer*, October 26, 1907, p. 2.

2. *The New York Times*, February 27, 1915, p. 18: Col. 2; *The Wheeling Intelligencer*, September 18, 1907, p. 2, February 3, 1908 (clipping in Dayton Papers), and February 17, 1915, p. 1; Younge v. U.S., 223 Fed. 941 (1915).

3. *Letter: Dayton to Attorney General, September 20, 1915, File #165095-63, Justice Department Records, National Archives. Cited hereafter as Justice Department.

4. *245 U.S. 229, *Cases and Points*, Brief for Petitioner (October term, 1916), 24: 26.

5. Edwin E. Witte, "Criticisms of the Manner in which the Courts Allow Injunctions to be used in Labor Disputes," Appendix G., Report on Injunctions (February, 1915), p. 14. Unpublished private papers gathered for the Commission on Industrial Relations, New York State School of Industrial and Labor Relations, Cornell University. Cited hereafter as Witte Papers; *Mitchell v. Hitchman Coal & Coke Co. 214 Fed. 685 (1914), pp. 698-99.

6. *Ibid., pp. 703-04.

7. Lawrence R. Lynch, "West Virginia Coal Strike," *Political Science Quarterly* 29 (December, 1914): 626-63; *The Wheeling Intelligencer*, July 24, 1912, p. 1, and August 31, 1912, p. 2; *testimony: William E. Glasscock, U.S., Congress, Senate, *Hearings before the Committee on Education and Labor pursuant to S. 37, Conditions in the Paint Creek District, West Virginia*, 63d Cong., 1st sess., 1913, 3 vols., pp. 372-73. Cited hereafter as *Conditions in the Paint Creek District*.

8. *The Wheeling Intelligencer*, August 20, 1912, p. 1, and June 10, 1913; *The Wheeling Majority*, July 4, 1912, p. 6; Iris Weed, "Digest of Report on Investigation of Paint Creek Fields of West Virginia, March 9, 1914," Department of Labor Records, National Archives. Cited hereafter as Labor Department.

9. *The Wheeling Intelligencer*, September 10, 1912, p. 1; testimony: A. M. Belcher, *Conditions in the Paint Creek District*, p. 1672.

10. *Charles B. Crawford, "The Mine War on Cabin Creek and Paint Creek, West Virginia in 1912-1913" (Master's thesis, University of Kentucky, 1939), pp. 37-38; *Struggle in the Coal Fields: the Autobiography of Fred Mooney*, ed. J. W. Hess (Morgantown: West Virginia University Library, 1967), p. 21.

11. Testimony: William E. Glasscock, *Conditions in the Paint Creek District*, pp. 377, 403; *The Wheeling Intelligencer*, September 11, 1912, p. 9.

12. *Letter: William E. Glasscock to Dear Sir, September 11, 1912, *Conditions in the Paint Creek District*, p. 520; *Letter: M. T. Davis et al. to William E.

Glasscock, September 13, 1912, ibid., pp. 521, 523.

13. Testimony: William E. Glasscock, ibid., pp. 539-30; *The Wheeling Intelligencer*, September 13, 1912, p. 9; *Clarksburg Telegram* (West Virginia), September 21, 1912 (clipping in William E. Glasscock Papers, West Virginia Collection, West Virginia University Library). Cited hereafter as Glasscock Papers.

14. Testimony: Thomas Cairns, *Conditions in the Paint Creek District*, p. 2051; *Report of West Virginia Mining Investigation Commission, Appointed by Governor Glasscock on the 28th Day of August, 1912* (Charleston: Tribune Printing Co. 1912). Reprinted in ibid., pp. 380-91.

15. *Testimony: George Williams, ibid., pp. 1826, 1857, 1861.

16. Testimony: T. T. Davis, ibid., pp. 1263-64; testimony: D. W. Shipley, ibid., p. 1781; warrant for arrest of Mary Jones, Coal Strikes, Records 1912-1913, West Virginia Collection, West Virginia University Library.

17. *The Wheeling Intelligencer*, December 23, 1912, p. 13, February 22, 1913, p. 18, and April 10, 1913, p. 12; *Biennial Report, Bureau of Labor of West Virginia 1913-1914* (Charleston: Tribune Printing Co., 1914), p. 162; "Governor's Message," January 2, 1913, Glasscock Papers.

18. *The Wheeling Majority*, October 17, 1912, p. 7; *The Wheeling Intelligencer*, February 5, 1913, p. 8, and *March 5, 1913, p. 11.

19. *The Wheeling Intelligencer*, March 19, 1913, p. 1, March 20, 1913, p. 1, and *March 22, 1913, p. 1.

20. *Ibid., February 5, 1913, p. 8, March 22, 1913, p. 1, and June 4, 1913, p. 1; Frederick Allan Barkey, "The Socialist Party in West Virginia from 1898 to 1920: a Study in Working Class Radicalism (Ph.D. diss., University of Pittsburgh, 1971), p. 148; *David A. Corbin, "Betrayal in the West Virginia Coal Fields: Eugene V. Debs and the Socialist Party of America, 1912-1914," *The Journal of American History 64*, no. 4 (March, 1978): 1000.

21. *The Wheeling Intelligencer*, April 18, 1913, p. 10.

22. *Ibid.

23. *Ibid., April 25, 1913, p. 1, April 23, 1913, p. 1, April 26, 1913, p. 1, April 29, 1913, p. 1, and May 1, 1913, p. 4.

24. *Ibid., April 26, 1913, p. 1, June 13, 1913, p. 1, and April 29, 1913, p. 1; testimony: Charles H. Boswell, *Conditions in the Paint Creek District*, pp. 2104-05.

25. *The Wheeling Intelligencer*, May 31, 1913, p. 1, June 25, 1913, p. 4, July 1, 1913, p. 1, July 30, 1913, p. 1, and August 1 [really August 2], 1913, p. 1.

26. Ibid., June 30, 1913, p. 1, and June 27, 1913, p. 1, and July 1, 1913, p. 1; *The Fayette Journal* (Fayetteville, W. Va.), May 15, 1913, p. 1.

27. Thomas E. Posey, "The Labor Movement in West Virginia 1900-1948" (Ph.D. diss., University of Wisconsin, 1948), p. 94; *Report of the Secretary of Labor 1914*, (1915), pp. 33-34; *Biennial Report, Bureau of Labor of West Virginia 1913-1914*, pp. 76-77, 84; *Testimony: D. C. Kennedy, *West Virginia Coal Fields*, p. 467.

28. *The Wheeling Intelligencer*, September 26, 1913, p. 4.

29. *Ibid., May 20, 1913, p. 1.
30. Iris Weed, "Digest of Report on Investigation of Paint Creek Fields of West Virginia, March 9, 1914," Labor Department; Robert S. Rankin, *West Civil Law Fails: Martial Law and Its Legal Basis in the United States* (Durham, S. C.: Duke University Press, 1939), pp. 111-13.
31. Mrs. Mary Jones, *Autobiography of Mother Jones* (Chicago: Charles H. Kerr & Co., 1925), p. 164; *Unidentified document titled: West Va. Resolutions, Justice Department.
32. *The New York Times*, June 5, 1913, p. 7; Col. 6; *The Wheeling Intelligencer*, May 5, 1913, p. 1; U.S., Senate, Committee on Education and Labor, *Report, Investigation of Paint Creek Coal Fields of West Virginia*, 63d Cong., 2d sess., 1914, pp. 1-21.
33. Testimony: John Nugent, C. L. Green, Bishop Donohue, W. D. Ord, *Conditions in the Paint Creek District*, pp. 1704-05, 1804-05, 1816, 1818, 1822, 2077-79, 2084; U.S. Immigration Commission, *Reports of the Immigration Commission: Immigrants in Industries*, vol. 6, pt. 5, Senate Doc. no. 633, 61st Cong., 2d sess., 1911, p. 207.
34. *Letter: Dayton to Attorney General, September 20, 1915, File #165095-63, Justice Department; *The New York Times*, June 8, 1913, p. 1, Col. 5.
35. *The New York Times*, June 9, 1913, p. 1; Col. 1.
36. *Letter: J. C. McReynolds to Albert B. Cummins, July 2, 1913, File #167424-11, Justice Department; *Letter: Harold A. Ritz to Attorney General, June 14, 1913, File #167434-9, ibid.; letter: [illegible, perhaps Maynard F. Stiles] to Attorney General, June 13, 1913, File #167424-8, ibid.
37. *Letter: William B. Barnhardt, Esq., to Attorney General, June 13, 1914, File #167-24-14, ibid.; letter: Assistant to the Attorney General [signature illegible] to William G. Barnhart, Esq., June 18, 1914, ibid.
38. Letter: Harold A. Ritz to Attorney General, May 17, 1913, File #165095-7, ibid.; *The New York Times*, June 10, 1913, p. 9, Col. 4.
39. *The Wheeling Intelligencer*, June 9, 1914, p. 1; *The Wheeling Majority*, January 22, 1914, p. 1.
40. Alston C. Dayton, *Finding of Facts in the Case of the United States v. James Oates et al.*, April 25, 1914, Appendix to United States Circuit Court of Appeals, Fourth Circuit, no. 1256, *Paul Scoric, Plaintiff in Error vs. the United States of America, Defendant in Error, Brief on behalf of the Defendant in Error*, pp. 20-28. Pardon Attorney Records, National Archives. Cited hereafter as Pardon Attorney Records. The document itself cited hereafter as Dayton, *Finding of Facts*; *The Wheeling Intelligencer*, October 8, 1913, p. 6 and February 28, 1914, p. 7; *The Pittsburgh Dispatch*, May 16 (or 17), 1914. [Clipping in Monongah Mine Disaster (1907-1909) file, West Virginia Collection, University of West Virginia Library.]
41. Dayton, *Finding of Facts*, p. 22.
42. *Letter: Dayton to S. W. Walker, May 19, 1914, Pardon Attorney Records.
43. *The Wheeling Majority*, December 11, 1913, p. 1, and January 22, 1914, p. 1.

44. *Ibid., December 11, 1913, p. 1; Dayton, *Finding of Facts*, p. 23.

45. *Letter: Stewart W. Walker to Attorney General, January 23, 1914, Pardon Attorney Records; *letter: William Wallace, Jr., Assistant Attorney General, to Walker, January 28, 1914, ibid.

46. Dayton, *Finding of Facts*, pp. 3, 23.

47. *The Wheeling Majority*, January 29, 1914, p. 1, and February 12, 1914, p. 3; letter: Dayton to Attorney General, September 20, 1915, File #165095-63, Justice Department; *The Wheeling Intelligencer*, June 30, 1914, p. 7.

48. *The Wheeling Majority*, February 2, 1914, p. 3.

49. Ibid., February 19, 1914, p. 1; letter: Woodrow Wilson to Attorney General, February 19, 1914, File #165095-18, Justice Department; letter: J. C. McReynolds to The President, February 26, 1914, ibid.

50. *The Wheeling Majority*, February 12, 1914, p. 1, and February 19, 1914, p. 1; *The Wheeling Intelligencer*, February 19, 1914, p. 1; *Dayton, *Finding of Facts*, p. 26.

51. Letter: John P. White to President, November 21, 1916, Pardon Attorney Records; *The Wheeling Intelligencer*, June 9, 1914, p. 1; *The Wheeling Majority*, March 26, 1914, p. 1.

52. *Dayton, *Finding of Facts*, p. 26; *The Wheeling Intelligencer*, April 4, 1914, p. 6, and March 26, 1914, p. 1; *The Wheeling Majority*, February 18, 1915, p. 6.

53. Homer Cummings and Carl McFarland, *Federal Justice: Chapters in the History of Justice and the Federal Executive* (New York: The Macmillan Co., 1937), p. 447; *The Wheeling Majority*, April 16, 1914, p. 1; *The Wheeling Intelligencer*, April 18, 1914, p. 6.

54. *The Wheeling Intelligencer*, pp. 1, 6; *The Wheeling Majority*, April 16, 1914, p. 1, and April 23, 1914, p. 1.

55. *The Wheeling Majority*, April 30, 1914, p. 1; *The New York Times*, April 26, 1914, sec. 3, p. 15, col. 4.

56. Application for Executive Clemency: Fannie Sullens, November 22, 1916, Pardon Attorney Records; *letter: Dayton to S. W. Walker, May 19, 1914, ibid.

57. Bittner et al. v. West Virginia-Pittsburgh Coal Co., 214 Fed. 716 (1914), p. 717; Mitchell et al. v. Hitchman Coal & Coke Co., 214 Fed. 685 (1914); letter: C. E. Smith, U.S. Marshal, to Attorney General, September 23, 1914, File #165095-47, Justice Department; *The Wheeling Majority*, February 18, 1915, p. 1.

58. *The Wheeling Majority*, August 9, 1917, p. 1; U.S. Senate, Committee on the Judiciary, *Hearings on S. 1482, Limiting Scope of Injunctions in Labor Disputes*, 70th Cong., 1st sess., 1928, pp. 633, 635. Cited hereafter as *Limiting Scope of Injunctions; The Wheeling Intelligencer*, April 1, 1914, p. 1, and June 13, 1914, p. 1.

59. Oates v. U.S., 223 Fed. 1013 (1915); letter: John P. White to President, November 21, 1916, Pardon Attorney Records; *The Wheeling Majority*, September 16, 1915, p. 1.

60. Schwartz v. U.S., 217 Fed. 866 (1915); Scoric v. U.S., 217 Fed. 817 (1915).

61. *The Wheeling Intelligencer*, June 13, 1914, p. 1, and February 9, 1915, p. 1; letter: The Ohio Valley Trades and Labor Assembly to Dear Sir and Brother, August 21, 1915. Enclosed in Dayton's letter to Attorney General, September 20, 1915, File #165095-63, Justice Department.

62. *U.S., House of Representatives, Committee on the Judiciary, *Official Conduct of Judge Alston G. Dayton*, Report no. 1490, 63d Cong., 3d sess., 1915, pp. 2-8.

63. *Ibid.

64. *Ibid.; *The Wheeling Intelligencer*, March 4, 1915, p. 1; *The Wheeling Majority*, March 11, 1915, p. 8.

65. Edwin E. Witte, *The Government in Labor Disputes*, (New York: McGraw-Hill, 1932), pp. 128-29.

66. Copies of threats, undated, Pardon Attorney Records; letter: C. E. Smith, U.S. Marshal, to Attorney General, September 23, 1914, File #165095-47, Justice Department.

67. *Letter: Dayton to Attorney General, September 20, 1915, File #165095-63, ibid.

68. Ibid.

69. *Letter: Dayton to Attorney General, December 1, 1916, File #165095-80, ibid. *letter: [illegible, perhaps Wm. Wallace], Assistant Attorney General, to Dayton, December 13, 1916, ibid.

70. Letter: John P. White to President, November 21, 1916, Pardon Attorney Records; *letter: J. P. Tumulty, Secretary to the President, to Attorney General, November 21, 1916, ibid.; *letter: T. W. Gregory to President, November 22, 1916, ibid.

71. *The Wheeling Intelligencer*, February 3, 1908 (clipping in Dayton Papers); Felix Frankfurter and Nathan Greene, *The Labor Injunction* (New York: The Macmillan Co., 1930), p. 76.

72. Edwin E. Witte, "The Actual Practice in Injunction Cases Arising in Connection with Labor Disputes," Appendix B., To the U.S. Commission on Industrial Relations (1915). Witte Papers.

73. John P. Frey, *The Labor Injunction: An Exposition of Government by Judicial Conscience and Its Menace* (n.p., 1923), pp. 86-87.

74. U.S., Senate, *Final Report and Testimony Submitted to Congress by the United States Commission on Industrial Relations*, Senate Doc. no. 415, 64th Cong., 1st sess., 1916; Graham Adams, Jr., *Age of Industrial Violence 1910-1915: the Activities and Findings of the United States Commission on Industrial Relations* (New York: Columbia University Press, 1966), p. 208.

75. Stanley I. Kutler, "Labor, the Clayton Act, and the Supreme Court," *Labor History* 3, no. 1 (Winter, 1962): 19-37.

76. *Letter: Stewart W. Walker to Attorney General, November 24, 1916, File #165095-74, Justice Department; *letter: John W. Davis, Acting Attorney General, to President, December 6, 1916, Pardon Attorney Papers.

77. Letter: John W. Davis, Acting Attorney General, to President, December 6, 1916, Pardon Attorney Papers; *memo: T. W. Gregory to Mr. Finch, December 9, 1916, ibid.

78. *The Wheeling Intelligencer*, January 13, 1916, p. 1.
79. Ibid.; *Ibid., May 25, 1916, p. 1; Charles Henry Ambler and Festus P. Summer, *West Virginia, the Mountain State*, 2d ed. (Englewood Cliffs, N.J.: Prentice-Hall, 1958), p. 386; *The Wheeling Majority*, February 16, 1916, p. 8, and March 1, 1917, p. 1.
80. Hitchman Coal & Coke Co., v. Mitchell et al., 245 U.S. 229 (1917), pp. 250-51.
81. Ibid.
82. Ibid., p. 273; Edwin E. Witte, "' Yellow Dog' Contracts," *Wisconsin Law Review* 6 (1931): 21-32.

Chapter Two: WAR

1. *The Wheeling Majority*, October 11, 1917, p. 2.
2. *The Wheeling Intelligencer*, July 5, 1915, p. 1, and April 25, 1916, p. 1.
3. *The Wheeling Majority*, September 23, 1915, p. 8, and *April 4, 1918, p. 12.
4. *The Wheeling Majority*, May 24, 1917, p. 8; *May 28, 1918, p. 5; July 12, 1917, p. 1; and May 23, 1918, p. 6; *The Charleston Gazette*, May 21, 1920, p. 6; report of Secretary-Treasurer Fred Mooney, January 8, 1918, attached to letter addressed to Mooney from Cornwell, January 11, 1918. John Jacob Cornwell Papers, West Virginia Collection, West Virginia Library. Cited hereafter as Cornwell Papers.
5. *The Wheeling Majority*, February 27, 1919, p. 1.
6. *Ibid.; C. H. Quenzel, "A Fight to Establish the State Police," *Journal of Criminal Law & Criminology* 34 (May-June): 62, 67; *The Charleston Gazette*, April 17, 1921, p. 4.
7. *The Wheeling Majority*, February 20, 1919, p. 7; *letter: Cornwell to L. J. Foreman, November 5, 1919, Cornwell Papers.
8. Harry Garfield, *Final Report of the United States Fuel Administrator 1917-1919*, 1921, pp. 209-10, 217. Cited hereafter as *Final Report, Fuel Administrator*; memorandum: "Suggestions as to Putting into Effect the Provisions of the Lever Bill with Respect to Coal and Coke," August 10, 1917, Harry A. Garfield Papers, Library of Congress. Cited hereafter as Garfield Papers.
9. *Final Report, Fuel Administrator*, p. 215; *Reports of the Department of Labor 1918: Report of the Secretary of Labor and Reports of Bureaus*, House Doc. no. 1449, 65th Cong., 3d sess., 1919, pp. 102, 110.
10. William Jett Lauck and Claude S. Watts, *The Industrial Code: A Survey of the Postwar Industrial Situation, a Review of Wartime Developments in Industrial Relations, and a Proposal Looking to Permanent Industrial Peace* (New York: Funk and Wagnalls Co., 1922), p. 118.
11. *The Wheeling Majority*, November 22, 1917, p. 1.

12. Testimony: Percy Tetlow, *Conditions in the Coal Fields*, p. 1430; *Final Report, Fuel Administrator*, pp. 167, 218.
13. Letter: W. B. Wilson to John L. Lewis, January 22, 1920, Labor Department; manuscript: "Profiteering in American Industry as the Cause of High Prices," W. Jett Lauck Papers, University of Virginia Library. Cited hereafter as Lauck Papers.
14. *Manuscript: "Profiteering in the Bituminous Coal Industry," Lauck Papers; Basil M. Manly, "A Survey of American Industrial Conditions," ibid.; Alexander M. Bing, *Wartime Strikes and Their Adjustment* (New York: E. P. Dutton & Co., 1921), p. 285.
    For a different assessment, see Paul H. Douglas, *Real Wages in the United States, 1890-1926* (Boston: Houghton Mifflin Company, 1930), pp. 11, 219, 587; Eli Ginzberg and Hyman Berman, *The American Worker in the Twentieth Century, a History through Autobiographies* (New York: Free Press of Glencoe, 1963), p. 150.
15. *Letter: Winding Gulf Operators Association to H. A. Garfield, July 30, 1918, Fuel Administration Records, National Archives; letter: Garfield to T. L. Lewis, November 15, 1918, ibid.
16. Bing, *Wartime Strikes and Their Adjustment*, p. 159; *The Wheeling Majority*, March 14, 1918, p. 8.
17. *245 U.S. 229, *Cases and Points*, motion for contempt, affidavit of W. H. Koch (1917), 24, pp. 21-26.
18. I believe the role of the war in establishing the UMW in West Virginia has been exaggerated. Ambler and Summer, *West Virginia*, p. 450, claims a total wartime membership of 50,000; *Autobiography of Fred Mooney*, pp. 60, 62; Report of Secretary-Treasurer Fred Mooney, January 8, 1918. Attached to letter addressed to Mooney from Cornwell, January 11, 1918, Cornwell Papers; *The Wheeling Majority*, March 14, 1918, p. 5, May 30, 1918, p. 1, and February 13, 1919, p. 1; *The New York Times*, November 12, 1919, p. 1; col. 7; Report on Coal Fields of West Virginia, Headquarters First Provisional Reinforced Regiment, First Division, Charleston, West Virginia, November 13, 1919, Cornwell Papers; *Biennial Report of the Bureau of Labor of West Virginia 1919-1920* (Charleston: Tribune Printing Co., 1920), pp. 97-99.
19. Gregory, T. W., Directions to United States Marshals and United States Attorneys for the Enforcement of the President's Proclamation of April 6, 1917, as to Alien Enemies, April, 1917, Glasser File, Justice Department.
20. *Telegram: Smith to Attorney General, May 22, 1917, File #186210, ibid.; telegram: Wilson to Bielaski, May 23, 1917, File #186210-2 ibid.; memorandum for Mr. Herron, May 23, 1917, signed A.B.B., ibid.
21. *Telegram: Kelly to Attorney General, January 23, 1918, File #9-16-12-2221-5, ibid.; *memorandum for O'Brien [probably from Kelly, illegible], February 1, 1918, ibid.
22. *John B. Wilson, special agent, Report on John Mohorwick, December 9, 1917, File #9-16-12-2007, ibid.; letter: Stuart M. Walker, U.S. Attorney, to Attorney General, December 29, 1917, ibid.; telegram: Walker to Attorney

General, January 9, 1918, ibid.; telegram: Gregory to U.S. Attorney, January 16, 1918, ibid.

23. Letter: U.S. Attorney to D. E. French, August 5, 1917, File #HCR-1759, ibid.; *letter: John Lord O'Brien to Stuart W. Walker, Esq., April 30, 1919, File #186233-77-33, ibid.

24. *The Wheeling Majority*, July 12, 1917, p. 1, and *July 25, 1918, p. 1.

25. Glasser manuscript, Justice Department. In this section I depend heavily on careful research carried out by Abraham Glasser, an attorney in the Justice Department. In the late 1930s, Glasser researched the use of federal troops in suppressing civil disorders during the First World War. He had access to classified documents. He pulled together all the pertinent documents and wrote an unfinished manuscript.

26. Ibid.; Abraham Glasser, Memorandum for Mr. Little, April 8, 1939, Glasser File, ibid.; *Federal Aid in Domestic Disturbances 1903-1922*, Senate Doc., no. 263, 67th Cong., 2d sess., 1922, p. 302.

27. *Federal Aid in Domestic Disturbances 1903-1922*, Senate Doc., no. 263, 67th Cong., 2d sess., 1922, pp. 219-21; Milton Rich, *The Presidents and Civil Disorder* (Washington, D.C.: The Brookings Institution, 1941), pp. 201-06.

28. Letter: A. Glasser to McFarland, June 30, 1938, Glasser File, Justice Department; Baker, Memorandum for the Chief of Staff, June 2, 1917, ibid.; Glasser manuscript, ibid.

29. Dispatch to the Adjutant General of the Army, June 26, 1917, Glasser File; letter: Secretary of War to Governors, July 10, 1917; *letter: Cornwell to Baker, August 31, 1917; *letter: Baker to Cornwell, September 6, 1917, all in ibid.

30. Glasser manuscript, ibid.; William Preston, Jr., *Aliens and Dissenters: Federal Suppression of Radicals, 1903-1933* (New York: Harper Torchbooks, 1963), pp. 104-08.

31. *Telegram: Adjutant General to Commanding Generals, September 29, 1919, Glasser File, Justice Department; telegram: Secretary of War to Governors, September 20, 1919, ibid.; *The New York Times*, October 16, 1919, (clipping in Glasser File) ibid.; Glasser manuscript, ibid.

32. Letter: Keeney to the President, November 3, 1919. Attached to letter: Kelly to Attorney General, November 4, 1919, File #16-130-83, Justice Department; *Report and Digest of Evidence Taken by Commission Appointed by the Governor of West Virginia in Connection With the Logan County Situation* (Charleston: Tribune Printing Co., 1919), pp. 9-16. Cited hereafter as *Logan County Commission*, 1919; George T. Swain, *Facts About the Two Armed Marches on Logan* (Charleston: George T. Swain, 1962), p. 3; Ambler and Summer, *West Virginia*, pp. 386, 460.

33. Winthrop D. Lane, *Civil War in West Virginia: A Story of the Industrial Conflict in the Coal Mines* (New York: B. W. Huebsch, 1921), p. 86; *Autobiography of Fred Mooney*, pp. x, 1, 45-46, 54, 88; John L. Spivak, *A Man in His Time* (New York: Horizon Press, 1967), p. 63.

34. Winthrop D. Lane, *New York Post*, February 25, 1921 (clipping in Scrapbooks, West Virginia Case 1920-1922, Lauck Papers); *The Wheeling*

Majority, September 11, 1919, p. 1.

35. *Statement by Cornwell [probably a press release], n.d.; Cornwell Papers; telegram: Cornwell to Newton D. Baker, September 6, 1919, ibid.; telegram: Cornwell to General Leonard Wood, September 6, 1919, ibid.; testimony: Keeney, U.S., Senate, Committee on Education and Labor, *Hearings pursuant to S. 80, to Investigate the Recent Acts of Violence in the Coal Fields of West Virginia and Adjacent Territory and the Causes which Led to the Conditions which Now Exist in Said Territory*, 67th Cong., 1st sess., 1921-1922, 2 vols., pp. 169-70. Cited hereafter as *West Virginia Coal Fields*.

36. Letter: Cornwell to Major T. B. Davis, September 20, 1919, Cornwell Papers; letter: Cornwell to Keeney, October 1, 1919, ibid.; letter: Keeney to Cornwell, November 6, 1919, ibid.; operative report, October 16, 1919, ibid.; *The Wheeling Majority*, December 4, 1919, p. 4.

37. Operative report, October 16, 1919, Cornwell Papers; letter: Mooney to Miners of the Guyan River and Norfolk & Western Fields [n.d., but September 21, 1919 approximately], ibid.; *Logan County Commission*, 1919, pp. 47-58.

38. *Statement: Cornwell, September 26, 1919, Cornwell Papers.

39. Perlman and Taft, *History of Labor*, 4: 472.

40. *Alinsky, *John L. Lewis*, p. 31.

41. *Ibid., pp. 31-32; Bing, *Wartime Strikes and Their Adjustment*, p. 154; *The New York Times*, November 1, 1919, p. 1, col. 5.

42. Operative report, October 21, 1919, Cornwell Papers; letter: Cornwell to Keeney, October 18, 1919, ibid.; telegram: Cornwell to Keeney, October 24, 1919, ibid.; telegram: Keeney to Cornwell, October 24, 1919, ibid.

43. *Letter: Wood to Cornwell, October 24, 1919 [letter quotes from Cornwell's letter to Wood, October 22, 1919], ibid.

44. *Letter: J. G. Bradley to Cornwell, October 30, 1919, ibid.; proclamation, October 30, 1919, ibid.; letter: Cornwell to Keeney, November 3, 1919, ibid.

45. *Letter: Cornwell to Keeney, November 3, 1919, ibid.; telegram: Cornwell to Wood, October 30, 1919, ibid.; letter: [probably by Cornwell, unsigned carbon] to Mayor Thomas B. Davis, October 30, 1919, ibid.; *The New York Times*, November 1, 1919, p. 1, col. 6, and November 12, 1919, p. 1, col. 7.

46. *Letter: Cornwell to The Sheriffs of the Respective Counties and the Mayors of the Various Municipalities, October 30, 1919, Cornwell Papers.

47. *Letter: Hastings to Cornwell, November 1, 1919, ibid.

48. *Letter: Cornwell to Hastings, November 3, 1919, ibid.

49. *The Wheeling Register*, November 3, 1919 [clipping attached to letter: Handlan to Cornwell, November 3, 1919, ibid.].

50. *Letter: Keeney to Cornwell, November 6, 1919, ibid.

51. *Perlman and Taft, *History of Labor*, p. 472; *The New York Times*, November 9, 1919, p. 1, col. 8, and November 12, 1919, p. 1, col. 7.

52. *The New York Times*, November 6, 1919, p. 1, col. 6; November 12, 1919, p. 1, col. 7; *November 14, 1919, p. 3 col. 1, and November 15, 1919, p. 1 col. 6; telegram: Walker to Attorney General, November 17, 1919, File

#16-130-83, Justice Department.

53. Telegram: Walker to Attorney General, December 1, 1919, ibid.; letter: Koch to Cornwell, November 11, 1919, Cornwell Papers; *The Wheeling Majority*, November 6, 1919, p. 1.

54. Telegram: Gilbert to Cornwell, October 30, 1919, Cornwell Papers; telegram: Palmer to Cornwell, November 3, 1919, ibid.; telegram: Cornwell to Palmer, November 3, 1919, ibid.; *letter: Walker to Attorney General, November 7, 1919, File #16-130-83, Justice Department.

55. *The New York Times*, November 14, 1919, p. 3, col. 1; telegram: Walker to Attorney General, November 13, 1919, File #15-130-83, Justice Department; telegram: Palmer to Cornwell, November 13, 1919, File #16-130-83, ibid.; *telegram: Cornwell to Palmer, November 13, 1919, Cornwell Papers; *letter: Walker to Attorney General, November 13, 1919, File #16-130-83, ibid.; Justice Department; telegram: Walker to Attorney General, November 17, 1919, File #16-130-83, ibid; telegram: Walker to Attorney General, December 1, 1919, File #16-130-83, ibid.

56. Letter: S. J. Jones to Cornwell, December 4, 1919. Cornwell Papers; letter: H. D. Carroll to Cornwell, December 5, 1919, ibid.; letter: Cornwell to Clarence E. Martin, November 25, 1919, ibid.; letter: G. M. Scott to Attorney General, November 28, 1919, File #16-130-83, Justice Department; letter: Ames to T. L. Lewis, February 2, 1920, ibid.; agreement, February 4, 1920 between District No. 29 of the UMW and the New River Coal Operators Association, ibid.

57. Diary, Garfield Papers.
    United States Bituminous Coal Commission, 1920, Majority Report. Reprinted in *Red Jacket Consolidated Coal and Coke Company, et al. plaintiffs, versus John L. Lewis et al., Transcript of the Record.* District Court of the United States for the Southern District of West Virginia (Charleston, 1923), 3: 1501a, 1579a. Cited hereafter as Red Jacket v. John L. Lewis.

Chapter Three.   OF LAWS AND MEN

1. *Letter: William D. Ord to John J. Cornwell, May 8, 1920, Cornwell Papers.

2. Testimony: Langdon C. Bell, *Conditions in the Coal Fields*, pp. 1836-37, 1840-41.

3. Ibid., pp. 1837, 1885.

4. Winthrop D. Lane, *New York Evening Post*, March 13, 1921 (clipping in Scrapbooks, West Virginia Case 1920-1922, Lauck Papers).

5. *Complainants' Exhibit, Red Jacket Affidavit of C. L. McKinnon, Red Jacket v. John L. Lewis. This particular affidavit is filed with the papers on the case at the District Court of the United States for the Southern District of West Virginia in Charleston, West Virginia.

The individual employment contract also was used in Mercer and McDowell counties by other companies. Considering the important role the United States Steel Corporation played in Mercer and McDowell counties, and its connection through Isaac T. Mann with the Red Jacket Company, undoubtedly United States Steel was behind the decision to use the individual employment contract throughout southern West Virginia. See Chapter 5 for additional discussion.
*Copy of contract [n.d.], Cornwell Papers.

6. *Letter: T. L. Felts to George Bausewine, Jr., May 17, 1920, *West Virginia Coal Fields*, p. 215.
    There was a dispute at the time as to the genuineness of this and other documents found on the body of Albert Felts after the Matewan incident. Winthrop D. Lane, a very able reporter who covered the labor struggle in West Virginia, believed they were genuine.

7. *18 Fed. (2d) 839. Reprinted in *Limiting Scope of Injunctions*, pp. 640, 642, 647.

8. *Ibid., pp. 641-44.

9. *Ibid., p. 643; Stanley I. Kutler, "Chief Justice Taft, Judicial Unanimity and Labor: The Coronado Case," *The Historian* 24, no. 1. (November, 1961): 76.

10. Testimony: Thomas L. Felts, *West Virginia Coal Fields*, pp. 892-93.

11. *The Charleston Gazette*, May 21, 1929, p. 7; *Testimony: Sid Hatfield, *West Virginia Coal Fields*, p. 206.

12. *Ibid., pp. 206-07, 209-10; *The Charleston Gazette*, November 27, 1920, p. 2.

13. Testimony: Sid Hatfield, *West Virginia Coal Fields*, pp. 216-17; *The Charleston Gazette*, August 2, 1921, p. 1.

14. Testimony: C. E. Lively, *West Virginia Coal Fields*, pp. 358, 361, 364-65.

15. Testimony: Mrs. Sid Hatfield, ibid., pp. 733-34; testimony: Ed Chambers, ibid., p. 739: *The Charleston Gazette*, August 2, 1921, p. 2; *Autobiography of Fred Mooney*, p. 88.

16. *Letter: John J. Cornwell to Fred Mooney, July 19, 1920, Cornwell Papers; letter: A. Mitchell Palmer to Fred Mooney, June 15, 1920, File #16-130-83, Justice Department.

17. Complainants' Exhibit, Red Jacket Affidavit of C. L. McKinnon, Red Jacket v. John L. Lewis. This particular affidavit is filed with the papers on the case at the District Court of the United States for the Southern District of West Virginia in Charleston, West Virginia.

18. Testimony: Fred Mooney, *West Virginia Coal Fields*, pp. 56, 60; testimony: Neil Burkinshaw, ibid., pp. 5-8; *testimony: Harry Olmstead, ibid., pp. 259-60.

19. Telegram: James W. Weir to John J. Cornwell, June 29, 1920, ibid.; testimony: Langdon C. Bell, *Conditions in the Coal Fields*, pp. 1835-36.

20. *Letter: Jas. D. Francis to John J. Cornwell, with attached document, July 17, 1920, Cornwell Papers.

21. Testimony: G. T. Blankenship, *West Virginia Coal Fields*, pp. 487-488; letter: William N. Cummins to G. T. Blankenship, May 25, 1920, Cornwell

Papers; letter: G. T. Blankenship to Williams N. Cummins, June 3, 1920, ibid.; letter: William D. Ord to John J. Cornwell, June 6, 1920, ibid.; *letter: G. T. Blankenship to John J. Cornwell, June 9, 1920, ibid.

22. Testimony: Fred Mooney, *West Virginia Coal Fields*, p. 19; report: James Purcell to H. L. Kerwin, July 17, 1920, File #170-1202, Labor Department; *letter: William D. Ord to John J. Cornwell, June 15, 1920, Cornwell Papers; letter: John J. Cornwell to William D. Ord, June 17, 1920, ibid.

23. *Letter: Jackson Arnold to James D. Francis, June 24, 1920, ibid.

24. *Letter: L. E. Armentrout to John J. Cornwell, July 16, 1920, ibid.; *telegram: Harry Olmstead to James W. Weir, July 22, 1920, ibid.; *letter: Jackson Arnold to John J. Cornwell, August 27, 1920, ibid.

25. *The Charleston Gazette*, August 29, 1920, p. 1; *governor's statement requesting troops [n.d., but in fact issued August 27, 1920], Cornwell Papers; *The Charleston Gazette*, August 30, 1920, p. 1; letter: Fred Mooney to John J. Cornwell, July 20, 1920, Cornwell Papers; letter: Jackson Arnold to John J. Cornwell, October 24, 1920, ibid.

26. *The Charleston Gazette*, June 22, 1920, p. 1; telegram: Jackson Arnold to Governor, May 21, 1920, Cornwell Papers; letter: James Damron to T. L. Felts, June 16, 1920, ibid.

27. *Letter: James Damron to John J. Cornwell, September 14, 1920, ibid.; *letter: James Damron to John J. Cornwell, September 2, 1920, ibid.

28. *Letter: S. Burkhardt to John J. Cornwell, August 31, 1920, ibid.; *telegram: S. Burkhardt to John J. Cornwell, September 1, 1920, ibid.

29. *Letter: John J. Cornwell to James Damron, September 8, 1920, ibid.; *letter: James Damron to John J. Cornwell, September 14, 1920, ibid; *The Charleston Gazette*, September 7, 1920, p. 1.

30. *Letter: John J. Cornwell to James Damron, September 8, 1920, Cornwell Papers.

31. *Letter: James Damron to John J. Cornwell, September 14, 1920, ibid.

32. Report of D. Randolph Bias's interview with James Damron, enclosed with letter: Harry Olmstead to John J. Cornwell, September 3, 1920, ibid.; *letter: Governor to Dr. T. E. Romine, August 27, 1920, ibid.

33. Winthrop D. Lane, *New York Post*, February 24, 1921 (clipping in Scrapbooks, West Virginia Case 1920-1922, Lauck Papers).

34. *Testimony: C. Frank Keeney, *West Virginia Coal Fields*, p. 184.

35. *Letter: James Damron to John J. Cornwell, September 14, 1920, Cornwell Papers.

36. Letter (copy): C. F. Keeney to Newton D. Baker, September 4, 1920 [report of operative No. 19, October 4, 1920], ibid.; *["Editorial"], *Coal Mining Review* (September 15, 1920), p. 10.

37. *Letter: William N. Cummins to John J. Cornwell, October 6, 1920, Cornwell Papers.

38. *Ibid.; letter: Jackson Arnold to John J. Cornwell, October 23, 1920, ibid.; letter: James Damron to The County Court of Mingo County, and G. T. Blankenship, Esq., Sheriff of Mingo County, October 15, 1920, ibid.; telegrams (2): J. W. Weir to John J. Cornwell, October 19, 1920, ibid.;

testimony: Harry Olmstead, *West Virginia Coal Fields*, pp. 265-66.

39. Letter: S. D. Stokes to James Damron, December 23, 1920, ibid., pp. 220-21; *The Charleston Gazette*, October 28, 1920, p. 10.

40. Rankin, *When Civil Law Fails*, pp. 128-29; Proclamation of Governor Cornwell, November 27, 1920, *West Virginia Coal Fields*, pp. 272-73; letter: James Damron to John J. Cornwell, September 14, 1920, Cornwell Papers; letter: Governor to Dear Sir, October 26, 1920, ibid.

41. *The New York Times*, February 8, 1921, p. 24, col. 4. *letter: Howard Sutherland to John J. Cornwell, February 17, 1920, Cornwell Papers.

42. War Plan White, Memorandum for the Adjutant General of the Army, May 27, 1920, Glasser File, Justice Department; Glasser manuscript, ibid.; *Federal Aid in Domestic Disturbances 1903-1933*, p. 317. Here the figure is 29, Glasser uses the figure 30.

43. *Quoted from restraining order, April 8, 1922, Red Jacket consolidated cases, *Limiting Scope of Injunctions*, p. 596. The text of Wadill's injunction of November 3, 1920, is not available, but form and wording would be essentially the same. *letter: William N. Cummins to E. K. Beckner, November 15, 1920, Cornwell Papers; preliminary statement, Bituminous Operators Special Committee to United States Coal Commission, *Conditions in the Coal Fields*, p. 2000.

44. Letter: Alfred Bettman to Roger Baldwin, August 1, 1922, Felix Frankfurter Papers, Box #44, Library of Congress. Cited hereafter as Frankfurter Papers.

45. *Testimony: Jackson Arnold, *West Virginia Coal Fields*, p. 551.

46. Testimony: Percy Tetlow, *Conditions in the Coal Fields*, p. 1445; statement by Bituminous Operators' Special Committee to the United States Coal Commission, August 1923, ibid., p. 2012; Ambler and Summer, *West Virginia*, pp. 387, 460; Posey, "The Labor Movement in West Virginia," pp. 207-08; Spivak, *A Man in His Time*, p. 87.

47. Testimony: Langdon C. Bell, *Conditions in the Coal Fields*, pp. 1835-36.

48. Testimony: J. R. Brockus, *West Virginia Coal Fields*, pp. 332-33.

49. Testimony: Harry Olmstead, ibid., p. 273; Rankin, *When Civil Law Fails*, p. 133; *The Charleston Gazette*, July 16, 1921, p. 1.

Chapter Four: **THE MARCH**

1. *Testimony: C. A. Medley, State v. J. E. Wilburn, Miners' Treason Trial Papers, 1921-1923, pp. 673-74, West Virginia Collection, West Virginia University Library. Cited hereafter as Miners' Treason Trial.

2. *Testimony: Jack Brinkman, State v. Walter Allen, ibid., pp. 757-59.

3. Letter: Elliott Northcott to the Attorney General, December 18, 1922, File #205194-50-306X, Justice Department; report: C. A. Martin, to Director Military Intelligence, Washington, D. C., September 4, 1921, Adjutant General File, War Department, Modern Military Records, National

Archives. Cited hereafter as Adjutant General File; testimony: W. R. Thurmond, *West Virginia Coal Fields*, p. 867; operative report, October 20, 1919, Cornwell Papers; *Baltimore Sun*, May 16, 1922 (clipping in Scrapbooks, West Virginia Case 1920-1922, Lauck Papers).

4. Letter: Fred Mooney to the Local Unions of District No. 17 [n.d.], State v. Walter Allen, Miners' Treason Trial; testimony: Major Thomas Davis, ibid., pp. 238, 243; Philip Murray, "West Virginia Report to the 28th Consecutive and 5th Bienniel Convention of the UMWA, September, 1921," Red Jacket v. John L. Lewis, 2: 2317.

5. *Testimony: A. O. Stanley, State v. Walter Allen, Miners' Treason Trial, p. 639; letter: C. F. Keeney, James Riley, H. L. Franklin, Fred Mooney, to Labor, Organized and Unorganized, August 1, 1921, ibid.

6. *District Mines Information Bureau, "Battle of Blair Mountain Before and After" [n.p., n.d.], p. 3., Ephraim F. Morgan Papers, West Virginia Collection, West Virginia University Library. Cited hereafter as Morgan Papers.

7. *Washington Post* (Washington, D.C.), April 29, 1922 (clipping in Scrapbooks, West Virginia Case 1920-1922, Lauck Papers); *testimony: E. F. Morgan, State v. Walter Allen, Miners' Treason Trial, pp. 189-90.

8. Report: Colonel C. A. Martin, Intelligence Officer, to Director Military Intelligence, Washington, D.C., September 4, 1921, Adjutant General File; *letter: E. F. Morgan to Anderson Fauber, et al., August 17, 1921, Morgan Papers.

9. *Letter: E. F. Morgan to C. O. Bruere, September 13, 1921, ibid.; *statement: E. F. Morgan, September [n.d.], 1921, ibid.

10. Testimony: Don Chafin, State v. Walter Allen, Miners' Treason Trial, pp. 212-14.

11. Testimony: Fred Mooney, ibid., pp. 1183-87; testimony: E. F. Morgan, State v. J. E. Wilburn, ibid., p. 623.

12. Statement: E. F. Morgan, September [n.d.], 1921, Morgan Papers; *letter: E. F. Morgan to E. E. Smith, September 1, 1921, ibid.

13. *Autobiography of Fred Mooney*, pp. 91-95; *testimony: Fred Mooney, State v. Walter Allen, Miners' Treason Trial, pp. 1177-79. The quote is primarily from Mooney's *Autobiography*. Mooney's testimony in the *Allen* trial has been used to supply a few details. A few words have been changed to make transitions clearer. Mooney refers to Droddy Creek; it should be Drawdy Creek.

14. Testimony: Don Chafin, State v. Walter Allen, Miners' Treason Trial, p. 217.

15. Ibid., pp. 220-23, 230, 232; testimony: Ephraim F. Morgan, State v. J. E. Wilburn, ibid., p. 628; memorandum: J. R. Brockus, August 28, 1921, Adjutant General File; *testimony: J. R. Brockus, State v. Walter Allen, Miners' Treason Trial, pp. 619-20.

16. Memorandum: J. R. Brockus, August 28, 1921, Adjutant General File.

17. *Letter: John H. Charnock to Morgan, August 30, 1921, Morgan Papers.

18. Letter: E. F. Morgan to Warren G. Harding, August 29, 1921, ibid.

19. Telegrams: John W. Weeks to Morgan, Morgan to John W. Weeks, August 30, 1921, ibid.; T. C. Townsend, *Martinsburg West Virginia Evening Journal*, September 15, 1923. Reprinted in *Conditions in the Coal Fields*, p. 1183; telegram: H. D. Hatfield to Harry B. Dougherty, August 31, 1921, File #205194-50, Justice Department; A Proclamation by the President of the United States, August 30, 1921, Morgan Papers.

20. **Autobiography of Fred Mooney*, pp. 98-99.

21. *Telegram: Bandholtz to Adjutant General, U.S. Army, September 1, 1921, Adjutant General File; *testimony: David Fowler, Red Jacket v. John L. Lewis, 2: 2863; *transcript of telephone conversation between Bandholtz and Major Gasser, September 2, 1921, Adjutant General File.

22. *Testimony: Jack Brinkman, State v. Walter Allen, Miners' Treason Trial, pp. 770-71; testimony: Henry Cole, ibid., p. 891; testimony: Sam Marlow, ibid., p. 559; Testimony: Ike Wilburn, State v. J. E. Wilburn, ibid., p. 461.

23. *Testimony: Ira Wilson, State v. Walter Allen, ibid., p. 115; testimony: Jack Brinkman, State v. Walter Allen, ibid., pp. 759-761; *New York Call*, May 4, 1922 (clipping in Scrapbooks, West Virginia Case 1920-1922, Lauck Papers).

24. *Testimony: Jack Brinkman, State v. Walter Allen, Miners' Treason Trial, pp. 762-66.

25. Testimony: Ephraim F. Morgan, ibid., p. 197; *testimony: William E. Eubanks, ibid., pp. 630-31; William E. Eubanks, Report of Operations, September 4, 1921, Morgan Papers.

26. *William E. Eubanks, Report of Operations, September 4, 1921, Morgan Papers.

27. Testimony: Jack Brinkman, State v. Walter Allen, p. 767; testimony: W. F. Harlis, ibid., p. 437; message: E. L. Bock, September 1, 1921, Morgan Papers.

28. Testimony: Major Charles T. Smart, State v. Walter Allen, Miners' Treason Trial, pp. 804-05; Wiliam E. Eubanks, Report of Operations, September 4, 1921, Morgan Papers; testimony: D. F. Pauley, M.D., State v. Walter Allen, Miners' Treason Trial, p. 248; testimony: L. F. Milliken, M.D., ibid., p. 469; *testimony: Ira Wilson, ibid., p. 121.

29. Report: John H. Charnock to Morgan, September 10, 1921, Morgan Papers; *West Virginia Federationist*, September 15, 1921, p. 4.

30. *Statement: Governor Morgan, September 8, 1921, Morgan Papers. *Phillip Murray, "West Virginia Report to the 28th Consecutive and 5th Bienniel Convention of UMWA, September, 1921," Red Jacket v. John L. Lewis, 2: 2319.

31. *Testimony: Captain John J. Wilson, Red Jacket v. John L. Lewis, 2: 2955, 2961; Report on conditions in Logan: Major C. F. Thompson to Commanding General, Provisional Brigade, September 6, 1921, Adjutant General File.

32. Testimony: Captain John J. Wilson, Red Jacket v. John L. Lewis, 2: 2953-54; testimony: Major Charles T. Smart, State v. Walter Allen, Miners' Treason Trial, pp. 801-03, 808; telegram: Bandholtz to Commanding

General, Fifth Corps Area, September 5, 1921, Adjutant General File.

33. Transcript of telephone conversation between Bandholtz and Major Gasser, September 2, 1921, Adjutant General File; memorandum: S. F. Bottoms, September 5, 1921, ibid.; daily report, Bandholtz, September 9, 1921, ibid.; *Memorandum for the Chief of Staff: Amos A. Fries, August 25, 1921, ibid.

34. *Report: Colonel C. A. Martin, Intelligence Officer, to Director Military Intelligence, Washington, D.C., September 4, 1921, ibid.

35. *Maurer Maurer and Calvin F. Senning, "Billy Mitchell, the Air Service and the Mingo War," *Airpower Historian* 12 (1965): 39.

36. Ibid., pp. 40-41.

37. Ibid., p. 41; orders: Colonel Stanley H. Ford to C.O., Air Service Troops, September 2, 1921, Adjutant General File.

38. Telegram: Bandholtz to Commanding General, Fifth Corps Area, September 5, 1921, ibid.

39. Letter: Bandholtz to Morgan, September 6, 1921, Morgan Papers; Preston, *Aliens and Dissenters,* p. 104.

40. *Letter: Morgan to Bandholtz, September 8, 1921, Morgan Papers.

41. Statement: Morgan, September 5, 1921, ibid.; letter: H. M. Daugherty to the President, October 22, 1921, File #205194-50, Justice Department; *memorandum: W. A. Bethel, attached to memorandum for Assistant Attorney General Crim, November 16, 1921, File #205194-50-295, ibid.

42. Memorandum: W. A. Bethel, attached to memorandum for Assistant Attorney General Crim, November 16, 1921, File #205194-59-295, Justice Department; letter: J. M. Wainwright to the Attorney General, February 28, 1922, File #205194-298, ibid.; *memorandum for Mr. Crim: Daugherty, March 3, 1922, ibid.

43. Daily report: Bandholtz, September 9, 1921, Adjutant General File; letter: W. Jett Lauck to Philip Murray, September 8, 1921, Lauck Papers; telegram: Bandholtz to Commanding General, Fifth Corps Area, September 5, 1921, Adjutant General File; *memorandum for the Attorney General: William J. Burns, October 24, 1921, File #205194-50-281X, Justice Department.

44. *Statement: Morgan, September 5, 1921, Morgan Papers.

45. Telegram: John L. Lewis to Morgan, September 19, 1921, ibid.; *telegram: Morgan to John L. Lewis, September 22 [?], 1921, ibid.

46. *T. C. Townsend, *Martinsburg West Virginia Evening Journal,* September 15, 1923. Reprinted in *Conditions in the Coal Fields,* p. 1185.

Chapter Five: **REFORM**

1. *Letter: Roger Baldwin to C. F. Keeney, March 31, 1920, American Civil Liberties Union Archives, New York Public Library. Cited hereafter as

ACLU Archives; letter: C. F. Keeney to Roger N. Baldwin, April 11, 1920, ibid.; letter: Jack Spivak to Albert DeSilver, May 2, 1920, ibid.; minutes, Executive Committee of the American Civil Liberties Union, May 24, 1920, ibid.

2. *Roger Baldwin Report on the situation in West Virginia, August 27, 1920, ibid.

3. Letter: Roger Baldwin to Harold W. Houston, September 7, 1920, ibid.; Donald Oscar Johnson, "The American Civil Liberties Union: Origins, 1914-1924" (Ph.D. diss., Columbia University, 1960), p. 311; Melvyn Dubofsky and Warren Van Tine, *John L. Lewis: A Biography* (New York: Quadrangle/The New York Times Book Co., 1977), p. 98; *United Mine Workers Journal*, April 1, 1921, p. 13; letter: Albert DeSilver to Harold W. Houston, November 12, 1920, ACLU Archives; letter: Roger Baldwin to Neil Burkinshaw, December 7, 1920, ibid.; letter: Albert DeSilver to Jack Spivak, May 21, 1920, ibid.

4 *Letter: H. W. Houston to Roger N. Baldwin, September 27, 1920, ACLU Archives; *The New York Times*, September 17, 1920, p. 22.

5. Letter: Roger N. Baldwin to Harold W. Houston, September 25, 1920, ACLU Archives; letter: Roger N. Baldwin to Harold W. Houston, October 16, 1920, ibid.; letter: Jackson H. Ralston to Albert DeSilver, October 7, 1920, ibid.; *letter: Albert DeSilver to Jackson H. Ralston, November 12, 1920, ibid.

6. Letter: Roger N. Baldwin to Harold Houston, December 4, 1920, ibid.; telegram: Houston to Roger N. Baldwin, December 10, 1920, ibid.; minutes, Executive Committee of the American Civil Liberties Union, May 23, 1921, ibid.; *Senate Resolution 80, *West Virginia Coal Fields*, p. 3; Johnson, "The American Civil Liberties Union," pp. 318-19.

7. Letter: W. Jett Lauck to Philip Murray, September 14, 1921, Lauck Papers.

8. *Roger N. Baldwin, Report on Publicity in Connection with the Senate Investigating Committee in West Virginia, September 18th-22d, 1921, ibid.; minutes, Executive Committee of the American Civil Liberties Union, September 18, 1921, ACLU Archives.

9. Letter: American Civil Liberties Union to Warren G. Harding, October 19, 1921, File #16-130-83, Justice Department; *letter: W. Jett Lauck to Philip Murray, September 28, 1921, Lauck Papers; statement: Operators Association of the Williamson Field, Williamson, West Virginia, to President Harding in Conference at the White House, September 9, 1921, State v. Keeney, Miners' Treason Trial; statement: Logan Coal Operators Association to President Warren G. Harding, September 9, 1921, ibid.

10. *Letter: Frank P. Walsh to Joseph Gallagher, October 27, 1921, Frank P. Walsh Papers, New York Public Library; *opening statement: Frank P. Walsh, *West Virginia Coal Fields*, p. 604.

11. Testimony: Philip Murray, *West Virginia Coal Fields*, p. 649.

12. Letter: W. Jett Lauck to H. W. Houston, October 15, 1921, Lauck Papers; *testimony: Samuel Untermyer, *West Virginia Coal Fields*, p. 711.

13. *U.S. Senate, *West Virginia Coal Fields, Personal Views of Senator Kenyon*

and Views of Senators Sterling, Phipps, and Warren, Report no. 457, 67th Cong., 2d sess., 1922. Reprinted in *Conditions in the Coal Fields*, pp. 1809-10.

14. Ibid., pp. 1811-13; *United Mine Workers Journal*, February 15, 1922, p. 6.
15. *Letter: Harold W. Houston to W. Jett Lauck, October 12, 1921, Lauck Papers; *United Mine Workers Journal*, October 14, 1922, p. 9.
16. *Memorandum: "United Mine Workers — Borderland Injunction," [n.d.], located in folder labeled: 1921 Handwritten Notes and Memoranda, Tray: B64, Box: Labor 1918-1930s, Lauck Papers; *testimony: W. Jett Lauck, *West Virginia Coal Fields*, p. 1445; Irving Bernstein, *A History of the American Worker 1920-1933: The Lean Years* (Boston: Houghton Mifflin Co., 1960), p. 131.
17. Minutes, Executive Committee of the American Civil Liberties Union, February 26, 1923, ACLU Archives; ibid., March 5, 1923; ibid., March 19, 1923.
18. *Letter: Alfred Bettman to Roger Baldwin, August 1, 1922, Frankfurter Papers; Johnson, "The American Civil Liberties Union," p. 329; minutes, Executive Committee of the American Civil Liberties Union, October 29, 1923, ACLU Archives.
19. Minutes, Executive Committee of the American Civil Liberties Union, September 27, 1920, ACLU Archives; ibid., December 13, 1920; telegram: Roger N. Baldwin to Harold W. Houston, December 1, 1920, ibid.
20. Minutes, Executive Committee of the American Civil Liberties Union, July 5, 1922; ibid., February 19, 1923; Johnson, "The American Civil Liberties Union," p. 330; *Pick and Shovel* (Fayetteville, W. Va.), February 21, 1923; *United Mine Workers Journal*, April 15, 1930, p. 8; testimony: Van Bittner, *Conditions in the Coal Fields*, p. 1267.
21. Minutes, Executive Committee of the American Civil Liberties Union, January 30, 1922, ACLU Archives; *letter: Elliott Northcott to Attorney General, December 18, 1922, File #180-337-619-1, Justice Department.
22. Letter: Elliott Northcott to Attorney General, September 20, 1923, File #227-596-4, Justice Department; letter: Harlan F. Stone to President Calvin Coolidge, October 18, 1923 [no file no.], ibid.
23. Perlman and Taft, *History of Labor*, p. 523.
24. *Letter: John J. Cornwell to A. B. Paxton, January 10, 1922, Cornwell Papers.
25. Letter: Z. T. Vinson to John J. Cornwell, December 12, 1919, ibid.; testimony: C. Frank Keeney, *West Virginia Coal Fields*, p. 196.
26. *Pick and Shovel* (Fayetteville, W. Va.), September 19, 1923; letter: Phil M. Conley to J. J. Cornwell, January 23, 1922, Cornwell Papers.
27. Letter with enclosures: Phil M. Conley to J. J. Cornwell, May 5, 1921, Cornwell Papers; letter: Phil M. Conley to J. J. Cornwell, March 9, 1922, ibid.; letter: J. J. Cornwell to George S. Wallace, May 5, 1920, ibid.
28. *Pamphlet: "West Virginia Has No Copyright on Lawlessness, Says American Constitutional Association," from *Allied Aids*, June, 1922. Exhibit with petition of C. F. Keeney for change of venue, State v. Keeney,

Miners' Treason Trial.

29. *Autobiography of Fred Mooney*, pp. 99, 118; *ibid., p. 107.

30. *Washington Post* (Washington, D.C.), April 29, 1922 (clipping in Scrapbooks, West Virginia Case 1920-1922, Lauck Papers).

31. Unidentified reprint of newspaper article, Morgan Papers; State of West Virginia v. Walter Allen, Indictment no. 3, Treason; Bill of Exception no. 15, Miners' Treason Trial; testimony of W. R. Thurmond, Logan Coal Operators Association, State v. William Blizzard entered into State of West Virginia v. Walter Allen, ibid.; *Autobiography of Fred Mooney*, p. 99.

32. *Judge J. M. Woods's ruling on the motion to exclude the evidence of the state and direct a verdict in the case of the State of West Virginia v. Walter Allen, September 11, 1922, Miners Treason Trial. While this quote is from the Allen rather than the Blizzard trial, the prosecution's argument is exactly the same in both cases. Here, Wood conveniently summarizes its argument.

33. *Washington Post* (Washington, D.C.), April 29, 1922 (clipping in Scrapbooks, West Virginia Case 1920-1922, Lauck Papers). James G. Randall, "Miners and the Law of Treason," *North American Review* 216 (1922): 321.

34. *Resolution adopted at a mass meeting held by citizens of West Virginia, on the Capitol grounds, Charleston, Sunday, August 7, 1921, relating to the industrial disturbances in Mingo County, and dealing with ways and means to establish peace in that coal field: An appeal to Governor E. F. Morgan, State of West Virginia v. Walter Allen, Miners' Treason Trial; *Washington Post* (Washington, D.C.), April 29, 1922 (clipping in Scrapbooks, West Virginia Case 1920-1922, Lauck Papers).

35. *Unidentified newspaper clipping, April 25, 1922, Lauck Papers.

36. *Randall, *"Miners and Law of Treason,"* p. 320.

37. *Verdict, September 16, 1922, State of West Virginia v. Walter Allen, Miners' Treason Trial; motion to set aside verdict and to grant a new trial, November 23, 1922, ibid.; *Autobiography of Fred Mooney*, p. 123.

38. Randall, *"Miners and Law of Treason,"* pp. 313-14; *Autobiography of Fred Mooney*, p. 123; Swain, *Facts About the Two Armed Marches on Logan*, pp. 43-44.

40. *Telegram: Herbert Hoover to H. M. Daugherty, October 13, 1921, File #16-130-83, Justice Department.

41. *United States of America ex. rel. Hitchman Coal & Coke Co. v. John L. Lewis, et al. Criminal Contempt Proceeding, No. 6589, Amended Petition, *Conditions in the Coal Field*, pp. 2129-30.

42. *Ibid., Judgement Order, pp. 2132-33.

43. Robert H. Zieger, *Republicans and Labor 1919-1929* (Lexington: University of Kentucky Press, 1969), pp. 218-25; U.S. Coal Commission, *Report of the United States Coal Commission, Labor Relations in Bituminous Coal Mining, Summary of Recommendations*, part 1, Senate Doc. no. 195, 68th Cong., 2d sess., 1925, p. 156.

44. *Report of the United States Coal Commission, Civil Liberties in the Coal Fields*, part 1, Senate Doc. no. 195, 68th Cong., 2d sess., 1925, p. 179.

45. Testimony: Percy Tetlow, *Conditions in the Coal Fields*, p. 1445.
46. *Autobiography of Fred Mooney*, pp. 127-28.
47. Testimony: Percy Tetlow, *Conditions in the Coal Fields*, pp. 1446-48.
48. Testimony: Van Bittner, ibid.; testimony: Henry Warrum, *Limiting Scope of Injunctions*, p. 616.
49. Testimony: Percy Tetlow, *Conditions in the Coal Fields*, p. 1460; notes for address by Van Bittner, Cleveland, Ohio, 1926, Van Amberg Bittner Papers, West Virginia Collection, West Virginia University Library.
50. Zieger, *Republicans and Labor 1919-1929*, pp. 232, 255.
51. *Testimony: John L. Lewis, *Conditions in the Coal Fields*, pp. 408-09.
52. Zieger, *Republicans and Labor 1919-1929*, pp. 256-58.
53. Carl Raushenbush, "The Use of Injunctions in Labor Disputes," *Editorial Research Reports* 1 (February 4, 1928): 113.
54. *S. 1452, A Bill to Amend the Judicial Code, *Limiting Scope Injunctions*, p. 1; letter: Edwin E. Witte to Roger N. Baldwin, December 24, 1931, George W. Norris Papers, Library of Congress. Cited hereafter as Norris Papers.
55. Letter: Edwin E. Witte to Roger N. Baldwin, December 24, 1931, Norris Papers; testimony: T. C. Townsend, *Limiting Scope of Injunctions*, p. 54; testimony: Morris I. Ernst, ibid., p. 158.
56. Theron Frederick Schlabach, "Edwin E. Witte: Cautious Reformer" (Ph.D. diss., University of Wisconsin, 1966), pp. 135-36; *Edwin E. Witte, "Memorandum in Support of the Several Provisions and Clauses of the Tentative Bill to Define and Limit the Jurisdiction of the Federal Courts, Based Mainly Upon Injunctions Issued by Federal Courts in Labor Cases Since 1920," Witte Papers.
57. *Interborough Rapid Transit Company Against William Green et. al., Brief for Defendants* (New York: The Workers Education Bureau Press, 1928), p. 282.
58. *Ibid., pp. 45-57. The quotation within Oliphant's brief is from Professor Hollander.
59. *Schlabach, "Edwin E. Witte," p. 140.
60. Edwin E. Witte, "The Federal Anti-injunction Act," *Minnesota Law Review* 16 (May, 1932): 639.
61. Richard L. Watson, Jr., "The Defeat of Judge Parker: A Study in Pressure Groups and Politics," *The Mississippi Valley Historical Review* 50, no. 2 (September, 1963): 213, 228.
62. Bernstein, *A History of the American Worker 1920-1933*, p. 407; *testimony: William Green, U.S., Senate, Subcommittee of the Committee of the Judiciary, *Hearing on the Confirmation of Honorable John J. Parker to be an Associate Justice of the Supreme Court of the United States*, 71st Cong., 2d sess., 1930, pp. 24-25; testimony: T. C. Townsend, ibid., p. 65; *United Mine Workers Journal*, May 15, 1930, p. 10.
63. Norman L. Zucker, *George W. Norris: Gentle Knight of American Democracy* (Urbana: University of Illinois Press, 1966), p. 104; *United Mine Workers Journal*, May 15, 1930, p. 9; *ibid., July 1, 1930, p. 3.
64. *Walter White, *A Man Called White: The Autobiography of Walter White* (New York: Viking Press, 1948), pp. 104-05; U.S., *Congressional Record*,

71st Cong. 2d sess., 1930, 72, part 8, 8105.

65. White, *A Man Called White*, p. 104.

66. Ibid., pp. 104-11; Herbert Hoover, *The Memoirs of Herbert Hoover*. Vol. 2: *The Cabinet and the Presidency, 1920-1933* (New York: The Macmillan Company, 1952), pp. 268-69.

67. Milton Lewis Farber, Jr., "Changing Attitudes of the American Federation of Labor Toward Business and Government, 1929-1933," (Ph.D. diss., Ohio State University, 1959), pp. 185, 189-90.

68. Papers relating to the nomination of John J. Parker to be an Associate Justice of the United States Supreme Court, 71st Congress, National Archives. These papers are restricted, no copying is permitted. However, the correspondence to the Judiciary Subcommittee strongly supports my interpretation that the rejection of Parker indicated Americans desired change in governmental institutions in general.

69. Farber, "Changing Attitudes of the American Federation of Labor," pp. 192-93; *United Mine Workers Journal*, April 15, 1930, p. 15.

70. Minutes, Executive Committee of the American Civil Liberties Union, May 5, 1923, June 4, 1923, and September 26, [no year given, probably 1923]; Farber, "Changing Attitudes of the American Federation of Labor," chaps. 1-3.

71. Zieger, *Republicans and Labor 1919-1929*, pp. 179, 262-64.

72. *United Mine Workers Journal*, May 15, 1931, p. 5; Schlabach, "Edwin E. Witte," pp. 146-47.

73. Edmund Wilson, "Frank Keeney's Coal Diggers," *The New Republic* 67 (July 8, 1931): 198.

74. Bernstein, *A History of the American Worker 1920-1933*, pp. 381-84.

75. *Autobiography of Fred Mooney*, pp. 144-45.

76. *Wilson, "Frank Keeney's Coal Diggers," pp. 195-96.

77. Farber, "Changing Attitudes of the American Federation of Labor," p. 193; letter: John P. Robertson, secretary to Norris, to Wilber Tillotson, November 4, 1932, Norris Papers.

78. *Letter: George W. Norris to Felix Frankfurter, March 27, 1931, Norris Papers; *letter: Felix Frankfurter to Roger Baldwin, December 9, 1931, ibid.

79. Letter: Roger N. Baldwin to George W. Norris, December 14, 1931, ibid.; letter: George W. Norris to Roger N. Baldwin, December 15, 1931, ibid.; Witte, "Federal Anti-injunction Act," pp. 640-42.

80. Witte, "Federal Anti-injunction Act," p. 642; *statement of Senator Norris, March 24, 1932, Norris Papers; Melvin James Segal, *The Norris-LaGuardia Act and the Courts* (Washington: American Council on Public Affairs, 1941), p. 16; *Lauf v. E. G. Shinner & Co., 303 U.S. 323 (1938), p. 330.

81. Witte, "Federal Anti-injunction Act," pp. 643-47.

82. Irving Bernstein, *A History of the American Worker 1933-1941: Turbulent Years* (Boston: Houghton Mifflin Co., 1970), pp. 21-35.

83. *Ibid., pp. 41-45; *United Mine Workers Journal*, February 1, 1934, pp. 7-8; *Alinsky, *John L. Lewis*, p. 71.

Index